"Much like my dear gr
fabric she ever comes a
for her children, grandc
Hensley has spent decades tucking away countless snippets of folk speech and uncommon sayings in the Appalachian mountains in drawers, notebooks, and in the back of her mind in hopes of have an opportunity to share them with others. Decades in the making, this collection is colorful and inviting, and tirelessly crafted into a book that should be handed down to future generations. *Say What You Mean: Mean What You Say* offers a colorful and comforting glimpse into the rich culture of mountain folk in the southeastern United States." - Cassie M. Robinson Pfleger, 2010 Conference Program Chairperson of the Appalachian Studies Association; Dahlonega, Georgia

"A delightful read overflowing with the wit and wisdom of mountain lore. Ms. Hensley's intimate understanding of Appalachia along with her deep abiding love of its people, heritage and customs inspires each and every page. Within you will discover a wellspring of uncommon knowledge and you will be wiser of mind and richer in spirit..." - Larry LaFollette, archivist for Southeast Kentucky Community and Technical College and President of the Harlan County Historical Society

"Judith Hensley's collection of mountain lore and wisdom is illustrative of her keen ear and vigor of mountain culture." - Roy Silver, Ph. D. Professor of Sociology, Southeast Kentucky Community & Technical College

Cover Design by Judith V. Hensley

Photo: Pine Mountain Settlement School; Pine Mountain Bledsoe Community in Harlan County, Kentucky

Say What You Mean:
Mean What You Say

By

Judith Victoria Hensley

Say What You Mean: Mean What You Say

All rights reserved.
Copyright © 2011 Judith V. Hensley
Second Printing:
Copyright © March 17, 2016 Judith V. Hensley
All rights reserved.

ISBN – 13: 978-1530617302
ISBN – 10: 1530617308

Printed by Create Space, An Amazon.com Company
Create Space, Charleston SC
www.CreateSpace.com/TITLEID

Available from Amazon.com, CreateSpace.com, and other retail outlets

All quotes in this book were recorded over the last thirty-six years from listening to people's conversations in areas of the Southeastern United States including: Kentucky, Tennessee, Virginia, West Virginia, North Carolina, South Carolina, and Georgia. All information is written purely to record the thoughts, speech, wisdom, and culture of the area. Occasionally there may appear several variations of the same thought, recorded as it was heard. Similarities to other collections are purely coincidental. The content is based entirely on what has been heard and recorded by the author.

This book may not be reproduced in whole or part, in any matter whatsoever without written permission, with the exception of brief quotations within book reviews or articles. It may not be stored in any retrieval system for any reason without written permission from the author.

DEDICATION

For Rachel Johnson Burkhart and Laura Johnson Curry; Jeanette and Jennifer McDaniels; Roxie Rowland; Ernest and Gladys Hensley; Robert and Geraldine Eads; Juanita Daniel; Rhonda Long Robinson; Sarah Boggs Conatser; and all of the friends who helped me listen, record, and recall a way of talking that is fading all too quickly from our remembrance.

DISCLAIMER

All information is recorded as documentation of what has been heard while listening to others in an effort to capture the poetry, imagery, idioms, similes, metaphors, euphemisms, humor, sarcasm, and bits of wisdom from the region. Any resemblance to other works of a similar nature is purely coincidental.

LETTER FROM THE AUTHOR

As an adult, I began to realize the uniqueness of the Appalachian culture and value the humor, imagery, and poetry of the language. A true Appalachian will use a simile, metaphor, or idiom in daily conversation to express the most mundane or common thoughts, spicing up the flow of conversation without planning or forethought. I catch myself using this pattern of speech daily, and am sorrowful for those who feel that they have "outgrown" the region, the speech, or their roots.

My first official notes about Appalachian language were for an Appalachian Studies class at Cumberland College in Williamsburg, Kentucky in 1974. From there my interest grew.

Simply by listening and recording, I have attempted to document the sound and flow of this section of Appalachia, the values, beliefs, and thought processes expressed in everyday language through a cross section of ages, vocations, gender, ethnicities, and communities. Changes creep into any culture slowly but surely. It is my desire to preserve things that are in place at this point in time before they are "disremembered". Every day I hear or say some unique phrase that I realize I don't have included in this body of work. I've added many even in the last days of proofreading, but this work could go on for many more years. The time finally came for me to stop and hope that someone else will continue to record what they hear into the future.

Say What You Mean:
Mean What You Say

Mountain people use beautifully poetic language that includes similes, metaphors, idioms, and euphemisms to color every day speech. Mountain language is more than dialect or accent. It is a lyrical embodiment of common sense, observations, humor, and emotions. Many of the sayings recorded in this section are common across the country and used widely in the region while others are quite unique to the mountain.

A

ability
- It just isn't in me.
- I will if I'm able.
- Some people are just born with it.
- He/she has a gift. (a talent)
- He couldn't catch a fish in a fish tank! (lacks ability)

abrupt
- He was brought up short.
- It was over before it started.
- He stopped before he started.

absence
- Absence makes the heart grow fonder.
- Out of sight, out of mind.

absurd
- That's nothing but hogwash!
- That's ridiculous.
- That's about like a hog in high heels!
- Don't be absurd! (don't say or do something ridiculous)

accident
- He came within two cents of killing himself!
- He came an Ace of dying.
- She came a hair of getting killed.
- He came a freckle of getting killed.
- He took a lick.
- She did it accidentally on purpose.
- There's an accident waiting to happen!

accolades
- That's a feather in your cap!
- A job well done is its own reward.
- If what you do you do for praise, you might as well do nothing.

accountability
- Am I my brother's keeper?
- You rode that horse in here. It's up to you to ride it out.
- I will take him to task.
- I can't help myself. (can't control my desires)
- I'll hold his feet to the fire.
- He's been taken to task.
- There's more who hold his book of accounts than me.

accurate
- That is dead on!
- You're on target.
- You've got the idea.
- You hit the bull's eye.
- You're right on track
- That hit the spot!
- That hit the mark.
- You are spot on.
- You're exactly right.
- You've hit the nail right on the head.

adult/adults
- We're all grown people here.
- Grown-ups are confusing.

- I don't want to grow up but my wife keeps telling me I have to.
- That child has adult tastes. (likes expensive things)
- Children take their cues from adults. (imitate)
- Children do what adults let them do. (permissible)
- Act like an adult!
- Act your age instead of your I Q

advantage
- She's trying to get the upper hand. (take control)
- We have the home court advantage. (playing by our rules; familiar territory)
- He took advantage of the situation. (opportunist)
- What advantage is it to me? (how does it benefit me?)
- Education is the best advantage a person can have.

advice (general)
- Even an old barn looks better with a new coat of paint!
- If you lie down with dogs, you'll get up with fleas.
- Don't corner anything meaner than you.
- To thine own self be true.
- Above all others, be true to yourself.
- It is good to know what side your bread is buttered on. (recognize those who care for you)
- It's better to be an old man's darling than a young man's fool.
- Find peace and you'll find the answer.
- Settle on an answer before you act.
- If you aren't careful you'll end up being a Jack of all trades and the master of none.

- Don't make rash decisions.
- Follow your dreams.
- Don't spread yourself too thin.
- Follow your heart.
- Don't be hasty.
- Keep it between the lines.
- Don't open Pandora's Box.
- Leave well enough alone.
- Don't open that can of worms.
- Curiosity killed the cat.
- Don't ever buy a pig in a poke.
- Be true to yourself.

affirmation
- He gave me the nod. (permission to do something)
- Roger Wilco! (I understand what you want me to do.)
- I've got the go ahead. (approval)
- We shook on it. (made a deal)
- It's a done deal. (has already been decided; approved)
- Count me in. (I want to be part of this plan.)
- You make me proud. (compliment)
- All systems are go. (Everything is ready.)
- Roger Wilco. Over and out. (I'm working on my own.)

age/aging
- He's older than dirt!
- I wonder if she rode a dinosaur to school when she was a kid?
- He's so old, his hinges are rusted. (arthritic movements)

- She's really breaking. (losing youthful looks)
- He's got a white top. (white hair)
- If you live long enough, you finally stop lying about your age and start bragging about it.
- He's robbing the cradle. (dating someone much younger)
- She's so old, a tree has less wrinkles.
- He's got fog on the mountain. (white hair)
- He's an old fogey. (doesn't want to be involved socially)
- She's an old stick in the mud. (old and no fun)
- He's got snow on the roof. (white hair)
- He's so old and hateful, if he smiled, his face would crack.
- How old am I? Old enough to sleep by myself. (an answer the question – How old are you?)
- You are old enough to know better!
- He's over the hill.
- Youth brings ambition. Age brings comfort.
- You're as old as you act.
- You're as old as you think you are.
- I don't know how I got over the hill without passing the top.
- She's all swiveled up. (dried up; wrinkled)
- She's buzzard bait. (very infirm, ready for the vultures)
- That old horse is nothing but buzzard bait. (useless)
- He's shriveled up like a prune. (diminished in size and stature compared to the person's youth)

- Age is a privilege that does not belong to all. I may be getting old, but that's better than the alternative.
- You're on the younger side of me.
- I'm getting old and I can surely feel it.
- You're no spring chicken any more.
- Age before beauty. (said as someone is allowed to enter a door in front of another person)
- He's sure showing his age.
- I'm too old a pony to put that saddle on and ride.
- That's so old; it must have come over on the ark!
- I'm just an old fart. (no fun)
- I'm just an old fuddy duddy.
- She's just an old fiddle fart.
- You know a body is getting old when they stop lying about their age, and start bragging about it!

aggravating
- You're about as aggravating as a sack of gnats.
- You aggravate the fire out of me!
- You aggravate the pooh out of me!
- He aggravates the devil out of me.
- Daggervatin' on it!
- I've never been in a more aggravating situation. (frustrating)
- You could aggravate the devil right out of hell!

agree/agreeable
- It's right as rain.
- It is a perfect fit!
- It should be agreeable to both parties.
- It is to both of their advantage.
- I heard that!
- They couldn't agree on the price of tea in China!

- They couldn't agree on the nose to put on their face!

agreement
- I believe we're of the same mind.
- We're on the same page.
- We're on the same wavelength.
- Your word is good enough to me.
- Yes.
- Yep
- Sure 'nuff
- For sure and certain
- Yes siree
- Yes sirree, Bob.
- We're honor bound.
- We're bound on it.
- We shook on it.
- He gave his word.
- We made a deal.
- We made a pact.
- He gave his word of honor.

ain't/cain't/hain't
- It ain't none of your business!
- I ain't goin' no place!
- I hain't in no mind to listen to your foolishness!
- Cain't shoved ain't in a bucket of paint.
- Now there hain't no such word as ain't.
- (Ain't can be substituted at any time for isn't, am not, or aren't.
- Cain't can be substituted at any time for can't or cannot.
- Hain't can be substituted at any time for hasn't or haven't.)

almost
- It's pret near as hot a day as I've ever seen.
- It's pret night lunch time.

- He's pit nite the friendliest feller I ever met.
- He's a hare away from the truth.
- It's nigh on to supper time.
- It's might near your birthday.
- It's tickin' on 4:00 o'clock.

alone
- Looks like it's just me and my shadow again.
- I got tired of being alone, so I sat down beside myself.
- Alone is not such a bad place to be.
- I may be alone, but at least I'm in good company.
- I'm never alone. There's always the three of us – me, myself, and I.
- You'll never feel alone if you just remember how much I love you.
- With the good Lord on your side, you're never alone.
- Let me alone. (Don't bother me.)
- That dress will cost a fortune let alone adding the price of shoes and a pocketbook to match. (let alone – besides)

ancestors
- My forebears came over on a ship from the old country.
- Our ancients were from across the waters.
- My roots are in the Mountains.
- Our forefathers were brave and strong.
- Our old ones lived long lives.
- The elders of a family should be heeded.
- My bloodline goes back to Ireland.
- My grandpap's grandpap fought in the Civil War.

anger/angry (Also see **mad**)
- He's hot under the collar.
- I could chew you up and spit you out!
- I could Jap slap you into next week.
- He'll jump down your throat.
- She was madder than a wet hen.
- He was madder than a hornet.
- She's easy to fly off the handle. (gets angry easily)
- He was madder than a hornet's nest.
- Don't go off half cocked.
- He was fit to be tied.
- She was spitting feathers.
- He is easily riled. (angered)
- He's on the warpath today.
- She's as ill as a hornet. (unpleasant)
- She was madder than a cat in cold water.
- I was madder than a cat on bath day.
- He was so mad; his face was as red as a turkey's gobbler.
- I'm so mad my ears could pop.
- You make my blood boil!
- He was madder than fire!
- He was as mad as a troll with an army on his bridge.
- You're worse than a sore tailed cat.
- He had smoke coming out of his ears.
- He was steaming!
- I'll be hopping mad if you don't do as I say!
- He's like a raging bull.
- I'd like to pinch your head off.

- She's seeing red.
- He blew his top.
- You really get my dander up!
- I'm so mad I could smoke a pickle.
- I could bite your head off!
- That really ticks me off!
- She was put out with me.
- You pushed the wrong button.
- He knows the right buttons to push.
- That really fries my taters!
- That really burns me up!
- He was foaming at the mouth.
- Don't get in such a stew!

angry expressions
- Bite me.
- Drop dead.
- Get out of my face.
- Take a hike.
- You hairy goomer!
- You're pushing the Hulk out of me!
- I wish you were dead!
- I'd like to knock you clean into next week!
- I don't think so!
- You can take this job and shove it.
- Try me if you think you're big enough!
- Why don't you kiss my grits?
- You can kiss it where the sun don't shine!

animal
- Did you see that critter run across the road?
- He's an animal! (sexually aggressive)

- It was a cattywumpus. (unknown animal)
- I saw a finnertail! (unknown animal)
- I saw an old J R. (unkown animal)
- I saw a wampus! (unknown animal)
- He's an animal when he's been drinking. (easily angered)
- He acts like a wild animal in a cage. (restless; pacing)
- You bring out the animal in me. (base instincts)

ankles
- What are your ankles for? To keep your calves from eating your corn.
- She has thick ankles. (unattractive)
- She's strapped the old ball and chain around his ankle. (a wife or girlfriend who's male counterpart is in a serious relationship with them)

answer
- I'm going to have to pin him down to get an answer.
- Don't answer me with a question!
- Can you riddle me that?
- Only God knows the answer to some questions.
- Find peace and you'll find your answer.
- God always answers prayers, but you may not always like the answer!
- I'll have to sleep on it, but you'll have your answer in the mornin'. (decision)
- Answer me the truth! (tell me)
- She wants her questions answered before they've ever been asked! (impatient)

anxious
- I'm on pins and needles waiting to hear if I got the job!
- I'm tied up in knots waiting to find out what the doctor says.
- I feel like I'm flying apart waiting for the telephone to ring.
- I'm all ajitter. (very nervous on the inside)

any
- I'll take ary one you give me. (any)
- Ever which one don't matter to me.

anyhow
- Leastways, that's what I've heard.
- Howsome ever, I'll come on over after work.
- Anyhoo, I thought it was a good idea.

apologize
- I take it back.
- I'm eating crow.
- I'm sorry as sorry can be.
- I'm askin' for forgiveness.
- I'm askin' your forgiveness.
- I'll not apologize.
- Apology accepted.
- He can apologize with a smile on his face while he has a knife stuck in your back!
- I was wrong and you were right.
- I'd rather die than apologize.
- I'll apologize when hell freezes over!

appearance/apparel/attire
- She looks mighty fine to me.
- You look fine!

- She's putting on the Ritz.
- She's all dolled up.
- He's dressed to the nines.
- He's all diked up.
- He showed up looking like a new penny. (rejuvenated; extremely happy)
- She's dressed to the hilt.
- He's dressed fit to kill.
- You're looking good!
- Nice threads!
- He's slicked up for his date.
- He's spruced up.
- She's dressed to the tea.
- She's all trussed up
- He looks like a dandy.
- He's been spit shined.
- She's putting on the dog to get someone's attention.
- He looks like he's stepping out tonight.
- She is quite fetching in that dress.
- She's all fancied up for something!
- He's decked out to impress someone!
- I look like a 'fore daylight haint!
- Clothes make the man.
- He's drop dead gorgeous in those threads.
- She could turn a few heads in her day.
- She's always got to look like the bell of the ball!
- Clothes DON'T make the man.
- She's all gussied up for some reason.
- She'd look good in a burlap sack.

- She'd look good with a brown paper bag on her head.
- Anybody's good looking with beer goggles on. (If you are drunk, everybody looks good.)
- He looks androgynous. (can't tell the gender for sure)
- Here I am, all dressed up, and no place to go.
- She's fixed up for Sunday Meetin'. (dressed for church)
- She's after more than a compliment dressed like that.
- Even an old barn looks better with a new coat of paint.
- She looks like she dresses out of the rag bag. (wrinkled, dirty, slovenly)
- She's pretty well exposed. (indecently exposed cleavage or legs)
- His pants are so tight you can see his makings.
- Where's the other half of that dress? (too revealing)
- Her pants are so tight they look like they've been painted on.
- Her britches are so tight, it looks like she's been melted and poured into them.
- Make sure to wear your best bib and tucker!
- I wouldn't be caught dead in that outfit!
- I wouldn't wear that to a dog fight.
- The more skin, the more sin.
- His clothes look like he's been in a fight with a bull dog and lost! (raggedy; deliberate holes cut in jeans)

appetite
- Do you have an appetite for anything? (preference of food)

- I don't have much of an appetite for anything. (no preference; not hungry)
- The smell of fresh baked bread whet his appetite for supper. (made him hungry)
- She has an appetite for rich things. (craves wealth)

appropriate/inappropriate
- It is only fitting that we pay our respects to the widow Jenkins.
- It's not fittin' for a young lady to act so! (unacceptable social behavior)

approval
- I couldn't have asked for a better son (or daughter).
- I want to be just like you when I grow up.
- That's just fine and dandy.
- I'm proud to be your Momma. (can be said from dad, wife, brother, etc.)

argue
- It's a war or words.
- He's going for the jugular! (saying deliberately cruel things)
- It's all over but the shouting.
- They are at loggerheads.
- They've locked horns.
- The gloves are off!
- I'll give you a piece of my mind!
- They were really going at it.
- They were at each other's throats.
- They are always at odds with each other.
- I have a bone of contention to pick with you.
- They are butting heads.

- Why don't you say what you really think?
- So, is that how you really feel?
- Don't raise your voice to me!
- Don't get into a stew!
- I have an axe to grind with you!
- He really chewed her out.
- It takes two to tango!
- It takes two to tangle.
- She always has to have the last word.

arrogant
- She thinks she doesn't have to lift a finger. (expects others to do all the work)
- He looks down his nose at everybody. (feels superior)
- She thinks her poop don't stink. (false sense of superiority)

ask
- I axed a question and she didn't answer.
- When you put it to me that way, the answer is yes.
- You have not because you ask not.
- Exactly what are you asking? (What are you really trying to find out?)

assassin
- He's nothing but a gun slug.
- They hired gun thugs to do their dirty work.
- He was a hired gun, brought in to cause trouble.
- He was shot by a bush whacker.

associations
- You're guilty by association.
- If you lay down with dogs, you'll get up with fleas.

- If you fly with the crows, you get shot with the crows.
- If you lay down with the devil, you'll wake up in Hell.
- If you stir in poop, you are bound to get some of the stink on you.

assurance
- He sure enough did!
- I'm telling you sure enough.
- I give my word on it.
- I'd hang my reputation on it.
- It's in the bag.
- No doubt about it.
- You can count on it.
- It will be just as I said, or I'll know the reason why!
- You don't have a thing in this world to worry about.

attentiveness
- Look sharp.
- Pay attention
- Prop yourself up.
- Focus!

attempt
- I'll give it a whirl.
- I'll give it my best shot.
- Ours is not to reason why, ours is but to do or die.
- You never know until you try.
- Why don't you have a crack at it?
- It's your turn to have a go.
- Nothing ventured, nothing gained

attire
- She looks like she dresses out of the rag bag. (wrinkled, dirty, slovenly)
- She's pretty well exposed. (indecently exposed cleavage or legs)
- His pants are so tight you can see his makings.
- Where's the other half of that dress? (too revealing)
- Her pants are so tight they look like they've been painted on.
- Her britches are so tight, it looks like she's been melted and poured into them.
- Make sure to wear your best bib and tucker!
- I wouldn't be caught dead in that outfit!
- He is all spruced up.
- I wouldn't wear that to a dog fight.
- The more skin, the more sin.
- His clothes look like he's been in a fight with a bull dog and lost! (raggedy; deliberate holes cut in jeans)
- Get out of those skin tight jeans!
- No child of mine is going out indecent into the world! (uncovered; too tight)
- She goes around slouchy looking all the time.

attractive
- He's the cat's meow.
- Is he for rent?
- She's hot enough to make a gay man straight.
- She's the bombdiggity.
- She's a brick house.
- She is drop dead gorgeous!
- I bet your momma's proud of you!

- He's smokin' hot.
- I could dip him in gravy and sop him up with a biscuit!
- Somebody grab a water hose. He's so hot, there's bound to be a fire.
- Wouldn't you like some fries with that shake?
- I wonder if THAT'S on the menu.
- Don't shake 'til you break what the good Lord gave you.

authentic
- She's the real deal. (genuine)
- He's the Real McCoy.
- She's the original.
- After the Good Lord made him, He broke the mold.
- After the Lord made her, He threw away the mold.

authority (or lack of)
- You don't buy my bread or pack my water.
- They don't pay my bills.
- He didn't hire me and he can't fire me.
- Who died and left you boss?
- Who's running this show?
- I want to speak to the man in charge.
- He don't put no pork chops on my table!

automobile
- That eight cylinder is a real gas hog .
- How long have you had that old puddle jumper?
- My new truck is a gas guzzler.
- That's a fine machine if I ever saw one!
- This car runs like a dream.
- How do you like my new ride?

- All I could afford was this old clunker.
- He thinks he's a big man riding in that jalopy.
- That used care is nothing but a pile of junk.
- I love your new set of wheels.

avoid
- Quit beating around the bush!
- I'll not be put off again!
- You can buzz around that flower patch all day long, but sooner or later you'll have to land.
- Don't pussyfoot around.
- You've been side stepping the real issue.
- You are trying to get around the truth.

B

babe/baby
- She's a baby boomer. (born in the 1950s)
- He's just a babe in arms. (very young)
- She's a babe in the woods. (innocent)
- He's a baby face. (looks very much younger than his age)
- Don't throw the baby out with the bath water. (keep the good, get rid of the bad)
- That's a fractious baby. (whiny, unhappy)

bad/bad behavior
- Ooooh! That's so bad, it's fine.
- You act like you were raised in a barn! (no manners)
- He's wild as a buck.

- You act like a monkey!
- They acted like they had been let out of a cage!
- You act like you've never been out in public before.
- Act your age!
- Act your age, not your I.Q.!
- Act like a little lady – not a tomboy.
- The classroom was a three ring circus.
- You act like the monkey that fell off the bed.
- Get out of my face if you don't know how to act any better than that!
- Too bad, too sad!
- Tough noogies.
- Get over yourself.
- That's the most gosh awful thing I ever heard!
- Things just went from bad to worse. (more complicated)
- You need an attitude adjustment.
- A trip to the woodshed would straighten you out! (spanking)

bag
- I take my lunch to school in a sack. (brown bag)
- I want my groceries in a paper poke. (shopping bag)
- He carries pop bottles in a burlap sack. (potato bag

bald
- He's sporting a convertible on top.
- He's a skin head.
- He's slick as an onion.
- He's roofless.
- He's as bald as a coot!

- Just call him baldy.

bargain (low prices)
- That's a steal!
- That's a real deal!
- That's the deal of a lifetime!
- That's the deal of the century.
- My house is full of bargains I never wear and never use. (Things bought just because they are cheap are often useless.)

barn
- Even an old barn looks better with a new coat of paint on it! (use cosmetics as you get older)
- Your barn door is open. (pants are unzipped)
- Your barn door is open and your horses are trying to escape.
  (vulgar rendition of the previous saying)
- Were you raised in a barn? (asked of children who have displayed inappropriate manners)

baseball
- You don't have to hit a baseball through her window to get her attention. (don't be so obvious)
- That's as American as apple pie and baseball.
- Take me out to the ball game!
- Three strikes and you're out. (you get three chances and no more)
- Don't walk him home! Make him work for it! (don't make it easy on him)
- Hey, batter, batter, batter, batter, Swing! (take a chance; do something!)

basics
- We need to get back to basics.
- We need to get down to the nitty gritty.

bathroom
- Where is your Johnny House ?
- I need to water the lilies.
- Can you point me to the Powder Room?
- Time to hit the bushes.
- I need the Ladies' Room .
- I need to use the facility.
- Where is your wash house?
- We have an outhouse.
- Throw it in the toilet.
- Do you need to go potty?
- I have got to find the Lou.
- The head stinks!
- I need to sit on the throne.
- I clean the porcelain throne.
- There's a little shack out back.
- I hope it's a two seater.
- Nope, it's a one holer.
- I need to take a leak.
- Save that cob for the outhouse.
- Save that catalogue for the toilet! (toilet paper)
- It's about time to dig a new toilet hole.
- I need to shake the dew off the lily.
- I have to see a man about a dog.
- I need to go shake hands with a politician.
- I need to take a run to the dry goods store.
- I need to shake hands with the governor.

- Mention my name and you'll get a good seat.

beat/beating
- She looks like someone beat her with an ugly stick. (hit)
- Now that's beating a dead horse. (pointless to discuss)
- Stop beating around the bush! (avoiding the main topic)
- I'd rather take a beating than apologize for something I didn't do.
- He's beating the bushes trying to find work. (searching everywhere)

beauty
- Beauty is more than skin deep.
- A girl like that gives beauty a bad name. (pretty but despicable; cruel)
- She's a sight for sore eyes. (lovely; beautiful)
- Beauty is as beauty does. (Behavior is more important than physical beauty.)
- Beauty is in the eye of the beholder.
- Beauty on the inside never fades.
- Only God can trade beauty for ashes.
- Inner beauty lasts when outer beauty is long gone.
- A think of beauty is a joy forever.

bed
- When you make your bed, you'll have to lay in it.
- Don't take that to bed. (take care of today's business today)
- Don't go to bed angry. (settle problems before you go to bed)
- That boy'd druther lay in the bed than eat. (lazy)

bed time partings
- Good night.
- Sweet dreams.
- Good night John Boy.
- See you in my dreams!
- Good night! Sleep tight! Don't let the bed bugs bite!
- See you in the morning!
- Sleep fast. Morning comes early.

before
- I've heard that afore.
- Think before you speak.
- Back whenever we didn't have computers or TV, people spent more time together. (before the time)
- Before you say no, just listen.
- His grandpa died back before I came into the family. (prior to becoming an in-law)

began/begin/beginning
- We're back to square one. (start over)
- Begin at the beginning.
- We will commence directly.
- I begin to understand.
- I've been involved since the get go.
- They're off to a flying start. (great beginning)
- We're back to the drawing board. (start over)
- We'll have to start from scratch. (begin again)
- I don't like to have to chew my backer twice. (start over)
- I don't intend to chew that pork chop twice.
- He commenced to talking and couldn't quit! (began)

believe
- I allowed that you did... (believed)
- He'd believe anything you say.
- I still believe in fairy tales and happily ever afters.
- I never allowed you did. (didn't believe)
- I have confidence in the fact.
- Believe half of what you see and nothing that you hear.
- Believe the impossible and you can make it happen.
- If you can believe it, you can do it.
- Anything is possible to the one who believes.
- I took it to heart. (believed something that has been told)

belly ache
- It feels like I've been eating little green apples.
- My belly feels like Montezuma's revenge.
- Little Mary ate a snake and woke right up with a belly ache.
- I think I ate rectal rockets for dinner.
- Oh, Lordy. Somebody slipped me a belly bomb.
- I've got the rumbley tumbleys.

bend/bends
- You might bend me, but you'll not break me! (I might have to learn to compromise, but I will never give in completely!)
- I bend over backwards for you and you don't appreciate it. (I do everything to please you and care for you.)
- He's got the bends. (severe belly ache; diarrhea)

- It's just another bend in the road. (life's road is unpredictable; seldom straight)
- She will bend him to her will. (manipulate; force)

beside
- He sidled right up beside of me. (got as close as he could)
- She's beside herself. (distraught)
- Pull up a seat and sit down beside yourself.

best
- I'd best be getting back to work. (I'd better…)
- Whatever you think is best… (I trust your judgment)
- The best is yet to come.
- The best is yet to be.
- You let him best you! (beat)
- I love you best. (more than anyone else does)
- You're the bestest friend in the whole entire world!

bet
- I bet you a dime for a dollar!
- Heads I win. Tails you lose! (unfair wager)
- It's a sure bet. (certain)
- I'll bet you a brass nickel!
- All bets are off. (no deal)
- You bet your sweet bippy! (why, certainly; of course)
- I'd bet my bottom dollar on it. (sure of the outcome)

betray/betrayed/betrayer
- You're a Benedict Arnold!
- You Judas Iscariot!
- You're a back stabber.

better
- We're in it for better or worse. (regardless of the outcome)
- For better or worse... (marriage vows)
- Don't get bitter. Get better!

between
- I'm betwixt and between houses right.
- He's between a rock and a hard place.
- I feel like my life is suspended somewhere between heaven and earth.

big
- The bigger they are, the harder they fall.
- What's the big deal?
- He thinks he's the big cheese.
- Big Brother is watching you.
- He's got the big head.
- His head is so big he can hardly get through the door!
- He thinks he's big. (important)
- You're a little fish in a big pond. (insignificant)
- I have bigger fish to fry. (more important matters to attend to)
- Dream big.
- You can't ever dream too big.
- She's the big giant head. (bossy)
- The big moment has arrived.
- This is the big day.

bird
- The early bird catches the worm.
- You are bird brained.
- A bird in hand is worth two in the bush.

- Everyone keeps staring at me like I have a big black bird on my head!
- That's killing two birds with one stone. (accomplishing two things with one effort)

birthplace
- Lee County, Virginia is my borning ground.
- The place of my birth is Blounte County, Tennessee.
- My borning place was at the head of the holler.
- I'll always find my way back home.
- Our old home place has fallen down.
- Corbin, Kentucky is my hometown.
- Where did the stork drop you off?

bite/bitten
- I believe I'll try a bite. (sample of food)
- I need to fix me a bite to eat before I do ary other thing. (snack)
- Don't bite the hand that feeds you. (Be kind to those who are kind to you.)
- His bark is worse than his bite. (sounds mean but isn't)
- I believe I'll take a bite out of that. (attempt something)
- Lies will come back to bite you in the butt.
- I've bitten off more than I can chew. (attempted something that is too complicated to complete)
- He's been bitten by the love bug. (falling in love)

black
- His mood was blacker than death.
- You have a black mark against you. (ill will from someone)

- It was a black out. (power outage; block on information)
- He's a black guard. (evil)
- He's not as black as he's been painted. (not so bad)
- It's black as Satan's heart out there.
- The house was blacker than a moonless night.
- It was blacker than burnt toast.
- It vanished into the black hole of Calcutta.
- Your clothes are as black as soot.
- Your socks are as black as tar.
- Her hair was blacker than a burnt shadow.
- That's blacker than a burnt homemade biscuit.
- His stomach was a black hole. (big eater)
- His head was a black hole. (empty
- I'll beat you black and blue.
- All cats are black in the dark. (commonality)
- His hair was as black as a raven's wing.
- It's a black day. (a tragedy)

blackmail
- He's holding that little bit of information over my head.
- She's holding that little bit of information for a rainy day.
- You can't use truth that's told openly to blackmail anybody.
- You can't use common knowledge for blackmail.
- Blackmail has a way of having the tables turned.

blast/blasted
- Dad blast it! (frustration)

- You couldn't blast me out of here with a keg of dynamite. (determined to stay in a designated place)
- He is a blast from the past. (a good memory)
- We'll have a blast! (good time)
- He got blasted. (drunk)
- He was blasted to smithereens! (utterly destroyed)
- I'll blast you into next week! (an angry threat)

bless/blessings
- With great blessing comes great responsibility.
- Count your blessings. (gratitude)
- He's my little blessing. (my child)
- May the sunshine always be at your back.
- May the road rise up to meet you.
- Bless his little heart! (this phrase can be added to the beginning or to the end of any comment and get away with it. "Bless his little heart; his mother never taught him how to act." "She's as ugly as a mud fence, bless her little heart." It turns a negative comment into an acceptable one.) "I'd like to bust his bottom, bless his little heart."
- Bless your little pea picking heart!
- Bless your pointy little head!
- Well, bless my time!
- That boy is such a blessing to his mother. (helpful)
- She will bless you out over that. (quarrel at you)
- I just got blessed out. (told off)
- Well, bless my soul! (said on hearing good news)
- Walk in the light.
- Peace be with you.

blind
- You are as blind as a bat! (can't see the obvious)
- Even a blind squirrel finds a nut once in a while. (continued trying pays off)
- When I talk to you, you act as if you are deaf, dumb, and blind! (being ignored)
- I've been blind-sided. (taken by surprise)
- He couldn't hit the broad side of a barn.

blood
- It's in your blood. (something a person feels passionately about)
- Blood is thicker than water. (family comes first)
- There is bad blood between them. (feud or disagreement)
- We've always had good blood between us. (friendly)
- He's a blue blood. (royal; wealthy)
- He'll want you to sign in blood. (a contract or covenant that can never be broken)

blue
- Her eyes were as blue as the sky.
- I'm lonesome, blue. (sad)
- I've got the blues. (melancholy)
- You're as blue as huckleberry pie. (poor circulation)
- He's as blue as a swimming hole. (hypothermia)
- Her lips are blue. (cold; bad circulation)
- You can talk to that boy until you are blue in the face and it won't do a bit of good. (you talk, he doesn't listen)
- They're kickin' the blue blazes out of the other team. (easily defeating)

- The idea came to me out of the clear blue. (unexpectedly)

bluff/bluffing
- He's all bark and no bite.
- His bark is worse than his bite.
- He always has his poker face on.
- He roars a lot, but he's harmless.
- She's a squawker.
- He's just quacking.
- He's a big talker.
- He's nothing but a big bag of wind.
- He's nothing but a blow hard.
- You're full of beans!
- You're full of baloney!

blurt
- She just blurts out any old thing without thinking it through.
- It seems like the wrong thing just spills out of my mouth.
- He's got the can't help its.
- She has hoof and mouth disease.
- I stuck my foot in my mouth.
- She stuck her foot in her mouth so far she just about bit her leg off.
- Take that foot out of your mouth so you can stick the other one in.
- She opens her mouth and whatever falls out, falls out.

boast
- He's all blow and no show.
- He's always tooting his own horn.

- Somebody else might brag on you if you'd give them a chance!
- He boasts a big house. (owns an admirable property)

body
- My bidey is tired.
- My bidey hurts all over more than anywhere else.
- Everybidey is welcome.
- Somebidey is at the door.
- Nobody loves me.
- You're nobody 'til somebody loves you.
- I wish I had a body like that.
- Now there's a body to write home about.
- His body is pure art work, chiseled by the hand of God.
- That girl's body is a work of art.
- The spirit is willing, but the body is weak.
- We are many members, but one body.

boldness
- She had the brass on her face to say it.
- He's got a lot of brass.
- He decided to take the bull by the horns.
- How dare you raise your voice to me!
- He has brass knockers.
- He had family jewels like a washtub.
- She was full of sass and vinegar.
- You've got a nerve to come here asking for anything!

bone
- I have a bone of contention to pick with you. (disagreement)
- I need to bone up on Algebra. (study, review)

- He's rotten to the bone. (poor character OR likably mischievous)
- I don't need you to throw me a bone. (do me a favor)
- You are bone of my bone and flesh of my flesh. (very close relationship)
- I'll make no bones about it. (say what I think and don't care if it offends anyone else)
- My car was bone dry. (completely out of fuel)
- My check book is bone dry. (out of funds)

bored/boring
- He's twiddling his thumbs.
- I'm so bored; I could fall off a log!
- She was so bored; she started finding people in the ceiling.
- He was as bored as a cat on the sidewalk watching cars.
- He was so bored, he started blowing spit bubbles.
- That show was kind of hokey.
- He only has one tone – monotone!
- That preacher could put a saint to sleep.
- I'm so bored I could dry up and die.
- I'm bored out of my mind.
- I'm bored to distraction.
- I'm bored as a gourd.
- His speech was a real snoozer!
- She is duller than dishwater.

boundary
- He owns a big boundary of land. (Large acreage.)
- The law has put a boundary on him. (Bounty)
- Know your boundaries. (your rightful place)

bounty
- There's a bounty on his head. (A monetary reward offered by the law for the capture of a criminal.)

bowels
- Don't get your bowels in an uproar! (Don't get so upset!)
- Don't get your bowels in a bind. (Don't get so upset.)
- His bowels are blocked. (constipated)
- I'd go to the bowels of the earth for you! (do the impossible to please you)
- I've been to the bowels of Hades and back. (been through a very traumatic experience)

boy
- Hey, boy! You'd better do as I say. (an unknown child or someone subservient to the speaker)
- Boy, oh boy! I sure am thirsty. (used for emphasis)
- He's more man than boy. (a teenager)
- That will separate the men form the boys! (said about a difficult task that must be done)
- Boys will be boys. (bad behavior is expected from boys)

braces
- He got braces. Now he's a brace face.
- I feel like a metal mouth with these braces on.
- You look like you have railroad mouth.
- I like the new grill!

bragging
- He sure likes to toot his own horn.
- She tried to steal his thunder.
- Let's make sure it works before we brag on ourselves.

- Who's got bragging rights? (credit for a successful endeavor)

brain (See also **dumb**)
- Her brother is so stupid, his brain moved out a long time ago.
- If you had a brain, you'd be dangerous.
- Don't sit down too hard. You might mash your brain.
- If your brains were gasoline, you wouldn't have enough to drive an ant half way around a b.b. on a motorcycle.
- If your brains were dynamite, you wouldn't have enough to blow your nose.
- If your brains were sitting next to a pea, it would be like sitting the moon next to the sun.
- If your brains were ink, you wouldn't have enough to dot an i.
- If you wanted to sell your brain for a transplant, you could probably get a million dollars for it, since it has never been used.
- If your brain was bug spray, you wouldn't have enough to kill a gnat.
- The biggest job your brain does is keeping your ears apart.
- If your brain were made of rocket fuel, you'd never get off the ground.
- When the Lord was handing out brains, you forgot to get in line.
- When the Lord was handing out brains, she thought someone said rain and put up her umbrella.

- If your brain was made of heat, you wouldn't have enough to keep a snake warm at high noon in the Sahara desert.
- If your brain was made of stone, it would be just another gain of sand on the beach.
- This road is so curvy, if you're riding in the back seat, it could pert near sling your brains out.

brave
- He has a stout heart. (courageous)
- Call him Brave Heart. (courageous)
- I can brave whatever storm comes with the Lord's help. (survive; overcome)

break
- Who's going to break the ice? (speak first)
- Break a leg. (good luck wish before a performance)
- She is breaking. (showing her age)
- Give me a break! (opportunity; stop demanding so much of me)
- This trip is going to break the bank. (cost a lot)
- Break it down. (simplify; dance)
- She's having a breakdown. (mental illness)
- They've had a breakdown in communication. (misunderstanding)
- The project had a breakdown. (fell apart; failed)
- You might as well break down and enjoy yourself! (stop being so formal or stiff)

break-up
- They've split up.
- He split.
- She shook him loose.

briar
- Whose briar patch have you been in? (trouble)
- Don't get all briared up! (worked up; angry; out of sorts.
- He's a briar. (hick; of rural origin)

brick/bricks
- She's dumber than a brick.
- She's a brick house. (voluptuous)
- I've been hitting the bricks. (looking for a job)
- Hit the bricks! (get out!)
- He got hit with a ton of bricks! (huge surprise)

bridge
- I'll cross that bridge when I come to it. (don't worry until necessary.
- This is a bridge to nowhere. (lost)
- Don't burn your bridges. (don't permanently break relationships)
- I'm burning all of my bridges behind me. (starting over, won't try to go back to the past)
- We need to bridge the gap. (make amends)
- We need to bridge the learning gap. (discrepancy between performance and expectation)

bright (also see **smart**)
- The room was as bright as the morning sun.
- It was as bright as a brand new light bulb.
- The day was as bright as the morning star.
- This is a bright child. (intelligent)
- She's as bright as a button. (stands out from the rest)
- You're about as bright as a burnt out light bulb.
- The sun was so bright, it hurt my eyes.

- Her smile was so bright, it filled the room. (radiant)

broke
- If it ain't broke, don't try to fix it! (don't meddle with what already works well)
- I'm so broke; I don't have any coins to jingle in my pocket.
- We are broker than convicts.
- I'm so broke next payday is already gone.
- I'm clean busted.
- I'm flat busted.
- You may be broke, but you'll never be flat busted.
- He's broke out all over. (rash; measles)
- He broke out of jail. (escaped)

brown
- He's brown as a biscuit. (very tanned)
- She's a brown nose. (flatters someone or does things for them in order to gain approval or favors)
- How now brown cow. (said to imitate someone with a northern accent and poke fun at it)

bubble/bubbles
- I'm lathering up my hair.
- This water is so hard it won't make a lather.
- Bubble, bubble, toil and trouble. (be careful about a decision you must soon make)
- He's always blowing bubbles. (playing instead of working)

budding
- The trees are putting out.
- She's a budding singer. (just starting)

bully/bullied
- He's henpecked. (dominated by his wife)

- She's punkin' me out. (picking on me)
- He tush hogged his way over everybody. (recklessly dominates)
- Sometimes you have to just hunker down and take it. (don't resist authority – even excessive authority)
- He goes around like a whipped pup. (may refer to an abused person – child or adult)
- He is cow towed. (dominated by a female)
- She doesn't open her mouth without his permission to speak. (dominated by a male)
- She doesn't dare have a thought without his permission. (may refer to someone too eager to please OR to someone who is fearful of disagreeing)
- He'll be riding you like a blue pack mule.

burned/burnt
- She sure burned him. (Broke his heart)
- He got burned. (Cheated in a bad deal)
- When he took that test, he burnt it up. (Did well)
- Lord, you're burnt up! (sunburned)
- What he said burnt her up! (made her angry)
- I'm as red as a lobster! (sunburned)

bus
- Jump on the bus, Gus! (Let's go!)
- He just got off the bus. (new in town)
- Do you have to get hit with a bus? (something obvious)

business
- Locks are his stock and trade. (what he does for a living)
- Mind your own business. (Don't be nosey in other people's affairs.)

- What business is it of yours? (Why do you want to know?) Keep your nose in your own business. (Take care of your own affairs and stay out of the affairs of others.)

busy
- She's busy a bee. (works all the time)
- We're as busy as a swarm of bees! (very busy)
- Her hands are busy all the time. (always working at something)
- I have too many irons in the fire. (too busy)
- He has too many pokers in the fire. (trying to be involved in too many things)
- He's busy as a beaver. (works hard)
- That pattern is too busy. (too complex; too bright; too many colors)

C

calf
- You'll have to lick that calf over again. (repeat something you've already done)
- She's as pretty as a spotted calf.
- Stop bawling like a calf separated from its momma. (whining and complaining about something)

call
- I'm calling the shots! (in control)
- Why don't you call a spade a spade? (be totally honest)
- He's calling the tune. (making important decisions)
- She got called in on the carpet. (reprimanded by a boss)

- I think I'll call it a day. (quit working for the day)

calm/calm down
- I am as calm as the ocean on a sunny day.
- She is as calm as a butterfly floating on the wind.
- He's as cool as a cucumber.
- She was as calm as steady water.
- She is always unfrazzled.
- No matter what happens, she remains unruffled.
- Breathe deep and count to ten.
- You need to cool your jets.
- Get hold of yourself!
- Pull yourself together.
- Take a chill pill.
- Sit down beside yourself and be still.

candle
- He's burning both ends of the candle. (working too hard)
- Life is like a candle in the wind. (quickly over)
- She can't hold a candle to her sister. (can't be compared to, inferior to)

cap
- I've never seen anything to cap it. (top it; beat it)
- Cap off that jar of mayonnaise. (put the lid on)
- Make sure you wear your cap. (hat)
- Put your noggin on! (knitted hat for a boy)
- She wears a fascinator. (knitted hat for a girl)
- He's a real cap buster! (likable person)
- Cap off that glass of milk. (finish drinking it)

care/carefree
- I was taking care of business.
- He's footloose and fancy free.
- She acts like she has not a care in this world.
- No worries.
- She goes lightly off on her way and lets the rest of us handle reality.
- He's as free as a bird. (carefree)

carry/carries/carrying
- Can you carry me to town? (give me a ride)
- Isn't that too heavy for you to tote?
- She carries herself well. (elegant walk)
- Don't carry that anger around with you.
- Don't sack your troubles in your pocket.
- She carries a fine tune. (sings well)
- He couldn't carry a tune in a bucket! (sings poorly)
- He's carrying that team on the back. (star player)

castle/castles
- She's building castles in the air.
- (setting unrealistic goals)
- A man's home is his castle. (his place where he's the boss)
- He's the King of his castle. (boss of his family)
- She's looking for a handsome prince complete with his own castle. (fantasizing about her prospective husband – a wealthy one)

cat/cats
- Scat Yeller! Tail's in the gravy. (Can be said to an animal that is underfoot or to a person that needs to get out of the way.)

- You're the luckiest cat I've ever seen – used up nine lives and still going strong. (a fortunate person; may be said to one who is accident prone)
- Who let the cat out of the bag? (told a secret)Letting the cat out of the bag is a lot easier than trying to put it back in! (It's difficult to keep a secret, once it's been told.)
- There's more than one way to skin a cat. (more than one approach to getting things accomplished)
- He's a fat cat. (wealthy)What's the matter? Cat got your tongue? (won't talk; shy)
- There's not enough room to sling a cat in this place. (tiny space)
- You can't sling a dead cat without hitting a church around here. (plenty of churches)
- There he sat, grinning like a Cheshire cat! (smug; self-satisfied)
- When the cat's away, the mice will play. (People behave differently with the lack of an authoritative figure.
- Curiosity killed the cat. (Trying to find an answer to something might prove to be dangerous!)
- All cats look black in the dark.

caution
- Measure once, cut twice.
- Never buy a pig in a poke.
- Anybody who buys a car checks under the hood first.
- Go easy.

certain/certainly
- No two ways about it.
- Sure enough.

- There's a sure fire way to get that job done.
- You can depend on it.
- You can bet your sweet bippy!
- For sure and certain it will happen.
- Without a doubt.
- I'll be there come hell or high water.

chain
- A chain is as strong as its weakest link.
- How's the old ball and chain? (refers to a spouse – usually the wife)

chance
- Take a chance on love.
- Sometimes you just have to take a chance.
- Let the chips fall where they may.
- Let it fall where it falls.
- You've got about one chance in a million!
- By happenstance, have you seen my hat? (perhaps)
- I ran into him by happenstance. (unexpectedly, unsought)

change
- A leopard can't change his spots.
- He couldn't change if he wanted to – and he doesn't want to.
- You'll never change!
- He hasn't changed since the day he was born!
- Don't change horses in mid stream.
- Change just for the sake of changes is not always a good thing.

character
- She's a jewel.

- She's a gem.
- He is an upright and honorable man.
- He's been brought up right.
- She is a well brought up young lady.
- I put no stock in him.
- He won't amount to a hill of beans.
- I wouldn't trust him any further than I could pick him up and throw him!
- He's a pistol!
- He's a corker!
- The apple doesn't fall far from the tree.
- Don't do as I do! Do as I say!
- He's a sorry, good for nothing biscuit eater!
- Speak of the devil!
- He casts a long shadow.
- He's the kind of feller that would kick you while you're down.
- I wouldn't touch her if she was dripping with diamonds.
- She's headed down the wrong road.
- She's keeping bad company.
- He's running with the wrong crowd.
- Birds of a feather flock together.
- One bad apple can spoil the whole bunch.
- Sorry is as sorry does.
- He's an old sneaky snake.
- He's nothing but a sneaky old rat.
- He's a no good bum.
- He's a skunk.

- The acorn doesn't fall far from the tree.
- I wouldn't have him if he was hanging in gold.
- You'll be judged by the company you keep.

charm
- He could charm the buttons off a snake.
- True charm is born – not learned in a school.
- It's easy to charm those who want to be.

chase
- I may not catch her, but I'll enjoy the chase. (pursue romantically)
- I chased him until he caught me. (enticed)
- Cut to the chase. (give the real reason)
- He's like a dog chasing his tale. (getting nowhere)
- She took out after him. (pursued in order to catch up with)

cheap
- Girls like that are a dime a dozen.
- That was a cheap shot. (unnecessary cruelty)

cheat/cheated/cheater
- He's such a cheater, I'm not even sure this baby I'm carrying is his! (unfaithful husband)
- I'm gonna have to turn my rooster into a hen if I want to keep him home.
- I've been hoodwinked.
- They sure took me to the cleaners.
- They saw you coming.
- I got the short end of that deal.
- I got fried like potatoes.
- I've been scalped.
- I've been duped.

cheek
- Turn the other cheek. (forgive; give someone another chance)
- She's awfully cheeky. (disrespectful)
- Pull your pants up. Your cheeks are showing. (buttocks)
- He said it with tongue in cheek. (insincere)

cheer
- You're awfully cheery this morning! (in a good mood)
- How can I cheer you up? (make you feel better)
- She brings cheer where ever she goes. (pleasant personality)
- Hi ho, cheer-i-o, and a way we go! (can be said before going anywhere)
- Spread a little cheer where ever you go.
- Sit down with me and let's share a cup of cheer.

chicken/chickens
- Don't count your chickens before they hatch. (Don't assume anything.)
- You are a chicken heart. (coward)
- That's chicken feed! (low cost)
- That old hen's little dittlers will come home to roost one of these days. (if you are deceitful, your lies will catch up with you)
- There's a chicken graveyard sittin' in my middle. (fondness for eating chicken)
- This chicken is finger lickin' good. (delicious)
- Lies, like chickens, come home to roost. (Lies catch up with the liar.)
- You big chicken liver! (coward)

child/children
- My rug rats are on the war path again!
- I've known you since you were a tadpole.
- The little cookie crumblers are in the kitchen.
- His offshoots look just like him.
- Her offspring are all intelligent.
- You little knot heads need to get in your seats!
- All of your little sprouts look like their parents.
- Can you get your young un to stop crying.
- Those acorns didn't fall far from the tree.
- Well, chillum, it's time for bed.
- Where are your munchkins going to school?
- You little devil!
- You little skunk!
- When they're young they tread on your toes; but they'll tread on your heart when they grow old.
- God protects the children, the innocent, and fools.
- Children and fools tell the truth.
- Hello there, whistle britches! (said to a younger child)
- Every mother's child is beautiful to her.
- He's a little tow headed thing. (blonde-white hair)
- Children can see what they cannot put into words.
- Blessed is the man whose quiver is full of children.
- Children are a blessing from the Lord, but sometimes I wish I hadn't been so blessed!
- I hope when you grow up and get married, your children treat you just like you have treated me. (said by a parent to an unruly child)

- I hope when you grow up and have children, they act just like you do and you get a dose of your own medicine. (said by a parent to an unruly child)
- You little booger!
- You little heathern! You little monkey!
- Don't cry honey child... (term of endearment; also said as "honey chile")
- You little yerker! (spoken to a misbehaving child)

choices
- It's up to you. (You decide.)
- I chased a squirrel down the wrong path. (made a bad choice)
- That's a real Hobson's choice. (if you want something, make it happen) or (there is no other alternative)

clean
- Clean your plate. (eat it all)
- He's as clean as a whistle. (very clean; nothing incriminating in his past)
- He has a clean bill of health. (very healthy)
- I'm making a clean break. (leaving something/someone behind and starting afresh without looking back)
- Our team made a clean sweep! (won everything)
- Cleanliness is next to godliness.
- We've got this place spick and span. (very clean)
- That's as clean as a hound's tooth. (very clean)
- He cleaned out his wallet. (spent all his money)

clear
- You can see spang through that t-shirt when it gets wet!
- It's as plain as the nose on your face. (obvious)
- Your idea is about as clear as mud. (totally unclear)
- Your meaning is perfectly clear. (understandable)
- She has such a clear complexion. (blemish free skin)
- It's a clear day. (fair weather)
- I'll clear the way for you. (remove any hindrances)
- Clear the table. (clean up after a meal)
- Clear your mind. (calm down; stop worrying)

clock
- Even a broken clock is on time twice a day! (Everyone is right occasionally.)
- He's watching the clock. (waiting for time to quit)
- She's on the clock. (working)
- He clocked out a long time ago. (left emotionally, or left work)

closet
- Look in the closnet.
- I got a new shift robe.
- I hid it in the chiffarobe.
- Your coat is in the wardrobe.
- Don't you wonder what skeletons are in his closet? (secrets)
- Everybody's got something in their closet they're trying to forget. (past hurts)
- He came out of the closet. (publicly announced being homosexual)
- I'd like to clean out her closet! (expose things she has hidden)

- My closet looks like the Good Will store. (too many clothes; old clothes)
- Stick it in the closet, lock the door, and throw away the key. (a significant event that needs to be covered up; never reveal information you have about a particular person or event)

clothes
- I've got to put my glad rags on. (dress up)
- I always get my sister's cast offs. (outgrown clothing)
- I grew up in hand me downs. (garments passed from an older sibling to a younger)
- I've got to strip. (Change clothes.)
- I like my new duds.

cloud/cloudy
- She's on cloud nine. (very happy)
- Every cloud has a silver lining. (look for the good in a bad situation)
- She believes in cotton candy clouds. (gullible)
- Your meaning is a little cloudy. (unclear)
- If the water is cloudy, don't drink it! (impurities in it)

clumsy
- He's like a bull in a China shop.
- Butterfingers!
- Watch out! Bush hog coming through.
- She's all thumbs.
- He's like a porcupine in a balloon shop.
- You're stomping around like a mule in a barn stall.
- He has two left feet.

coal
- He's working at the coal face. (where the real job is done – not in an office.
- She was raked over the coals. (reprimanded by a boss)
- Do you really want to rake over old coals? (bring up the past and cause trouble)

coffee
- I need a cup of Joe.
- Pass the java.
- That coffee is strong enough to get up and walk!

coiled
- That snake is quiled up and ready to strike.
- Hand me that quile of rope.

cold
- I feel like I'm thawing out of the deep freeze.
- A cold wind rode down from the North.
- I'm colder than a well digger's behind on a snowy day.
- It's colder than a well digger's butt on Christmas morning.
- I'm colder than kraut!
- I'm colder than a witch's chest in a brass bra.
- It was so cold it was like sliding naked down an icicle.
- It's cold enough to freeze a brass monkey to death.
- The cold cut through me like a knife.
- She's as cold as ice. (unemotional; unfeeling)
- It's cold enough to hang hog meat in here. (as cold as a butcher's refrigerator)

cologne
- Give me some of that good smellum stuff.
- I've run out of my smell good.
- Mmmm. Me smellum good!
- I need some man smelling stuff.

comb
- I went over it with a fine tooth comb. (took great pains to discover any errors or flaws)
- Comb those rats out of your head! (Get the tangles out of your hair!)
- I've been combing the woods looking for you. (searching for)
- I'd like to introduce that child to a comb!
- Her head looks like it's never seen a comb in her life. (matted, messy, nasty, or unkempt hair)

commotion
- Who started this big rumpus?
- A brawl broke out in the bar.
- Who started this ruckus?
- Stop that racket! (noise)
- What is this shenanigan?
- He started a bru-ha-ha.
- The hooligans are at it again.

communicate/communication
- Give me a ring. (call)
- Drop me a line. (write
- He sent word that he'd be here soon. (letter; message)

company
- Company's a comin'! (visitors are on the way)
- Come and keep me company. (pay a social visit)

- She's runnin' with bad company. (people who will get her in trouble)
- You are known by the company you keep. (Your reputation will be affected by the reputation of those you spend time with.)

comparison
- That's comparing apples to apples. (similar things)
- You can't compare apples to oranges. (unrelated things)
- He can't hold a candle to his dad. (not held in the same esteem)
- That boy doesn't know his head from a hole in the ground!
- Some people can't tell the difference between skunk weed and cabbage.

compassion
- Have compassion on one another. (be kind)
- Have you no compassion for their plight? (sympathize with someone during a difficult time)
- He has a heart of compassion. (helps the needy)
- Why is it that some people have no compassion for anyone else, but think they're entitled to get it when it's their turn to need it?

complete
- He's moved out – lock, stock, and barrel. (entirely)
- I'll take the whole kit and kaboodle. (the whole thing)
- I stayed for the whole shebang. (event)
- That new dress comes with bag and baggage. (accessories)
- Get it done! (finish a task)
- Get 'er done! (win a game)

complexion
- Her skin is as clear as a baby's hide. (blemish free)
- Her skin is as soft as a baby's behind. (youthful)
- Her face is as smooth as a baby's bottom. (clear)
- Her skin is as rough as sandpaper.

complicated
- Does she come with instructions?
- Well, you're durned if you do and durned if you don't. So what is a feller to do?
- It says to put the thingamabob in the whatchamacallit, but there are no pictures included.
- It's more than just a matter of want to.
- That's just adding fuel to the fire.

compliments
- Give my compliments to your mother and father. (greetings)
- You're as sweet as blackberry pie.
- You're as sweet as molasses.
- This cake would melt in your mouth.
- She's put together like a brick house.
- Your hair is soft as silk.
- He/she's hot.
- That's good enough to write home about! (delicious)
- My compliments to the chef! (great food)
- You're as cute as a bug's ear.
- Did it hurt when you fell from heaven?
- That's a left handed compliment. (a statement that on the surface sounds like a compliment, but was really an insult)
- My compliments to your folks. (greetings)

comprehend (or lack of comprehension)
- I can't wrap my head around it.
- I don't get it. (failure to understand)
- My head is too thick. This math is not sinking in.
- Gotcha!
- That doesn't make a lick of sense to me.

confess
- I need to get something off my chest.
- It will eat him up inside until he tells it all.
- You need to own up to the truth.
- He needs to take responsibility.
- You'll feel better when you let it out.
- I need to make a clean breast of it.

confidence
- She has no faith in herself.
- He knows what he's about.
- She lacks confidence.
- He's confident he can handle it. (take care of a task)
- She has no confidence in him. (doubts his abilities)

conflict
- You'd better not throw in with that bunch!
- Which side are you on?
- Mind your own bees wax.
- Mind your own business.
- They've stirred up a mess like a sack full of bobcats.
- I'm going to keep my oar out of the water.
- Keep your chickens at home.
- Keep your opinion to yourself or you'll be square dab in the middle of the mess.

confused/confusing
- I can't make heads or tails of it.
- I'm as confused as the kid who dropped his gum in the chicken lot! (gum and chicken droppings look similar in the dirt)
- She doesn't know a diaper from a dishrag.
- She acts addle pated.
- I have no idée what you're talking about.
- I'm bumfuzzled about the whole thing.
- I can get no sense out of it.
- That was a bewildering comment!
- I am befuddled as to what to do.
- I feel like I'm cruising on the big ship of fools.
- I can't straighten it out in my mind.
- Excuse me. I'm discombobulated at the moment. (distracted; confused about something I'm supposed to be doing at this moment; lost my train of thought)
- I can't wrap my head around it.
- I'm feeling foggy headed.
- It looks like a bird's leg in an oatmeal box to me.
- Her head stays in the clouds.
- It has got me stumped!
- I'm losing my marbles.
- She's running around like a chicken with its head cut off!
- You can't see the forest for the trees!
- It makes no sense to me.
- Thinking about it makes my head swim.
- I can't think straight.
- Her thoughts were muddied. (unclear)

- Her mind was muddied. (unclear; troubled)

consequences
- Time to face the music.
- You reap what you sew.
- Let the punishment fit the crime.

considering
- I'm contemplating my next step.
- I'm trying it on for size.
- I'm thinking about changing my ways.
- She's studying on it.
- Are you figuring on going?
- I will, if I take a mind to.
- I've been thinking on it.
- That would give a fellow pause. (a reason to stop and think carefully)
- I'm pondering the idea.
- I'm weighing it out in my mind.
- I'm looking at the pros and cons.
- Should I or should I not?
- I'm negotiating it in my brain. (trying to discover the best idea or the best plan of action)

constipated
- My pipes are clogged.
- If I don't go soon, my head is going to pop off.
- I'm backed up.
- My sewer is backed up.
- I feel like I've got some blockage in my gut.
- I need a good dose of working medicine.
- I'm all bound up.

contempt
- I wouldn't spit on him if he was on fire.
- Stick that in your pipe and smoke it!
- Take this job and shove it!
- I wouldn't help him if he was the last man on earth.

continually
- I've had this job forever and a day.
- She is with her children twenty-four /seven.
- Every day and all the time you'll find me at home.
- It's the same old, same old.
- I feel like I'm living in groundhog day.

control
- She took the bull by the horns.
- Don't worry. I've got the situation under control.
- He's a control freak.
- She has a Jezebel spirit.
- It's time for me to put my foot down!
- You'd better get control over that child while you can!

convenient
- That might come in handy to use again. (useful)
- The store across the street is right handy. (useful)
- It's as easy as one, two, three.
- It's as easy as pie.
- That'll do just fine.
- That's as handy as pockets on a shirt.
- That's as handy as a shirt full of pockets.

convince/convinced
- You'll have to do more than that to convince me.
- I was taken with the idea.

- The more I thought about it, the more sense it made.
- I'm not convinced, but I'm considering it.

cook
- You have cooked your own goose. (got yourself in trouble)
- Too many cooks spoil the pot. (too many opinions are not helpful)
- Hey! What's cookin'? (What's going on?)
- You're going to have to make friends with the cook. (said to someone who receives a very small portion of food at a restaurant or in someone's home)

coon
- I haven't seen you in a coon's age! (long time)
- The miners had to coon walk out after the rock fall. (feel their way along the tracks back to the opening of the coal mine)
- There he sat, like a coon on a log! (smug)
- They are as happy as two coons. (content with each other)

cooperate
- You'd better get yourself in gear.
- It takes a team to win a boat race.
- One for all and all for one.
- Trying to get them to cooperate was like trying to herd cats!

correct
- You are right on.
- You've got it down pat.

cough
- I thought he was going to cough up a lung.
- I coughed up an ovary

- She coughed her head off.
- You sound like a frog croaking.
- Cough it up! (pay up; confess; tell all)

country (rural)
- That boy is as country as cornbread!
- That girl is as country as gravy and biscuits.
- He's plain country.
- She's countrified.
- He's as country as whang!
- You can take the girl/boy out of the country but you can't take the country out of the girl/boy.
- I enjoy his country ways. (simple)
- This country mouse does not belong in the city.
- He's a big Goober. (country boy)
- He's/She's a hick. (country girl/boy)
- I'm in need of a good dose of country! (need a vacation)

courage
- He shows courage in the face of danger. (bravery)
- Take courage. (brace yourself for what you must face)
- Why don't you grow a backbone? (develop courage)

court
- I'd like to court your daughter. (date)
- It's a kangaroo court. (not official, no power to render a valid decision)
- Looks like we'll have to take that to court. (can't reach a decision)
- I'll see you in court. (ready to take legal action)

cover
- It's cold in here. You may need some more kivver. (bedding)
- Kivver me up, please. (tuck me in)
- He reads the Bible kiver to kiver oncet a year. (completely)
- Don't blow my cover. (false identity)
- He was born on the wrong side of the cover. (illegitimate)

cow
- Don't have a cow! (don't get upset)
- That cow will have to lick her calf twice! (do something again)
- That is a muley cow. (cow with horns)
- That's my cash cow. (money maker)
- Why buy the cow when you can get the milk for free? (refers to not marrying a promiscuous girl)
- You'll be waiting 'til the cows come home. (a long time)
- He's cow towed. (dominated by a female)
- Everything that comes out of a cow ain't milk!
- Girls who are too particular in finding a boyfriend are like the little butterflies who flit past all the pretty flowers and then land on a cow pie.
- Don't step in the cow pies. (cow poop)

coward
- You're a yellow bellied sap sucker!
- You lily livered coward!
- He's a yellow bellied coward!
- He's afraid of his own shadow.

- If trouble comes, she'll be the one who has to protect him!
- He's got a yellow streak right down his back.
- She's scared of every little thing

crazy
- He's as crazy as a bird in a room full of cats. (extremely nervous)
- He went berserk. (out of control angry)
- He's crazy like a fox. (sly)
- She's as crazy as a March hare.
- He's as crazy as a Mad Hatter.
- You're a nut.
- She has bats in her belfry.
- He's crazy as a bess bug.
- She's crazy as a loon!
- He's coo-coo.
- She's caught in a web of thoughts.
- He's nuttier than a fruit cake.
- The whole world has gone mad.
- You've gone off the deep end.
- His whole world is topsy turvey.
- You crazy Americans! You boil your tea to make it hot, then you put it in ice to make it cold. You put lemon in it to make it sour, and then put sugar in it to make it sweet!

creek
- He split the creek dry. (run or ride very quickly up the creek)
- We are up the creek without a paddle. (in trouble)
- Stay out of the creek! (avoid trouble)

- There's a crick running past their cabin.

critical/criticizing
- He was billyfying her.
- She was vilifying him.
- If you can't say something good, don't say anything at all.
- She has a critical spirit.
- He never sees anything right with the world.
- He was putting her down.
- He's an armchair critic.
- Stop bad mouthing her!

crooked
- That is the crookedest road I ever saw. (curvy)
- He's as crooked as a dog's hind leg. (dishonest)
- That picture is sigoggled. (uneven)
- He hung the curtain sigoggledy. (uneven)
- He is sigoogled. (cross-eyed)
- He is crooked. (dishonest in business; has the law bought off)
- Her teeth are crooked. (uneven)
- He had a crooked cat that caught a crooked mouse and they all lived together in a crooked little house. (refers to someone deceitful)
- That road is so crooked, you could meet yourself coming and going!
- That sign is hanging cock eyed.

crowded
- People were packed in the church like sardines.
- The theater was jam packed full.
- There wasn't room to turn around in.

- I couldn't breathe in there, it was so tight.

cry/cried/crying
- Cry baby!
- Bawl baby!
- Please stop bawling.
- There's no use crying over spilt milk! (what's done is done)
- She's cried "wolf" once too often. (insincerely needed help)
- She bawled like a baby.
- Go ahead and cry! The more you cry, the less you pee.
- You better stop that crying before I give you something to cry about!
- I cried myself to sleep.
- She cried until she was blue in the face.
- Crying does a body good every once in a while.
- She cried buckets of tears over him.
- The baby cried like a dying panther.
- Now, that would be a crying shame! (unfortunate)
- Why don't you cry me a river?
- I couldn't turn the tears off.
- I started crying and it was like a dam let loose.
- You are whining like a whipped pup.
- Cry me a hand full why don't you, and see if I care!
- If you cry me a river, I'll build you a bridge.
- She'll be dashing the tears away.
- She's squawling like a newborn baby.
- She's been on a crying jag. (crying over a period of days)

- She's crying crocodile tears. (insincere)
- She can cry at the drop of a hat! (easily)
- She can cry at the drop of a handkerchief! (easily)

cucumber
- He's as cool as a cucumber.
- She's as calm as a cucumber.
- I guess she'll be eating cucumber sandwiches. (moving up in society)

curvy
- That road is a real stomach churner.
- That is a snaky road.
- You can meet your own tail lights going down that road.

cuss (often used instead of the word curse)
- He's an ornery old cuss!
- She'll cuss you out and call you everything but a white child!
- Excuse my French.
- He was cussing a blue streak.
- He was cussing like a sailor.
- She was cussing up a storm!

cute
- That baby is as cute as a button.
- She's too cute for words.
- He's so cute I could sop him up with a biscuit! (refers to soaking bread in gravy and eating it)
- Pretty as a picture, busy as a bee,
  she's the cutest little thing,
  that you ever did see!
- You are not being cute. (clever comments that are inappropriate in the setting)

- Cute – very cute! (said in response to a smart aleck comment)

D

dance
- You've got to dance with the one who brung you. (be responsible for your choices)
- You don't have to dance with the devil. (You don't have to choose to do wrong.)
- Are you going to the frolick? (social dance)
- They are frolicking to the music.
- They are having a hoe down.
- She can really cut a rug!
- She's strutting herself around all over the floor!
- He can cut a jig!
- She was really puttin' on a show. (drawing attention to herself)
- He was really giving them a show. (using fancy dance moves)
- We are going out high stepping.
- Would you like to trip the light fantastic?
- She loves to kick up her heels.
- He's as loose as a long necked goose. (limber dance moves)

dandy
- She's a dandy. (a very good person)
- He's a dandy. (feminine acting)
- That's a dandy dog you've got there. (a fine specimen)
- He acts like a dandy. (fussy/fussbudget; homosexual)

danger
- Danger! Danger! Danger, Will Robinson!
- There's a bad moon rising.
- There's no danger in just looking.
- You're in danger of making him fall in love with you.
- She's drawn to danger like a hog to slop.

dare
- How dare you speak to me that way! (outrage)
- She's daresome to go against anything he says. (afraid; doesn't want to deal with the consequences)
- I dare you to walk up to him and say hello.
- I double dog dare you! (really dare you)
- I triple dog dare you! (really, really dare you)
- I dare say it was so. (true)

dark
- It was as dark as a moonless night.
- It was as dark as the grave.
- It was as dark as a starless night.
- The room was pitch black.
- He's in a dark mood. (sullen; angry; troubled)
- It was so dark you couldn't see a hand in front of your face.
- It was pitch dark outside.
- It was so dark you couldn't see the nose on your face.
- It was dark as a dungeon.
- His humor is a little dark. (macabre)
- Don't let anger take you to the dark side. (cause bitterness to take root in your heart and grow there)
- His people are dark complected. (skin color)

dash
- I need to dash out to the store for a minute. (quick trip
- This soup needs a dash of salt. (small amount)
- It's a dash to the finish line. (burst of speed)

dating
- They are sweethearts.
- They are courting.
- They are sparking.
- They've found their split apart.
- They are canoodling.
- They've found their better half.
- They claim each other.
- They are exclusive.
- They are going together.
- They are committed.
- They are testing the waters.
- They're a perfect fit.
- They are riding out together.
- He's out slue footing. (looking for a date)
- They've found their destiny.
- They are real fond of each other.
- They are made for each other.
- They are a match made in Heaven.
- I'm going to see a man about a dog.
- They are stepping out together.
- They are walking out together.
- They are going up to watch a double feature.
- They will soon be wearing the Mr. and Mrs.

dawn
- When the sunball peeks over the mountain, you should have your day well under way.
- You need to go out about smoky daylight.
- Just before daylight is the time I sleep best.
- Just before bird song is the quietest time of morning.
- He gets up at the butt crack of dawn.
- When the sun breaks over the mountains, it's time to be up and attending to chores.
- I've got to get up in the morning at day bust.

dead/death
- When the Weeper comes, you have to go. (the death angel)
- Speak kindly of the dead.
- He went skudoodle.
- She's gone to glory.
- He is reaping his reward.
- She passed off recently.
- God rest her soul.
- She's gone home.
- He kicked the bucket.
- Speak no ill of the dead.
- She croaked.
- Do not speak ill of the dead.
- May the dead rest in peace.
- He's pushing up daisies.
- She checked out a week ago.
- He's six foot under.
- He's finished for good.

- She passed away
- He bit the dust.
- Dead men tell no lies.
- He gave up the ghost.
- Old habits die hard.
- She up and died.
- She's gone on.
- She's gone on to glory.
- God rest his soul.
- He's gone on to be with the Lord.
- That cat is as dead as a door knob.
- You are dead meat! (in serious trouble)
- He's in bed, dead to the world. (fast asleep)
- He's deader than a doorknob.
- You look like death warmed over. (very sick)
- Dead men can't defend themselves.
- He's a dead duck! (going to be in trouble)
- I did my dead level best. (tried as hard as I could)
- My cell phone is as dead as a door nail. (useless)
- That project is dead in the water. (not going anywhere)
- She's dead from the neck up. (not smart)
- She fainted dead away. (out cold)
- The air was as still as death. (silent; no breeze)
- Her mood was like death. (solemn; serious)
- His love had her in a death grip. (abusive relationship)
- That hair style has been done to death. (too frequently)

- He's gone to meet his Maker.
- He's on his last legs. (almost dead.
- This spring, the old folks have been dropping like flies. (frequent; numerous deaths)
- She passed on a couple of months ago.
- He's gone home to be with the Lord.
- He is reaping his reward.
- He has changed his permanent address.
- He stripped out and left us.
- They're dead even. (tied)
- You'll catch your death! (dress for bad weather or you'll die of pneumonia)
- Only two things are certain in this life – death and taxes.
- Death comes to us all.
- Death is the great equalizer.
- I don't wish death on anyone… but… (said about someone you really don't like or who has treated you horribly)

deaf
- He's a deaf as a post!
- She's as deaf as a rock!
- She's deaf and dumb. (mute)
- He's deef.
- He's only deaf when it suits him. (selective hearing)

deceitful/deceiving
- He was gas lighting her.
- she was deliberately misleading him.
- He was leading her down the wrong path.

- He's always trying to use that hocus pocus to trick someone.
- All that glitters is not gold.
- She really pulled the wool over his eyes!

decided/decision/decisive
- His fate is decided.
- Case closed.
- I took a notion to bake an apple pie.
- You can't straddle the fence forever. (You must decide.)
- It is a cut and dried case.
- It is a done deal.
- I've made up my mind.
- I've got a mind to write him a letter.
- The last curtain call is over.
- Consider your options.
- Don't be hasty.
- I believe I will… (made a decision in favor of)
- The die is cast. (things are already in motion that can't be changed)
- Shake the dust off your feet and move on. (move forward without regrets)
- Don't look back. (consider future goals instead of past failures)
- If you are bound and determined to do it, go right ahead and you'll reap the whirlwind! (said when a person is making a bad decision against advice)
- I'm agreeable. (I agree with a major decision.)
- They turned me plumb against it. (pointed out the negativities)

- Hang 'em high and be done with it.
- Settle on an answer before you act.
- What's the worst that can happen? If it should, can you live with it? (advice to someone making a decision)
- Jump on in, feet first. (be fully committed)
- He went into it with his eyes open. (knew there would be difficulties)
- Don't buy a pig in a poke. (don't buy what you can't see)
- Don't make rash decisions. (hasty, emotional decisions that may not be wise)
- Poop or get off the pot. (make up your mind)
- Fish or cut bait. (make a decision; stop flirting with someone if you have no intention of forming a relationship)

deeds
- Let your good deeds go unspoken.
- Actions speak louder than words.
- The deeds of the wicked are oft done in darkness.
- A good deed is never lost.

deep
- She is really deep. (has much understanding; thinks philosophically or spiritually)
- Still waters run deep. (Quiet people may have great emotions beneath the surface.)
- You can't tell how deep a river is until you try to cross. (Looks can be deceiving.)
- He has a deep voice. (sings bass)
- There's a deep valley between them. (serious difference of opinion)

defeat/defeated
- I will not be cow tailed. (come in last)
- I won't give in.
- I'm done in.
- I won't go down without a fight!
- He went down swinging! (fighting until the end)
- He went down like a lead balloon. (suddenly; hard)
- I've hit rock bottom.
- There's nowhere to go from here but up!

defensive
- You have a chip on your shoulder the size of a house.
- She wears her feelings on her shoulders.
- He always expects a put down.
- He stays on the defensive. (expects negative things)

definitely
- Absolutely! You are more than welcome to come.
- Absotively posolutely! I will go with you.
- Without a doubt it happened just that way.
- Undoubtedly, he will be there.
- For sure and certain! I'll be there if it doesn't rain.

deflated (ego)
- Somebody let the air out of his tires.
- He got shot down.
- She put him in his place.
- She got brought up short.
- He put her back on the shelf.
- It's about time he got brought down to size.
- She popped his balloon.
- He got brought down a notch or two.
- He popped her bubble.

- It's about time somebody put him in his place.

delicious
- It was scrumdiddlyicious!
- Now that's a tasty morsel!
- Her meatloaf is delicioso!
- The salad is delectable.
- This meal is fit for a king!
- This cheesecake is absolute perfection.
- I could eat this three meals a day!
- That tastes so good, you can't sit still and eat it!
- This is so good, I think I'll marry the cook if she'll have me. (a compliment to the hostess)

dependable
- She has a steady hand.
- He's like clockwork.
- You can count on him.
- You can set your clock by him.
- With her in charge, you don't have to give it a second thought.

depressed
- She's in a funk.
- He's in a dark place.
- Don't despair.
- She's got the blues.
- She is downhearted.
- He's a gloomy Gus.
- He's down in the mouth.
- He's down in the mully grubs.
- She's got the can't help its.

- He's got that hang dog look.
- I've got a bad case of the "can't help myselfs."
- I'd be downright disheartened.
- She has a dark and gloomy spirit.
- She's caught in the Doldrums. (not going anywhere – stuck in a situation she doesn't want to be in)
- Gloom and doom. Gloom and doom is all she ever talks about.

desert
- After supper, I like a bite of sweetening.
- Stick your finger in my coffee and sweeten it up.
- You're all the desert I need.

desire/desiring
- I've been hankering for a mess of fried chicken.
- She is pining away over him.
- I'd give my eye teeth for a good cold drink of water right now.
- I'd give my right arm if I could take back what I said.
- I'm hungry for a new car.
- I'm longing for the day when I see him again.
- I'm yearning for the sight of home.
- I'm craving a day in the sunshine.
- You could do it if you had a mind to.

destroyed
- It was blown to smithereens.
- It looks like a wrecking crew has been here.
- I've got to do some chores. My house is destroyed!
- Your room is in complete shambles!

desert
- After supper, I like a bite of sweetening.

- Stick your finger in my coffee and sweeten it up.
- You're all the desert I need.
- Desert is always the best part of a meal.
- I'm saving room for desert.

determination
- Do or die.
- I'll do it or die trying.
- I'm going strong.
- I mean business!
- Pull yourself up by your bootstraps.
- I'll do it if it hair lips the governor.
- I'll do it if it hair lips Rachel.
- You just hide and watch, and see if I don't do it!
- I won't take no for an answer.
- You'll just have to buckle down and do it!
- He's hell bent for certain.
- Where there's a will there's a way.
- What part of "NO" don't you understand?
- Don't try to stop me. I'm bound and determined!
- I'll get it done if I have to move heaven and Earth.
- I'll be there, come hell or high water.
- You couldn't run him off with a stick. (deter a suitor)

devil
- The devil you know is better than the devil you don't.
- You little devil! (mean child)
- That's such a mess the devil wouldn't have it! (big mess)
- He likes to devil people. (tease)
- Old slue foot is always lurking about.
- The serpent deceived the children of Eden.

- Speak of the devil and there he is!
- The old dragon is always on the prowl.
- The enemy of my soul tempts me.
- Even the devil got his start as an angel. (Some people start out good and end up evil.)
- The evil one is working overtime in this day and hour.

diamond
- He's a diamond in the rough.
- Her eyes sparkle like diamonds.
- Diamonds are a girl's best friends.
- It's not official 'til I'm wearin' the diamond. (engagement)

diarrhea
- He's got the runs.
- She's got the trots.
- He's got the squirts.
- She's got the Johnny trots.
- She has the back door trots.

dickens
- He pinched the dickens out of her.
- What in the dickens is going on here?
- What a little dickens that one is! (mean child)
- If I don't get this job done, the boss will give me the dickens when he sees it undone. (get reprimanded)
- You scared the dickens out of me!

different/differences
- One turns one way, one turns t'other.
- They are as different as night and day.
- They couldn't be more polar opposite.
- We've had a difference of opinion. (quarrel)

- What difference does it make? (irrelevant)
- They've put aside their differences. (come to an agreement)
- That's a different kettle of fish! (different story than what I've been told)
- There goes a horse of a different color! (unique)

difficult/difficulty
- That's a tall order to fill.
- Life gets tegious. (tough; tedious)
- That's a long row to hoe!
- You are walking on thin ice.
- His back is against the wall.
- That's just the nature of the beast.
- I've painted myself into the corner.
- Teenagers are hard to live with.
- It's an uphill battle.
- It's like pulling teeth.
- That will be a tough time.
- That's like trying to nail Jell-O to a tree.
- She's a little fussbudget! (difficult to please)
- You are pushing my buttons. (deliberately trying to annoy)
- If it's not one thing, it's another! (a succession of difficult situations)
- We'll have to fight tooth and nail.
- The news of his death sure didn't go down easy.

dig
- You're trying to dig yourself out of a hole.
- Nice digs! (dwelling place)
- Dig a little deeper. (try harder)

- Reach into your pocket and dig a little deeper. (give more to a charity)

direct
- Don't beat around the bush.
- Get to the point.
- Point blank, tell me the truth.
- Don't sugar coat it.
- Don't mince words.

direction/directions
- He was standing smack dab in the middle of the road.
- It's about a mile as the crow flies.
- She couldn't find her way out of a paper bag.
- My folks live up the creek.
- When I got married, I moved down the creek.
- My friend lives over yonder.
- Over hyander is where we are going to put the barn.
- They live at the head of the holler.
- You'll find it just around the corner.
- Head over the hill. (go downhill)
- It's about a country mile. (long)
- You will come to a little snake in the road... (curve)
- There's an old mountain goat way to get there, but I'd say the path is grown over and might be hard to find. (a trail that hasn't been used in a long time)

dirty
- Your room looks like a pig's pen!
- You look like you've been drug up a stove pipe.
- You couldn't be dirtier if you'd been sucking a sow!

- That child goes around like a ragamuffin.
- She looks like an orphan child.
- What pig pen were you playing in?
- Behind your ears are so dirty, you could plant a garden back there.
- You're so dirty a fly would be ashamed to light on you.
- You could plant potatoes between those dirty toes.
- Your room looks like it's been hit by a cyclone.
- You're as nasty as a dumpster.
- What did you do – let a pig loose in there?
- That's plumb cyarny.
- You look like you've been wallowing in the pig pen.

disagreeable/disagreement
- He's an ornery old coot!
- And just suppose I take a notion not to?
- Quit beating around the bush.
- Don't air your dirty laundry in public.
- You are trying me.
- You are testing my patience.
- Get to the point.
- Do you want to bury the hatchet?
- You are always digging up bones. Everyone has a few skeletons in their closet. You'd better think twice if you don't want me to unlock your closet door.
- If you were to shake your family tree, it's untelling what might fall out.
- I bend over backwards to try and please you, but you can't be pleased.
- I didn't open my mouth against him.

- That goes against the grain!
- You are throwing yourself away.
- I don't think so! (I disagree.)

disappointment
- Her hopes were dashed.
- She was let down.
- It was no big deal.
- Things could've been better.
- Not so much. (in response to the question, "How do you like _____?" could apply to anything)
- It sure wasn't all it was cracked up to be.
- People went on and on about it, but I didn't think it was that great. (praised it)
- Try not to break down. (cry because of frustration)
- Been there, done that, never want to do it again!
- Let's don't and say we did!
- I've had better.
- I'm sorry it rained on your parade.
- All the air went out of his tires.

disastrous event (something gone wrong)
- Well, this is a pretty piece of business.
- Isn't this a pretty kettle of fish you've gotten us into?
- This is a fine mess we're in!
- This is a pretty pickle we're in.
- This is a quanundrum.
- That sure followed Murphy's Law. (whatever can go wrong will go wrong)

disbelief
- You don't say!

- Upon my honor!
- I pawn my honor!
- Surely not.
- My word!
- My foot!
- Tell me it isn't so!
- Oh, sure! (said in a negative tone)
- If I believed that you'd try to sell me swampland.
- I'm not falling for that!
- Crymanently!
- Crymanies! Do you think I'm that dumb?

discourage
- She poured cold water on his idea.
- You sure put the dampers on me!
- She certainly knocked the wind out of his sails!
- He put the kibosh on the project idea.

discover/discovered
- She found out the truth.
- I've finally seen through him.
- She's been uncovered.
- The jig is up.
- He's been found out.
- He's been caught on to.
- We need to get to the bottom of it.

disgusting
- That is double gross!
- You make me want to vomit!
- Gag a maggot.
- That would make a dog puke.

dish
- She's quite a dish. (pretty woman)
- You can dish it out, but you can't take it. (teasing; criticism)
- Don't dish it out if you can't take it. (don't be critical if you don't want to be criticized)
- What's the latest dish? (gossip; news)

dishonest
- That man is as crooked as a dog's hind leg!
- He's about as slippery as a greased dog.
- He's as slippery as a greased pig.
- She's as crooked as a creek bed.
- You're lower than a snake's belly in a wagon rut.
- I wouldn't trust her any further than I could throw her.
- You're as crooked as an oak tree.
- You're a goose egg.
- He's so crooked, you'll have to screw him in the ground when he dies.
- You lie like a rug!
- He was crooked from the beginning.
- He crooked me right out of my land!
- He's about as straight as a broken stick.
- You lie like Pinocchio.
- That boy is as crooked as a barrel of fish hooks!

displaced
- He was like poop in a punch bowl.
- She was a fish out of water.
- I felt like a bull in a china shop.
- He's like a fish in a pickle dish.

disrespect
- Don't sass me.
- No back talking.
- Don't disrespect me.

disturbance
- It caused quite a ruckus.
- What a racket! (lots of noise)
- What's the commotion?

dive
- He busted the swimming hole wide open. (verb form)
- What a dive! (unpleasant place to live or work)
- That was his swan dive. (last performance)
- He moved into some dive in the city. (apartment)

divorce
- Their marriage fell apart.
- They went under.
- Their marriage broke apart.
- They've dissolved their ties.
- They've split up.
- They've broken up.
- Their walls have broken down.
- There's a Jack for every Jenny, and your first one was a Jack ass.
- I'm getting rid of that man. He don't put no pork chops on my table. (doesn't provide for me)
- He hung her out to dry. (filed for divorce)

dizzy
- She's a dizzy dame. (scatterbrained)
- I'm feeling a little swirly jiggy.

- I'm as dizzy as a three legged dog chasing his own tail.
- You are dizzy. (silly)
- My head feels like a whirly gig.
- The ground is about to come up and smack me in the face.

do/doing
- They are having a big to do this week-end. (party)
- If you keep doing what you're doing, you'll keep getting what you got.
- How do you like my new do? (hair style)
- It was all I could do not to! (forced myself not to do something I shouldn't do)

doctor
- What's up doc?
- He's a life saver!
- That doctor's a quack.
- He's a regular horse doctor.
- That leech will run all kind of tests on you.
- He's a blood sucker!
- That doctor is knife happy. (frequently recommends surgery)
- I wouldn't take a good dog to that doctor.
- You know what they say about doctors. They bury their mistakes and the ones that survive live to sing their praises.
- The love doctor is in.
- Doctor, lawyer, Indian chief. You cannot have all leaders without some followers.

dog
- A dog is man's best friend.
- He's a regular water dog. (loves water sports)
- You can't turn a good dog down. (accept something given for free; a good deal)
- Unconditional love is spelled D - O - G!
- He took off like a scalded dog. (fast)
- You'd give a dog a bad name! (guilty by association)
- He walks around like a blind dog in a meat house. (unaware)
- He's a dirty dog. (untrustworthy)
- My dogs are barking. (feet are tired)
- Every dog has its day. (everyone gets a chance to succeed)
- The sun doesn't shine on the same dog's butt every day. (popularity doesn't last forever)
- You can't teach an old dog new tricks. (can't change old people or old ways easily)
- He's an egg sucking dog! (worthless)
- Call your dogs off! (someone sent to harass)
- It is a dog eat dog world. (take care of yourself)
- It's a dog's life. (difficult)
- It's raining cats and dogs! (pouring)
- Let sleeping dogs lie. (Don't agitate an already troublesome situation. Leave well enough alone.)
- That is a dog eared book. (worn; well read)
- He's a lap dog. (eager to please; wants attention; a favorite)
- Barking dogs seldom bite.
- If you lie down with dogs, you'll get up with fleas.

- You can't stick an old dog's head on a pup. (applies to pups and people – the young have to have time to learn what the old already know)
- He'd give a good dog a bad name. (ruin someone's reputation)
- He ran like a scalded dog! (very fast)
- You are whining like a whipped pup!
- You can't turn a good dog down.
- She's puttin' on the dog. (showing off; acting superior)
- I was sicker than a dog! (very sick; nauseated)

doll
- He wobbles around like a bobble-headed doll.
- She's a doll. (good person)
- The only date he can get is with an inflatable doll.
- They live in a doll house. (cute; small)

doomed
- Those who do not learn from history are doomed to repeat it.
- I'm doomed if I do, and doomed if I don't.

dominate/dominated
- He's hen pecked. (dominated by a wife)
- He's cow towed. (told what to do)
- He bows and scrapes to her whims. (tries to please)
- He is hag ridden. (dominated by a female)
- I've got him by the scruff of the neck. (completely control)
- He needs to cut the apron strings. (dominated by a mother)
- She wears the pants in her family.
- She wears the trousers in her family.

- When they get up of a morning, she puts the britches on. (implies role reversal of authority in man and wife)

dope
- Have you heard the latest dope? (gossip)
- He's hooked on dope. (prescription drugs)
- We don't use none of that dope on our garden. (chemicals; manmade fertilizer)
- He's a real dope. (stupid; gullible)

doubt
- It's doubtful that she'll even remember that she promised to do it, much less get it done.
- I don't reckon he will. (doubt of someone doing something)
- That will happen when pigs fly!
- Just hid and watch. That won't last two minutes!

down
- She's down in the mouth. (sad)
- He's down and out. (going through a hard time)
- She's down in the dumps. (sad)
- We're down to the wire. (almost at a deadline)
- She is a down to earth kind of girl. (simple, wholesome)

drain
- Dreen that glass of milk.
- I'm dreening my oil pan.
- Don't let it go down the dreen pipe.
- I am drained. (tired)
- All my money went down the drain. (lost)
- That relationship is down the drain. (over)

- I feel like someone pulled a stopper out of the bottom of my feet and let all my energy drain out. (very tired)
- This car payment is a real drain on my finances. (costly)
- This problem is a brain drain. (difficult/complicated)

dreams
- I dreamed a dream and it was sweet. (unlikely to happen, but wishful)
- She's building castles in the air. (dreaming about impossible things)
- She's chasing rainbows. (impossible to achieve)

dress - inappropriate (also see **attire**)
- You'll catch a cold where you can't take medicine.
- Scratch where it itches if it isn't in your britches.
- That outfit leaves nothing to the imagination.
- She's certainly advertising in that get up.
- She might as well wear a neon sign that says, "Cheap!"
- If she bends over, it's all over!
- Looks like her momma would teach her how to dress.
- She looks plumb trashy.
- He's showing his plumber's crack.
- He goes around slouchy with his pants falling off.

drink
- Always drink upstream. (to avoid drinking polluted water)
- Now there goes a tall drink of water! (tall person)
- That drink will sour on his stomach. (bad choice made)
- Drink 'til you founder! (get your fill)

- Whisky was not made for shot glasses. It was made for chug-a-lugging.
- Did you ever tank 10-69? (drink deer urine – a primitive hunter's practice after killing a deer)
- I don't drink and I don't chew. I don't go with them that do! (don't date people with bad habits)

driving
- Let's go cruising. (driving around for entertainment)
- Your lead footing it. (driving too fast)
- She's driving me to distraction. (getting on my nerves)
- You drive me crazy. (irritation; lustful)
- You could drive a preacher to drink.
- You can drive a horse to water, but you can't make him drink. (you can give someone advice, but they don't have to take it)
- Put the pedal to the metal. (drive faster)
- You're driving like my granny. (too slow)
- Lay rubber. (pull out fast)
- He was burning rubber. (speeding)

driving comments
- Why don't you just crawl up my back end? (being followed too closely)
- Move over Bozo!
- Where'd you get that driver's license – out of a Cracker Jacks box?
- Where did you learn to drive?
- If you don't stop criticizing my driving, I'm going to put you out beside of the road and let you walk home!

- If you got a driver's license, they must have been handing them out for free on the sidewalk.
- Road hog!
- Dim your lights, buddy! This ain't no runway!
- You're a back seat driver!

drummer
- He marches to a different drummer. (follows his own beliefs)
- His drummer plays to a different beat. (out of the ordinary)
- The drummer came by this week. (salesman)

drunk (also see **intoxicated**)
- He's drunk as a skunk.
- She's a bar fly.
- They were as drunk as Cooter Brown.
- He's three sheets to the wind.
- He's rip roaring drunk!
- He's drunker than a Lord!

dry
- I'm drier than a desert.
- It is drier than a popcorn fart.
- My mouth is as dry as toast.
- My throat is drier than dirt.
- I'm dry as a bone.
- I'm parched. (thirsty)
- I'm scorched.
- He left her high and dry. (abandoned)

duck
- He's a lucky duck!

- Walks like a duck, talks like a duck – must be a duck!
- Crap, crap, crap! Her mouth goes like a duck's butt all the time. (talks negatively)
- You need to get your ducks in a row. (set priorities)
- He took to it like a duck to water. (did something new very well.)
- He walks around like a duck looking for thunder.
- She drove her ducks to a dry pond. (made a bad decision; marriage that did not turn out well)

dumb
- She's a little dimwitted
- She's a blonde.
- That's a bird brained idea.
- He's as dumb as a bridge.
- That's the dumbest thing I ever heard!
- He's not the sharpest tool in the shed.
- He's a starn naked fool!
- You're a bungling idiot!
- He's a dumb thumick.
- Her gates are down, lights are on, and the bell is ringing, but the train's not coming.
- His wheels are spinning, but he's not going anywhere.
- He's dumber than a doorknob.
- I believe your light bulb has just about burnt out.
- Hello! No one's home.
- He's a real knuckle head.
- He is full of hair brained ideas.
- He is so stupid, his brain moved out a long time ago.
- He's so dumb, someone said the weather is chilly outside and he ran for a bowl and spoon!

- She's so dumb, she tripped over a cordless telephone.
- He's dumber than a knot on a log.
- She's dumber than a fence post.
- He's not playing with a full deck.
- He's too dumb to come in out of the rain.
- She doesn't know whether to use the bathroom, fall down, or wind her wrist watch.
- You're dumber than a cat under poop.
- His body has outgrown his brain.
- That boy doesn't know whether to pee, fall down, or go blind.
- The biggest job your brain does is keeping your ears apart.
- He's about half baked.
- If your brain was rocket fuel, you'd never get off the ground.
- He's so dumb, if you gave him a penny, he'd try to give you back change.
- If your brain were made of ink, you wouldn't have enough to dot an "i."
- She's dumber than a box of rocks.
- She's dumber than a coal bucket!
- He's not playing with a full deck.
- Her elevator doesn't go to the top floor.
- You are dumber than dirt.
- He's as thick as mud.
- His body has outgrown his mind.
- She's dumb as a brick.
- Her dough didn't rise to the top.
- He's about a brick shy of a load.

- I believe her light bulb has gone out.
- Not a one in that family will ever set the world on fire.
- That whole family crawled out of the short end of the gene pool.
- There are no brain surgeons in that bunch.
- If you had a brain, you'd be dangerous.
- He is so dumb, he got hit by a parked car.
- He's a few fries short of a happy meal!
- He wears his shoes on the wrong feet.
- His brain is like a b b rolling down a four lane highway.
- She's as blank as a clean sheet of paper.
- He's not firing on all cylinders.
- He's a little short of a cup.
- She's not the brightest color in the crayon box.
- He's not the brightest bulb in the pack.

durable
- It's built to last!
- He's tougher than nails.
- That car will outlive you!
- He's tougher than shoe leather.
- She's tougher than whip leather.

duty
- I always do my duty by my husband. (keep house, prepare meals, etc.)
- He's been called to active duty. (military service)
- It's my civic duty to vote. (responsibility)

- My call to duty is not the same as yours. (act in a responsible way)
- I took my post. (place of duty)

dynamite
- It'll take a lot of diddymite to blow that tree stump out of the ground.
- He's ready to blow like a keg of dynamite. (angry)

E

ear/ears
- He has long ears. (eavesdrops)
- How close to the floor do I have to put my ear to hear the devil?
- She has rabbit ears. (large ears)
- He has ears like a fox. (hears well)
- Lend me your ear. (listen to my idea)
- The money has already been earmarked for a project. (designated)
- He looks like Dumbo! (big ears)
- His ears stood up when he heard what they were saying. (eavesdropping)
- Her ears perked up. (listened to something she wanted to hear)
- When he talks, I let it go in one ear and out the other. (don't take it to heart)
- Will you be my ears? (listen for clues; eavesdrop with a purpose; tell me what goes on)

early
- The early bird catches the worm.

- Early to bed, early to rise, makes one healthy, wealthy, and wise.
- I'm up with the crows in the mornings.
- He gets up before the chickens.
- He gets up before the crack of dawn.
- Better early than late!

ease/easy
- Easy come, easy go!
- That's as easy as pie!
- That's a piece of cake!
- It's like taking candy from a baby!
- It's like shooting fish in a barrel.
- He's living the life of Riley.
- It's as easy as falling off a bike!
- It's easier said than done.

eat
- He eats like a pig. (no manners)
- The smell of that ham roasting really whetted his appetite. (made him hungry)
- You better eat before you cave in! (die)
- He ate a big bait of fresh salad greens. (large amount)
- If you don't eat, you'll dry up and blow away! (get too thin)
- He'll eat anything that doesn't crawl off his plate! (indiscriminate eater)
- If that boy got paid to eat, he'd be a rich man!
- We always make enough for a second helping.
- I'll take seconds on those potatoes!
- That smells so good, I can hardly wait to chow down!

- I could make a meal out of poke sallet! (can apply to any favorite food that a person likes well enough to eat it and nothing else with it)
- I guess I'll have to eat crow. (apologize)
- He'll have to eat those words. (admit he was wrong)
- If he wins that race, I'll eat my hat! (don't expect it to happen)
- She acted like she could eat him up alive. (adore)
- I'll eat you alive. (beat, defeat)
- Eat your heart out! (be envious)
- Any time you can get something to eat is a good time to eat.
- If somebody offers you something to eat, you take it! You don't have to be hungry to eat. You eat to keep from getting hungry.
- If you don't work and make you something to eat, old Pete will be sitting on the table! (hunger)
- She doesn't need a plate, just give her a trough!
- She eats like a bird. (eats very little; picky)
- I ate until I'm foundered. (overate)
- He didn't do more than smell his food. (ate little)
- She picked at her plate. (finicky)
- You'll eat those words! (retract; regret)
- He licked the platter clean!
- This is a Duke's mixture. (combination of foods; leftovers)
- He ate like a ravenous wolf. (starved)
- I've got an appetite like a bear waking up in the spring.
- I'm so hungry I could eat an elephant.

education
- She has a lot of book learning. (self-taught)
- He has book smarts. (reads a lot)
- He didn't have an education, but he had plenty of common sense.
- I had no formal learning. (self-taught)
- Boys, get an edumacation!
- You need to be edumacated.
- I wish I had more schooling.
- He got his letters from the university. (degree)
- Education is a great equalizer between social classes.
- The best way up the ladder is through education.
- Education brings change.
- True change starts with education the public.
- If you get an education, you can hold your head up in any crowd.
- Get an education so you will never have to be ashamed

effort
- I will do my level best. (maximum effort)
- I will do my dead level best.
- I know you can do better.
- I gave 100%. (all I had to give)
- My get up and go got up and went. (tried but failed)
- I'm tired of trying. (discouraged)
- Try, try again. (don't give up)
- Third time's the charm.
- Give it your best shot.
- Give it all you've got.
- You get an "A" for effort. (tried but didn't succeed)

- He didn't give half an effort. (didn't try)
- Can't you try a little harder?
- It took me some doing, but I managed to get my doctor's appointment changed.

egg/eggs
- Don't put all your eggs in one basket. (diversify)
- Why don't you go fry an egg? (leave me alone)
- He's a bad egg. (bad reputation)
- She's an egg head. (very smart, studious)
- I have a little nest egg tucked away. (secret savings)
- You have egg on your face! (mistaken and embarrassed about it)
- She's a good egg. (a good person)
- I'll break him from sucking eggs! (break a bad habit)
- Honey, that egg is already scrambled. (a mistake/decision that can not be undone)
- You'll not find a goose egg in a hummingbird's nest. (some things are illogical; won't happen; doesn't fit)

ego
- Contrary to what your parents may have told you, your name is not Sunshine, and the universe does not revolve around you!
- She always has to be the center of attention.
- He's a cocky simp of a man. (not as good as he thinks he is)
- Little Smarty went to a party.
  No one came but little Smarty!
- That boy is getting too big for his britches! (thinks more highly of himself than he has a right to)
- She thinks she's something the cat covered up. (important enough for a cat to bury)

- He thinks he's high and mighty.
- She thinks she can walk on water, but I know better.
- He's a real glory hound!
- If you could buy him for what he's worth and sell him for what he thinks he's worth, you'd be rich for the rest of your life.
- I'm being totally selfish. I've talked about "me" for the last hour. Why don't I stop and let you talk about me?
- He's a regular pack of smarties!
- He thinks his poop don't stink! (superior to others)
- He's a legend in his own mind.
- He thinks he's the Grand Poo Bah.
- He's about as slick as snot on a doorknob.
- He thinks he's something on a stick.
- She needs to eat a slice of humble pie.
- He'll be eating crow for a long time over that! (humbled)
- He's got a chip on his shoulder. (defensive)
- He thinks he's a Big Ike. (one with great authority)
- He thinks he deserves a standing ovation every time he passes gas.
- Someone needs to take him down a peg.
- Someone needs to put her in her place.
- Your mom might think you're going to be President, but trust me – you never will.
- She acts like she's the family princess.
- You're not worth as much as you think.
- She thinks she's all that and a bag of chips.

- He thinks he's better looking than a store front window.
- He thinks he's worth more than a store front window, but I didn't ask how much one costs.
- You don't ever fly so high that you don't have to come down.
- Get off your high horse! (opinion of one's self that is superior to others)

electricity
- Have you paid the juice bill? (electric bill)
- He got juiced. (electrical shock)
- Turn the power on. (plug in; flip a switch)
- Hit the switch. (flip the switch on or off)
- It felt like electricity coursing through my body. (pain)

elephant
- No one wanted to discuss the elephant in the room. (big problem that everyone knows and no one wants to deal with)
- She has a memory like an elephant.
- Oh, if only elephants could dance! (a comment about an impossible situation)
- I thunk I'll ride an elephunk, but, no it is an elepho. He thought it was an elephought. She says we can't ride that elephant. (who is right and who is wrong; does anyone know what they're talking about?)

eliminate
- Throw it in the yard. (get rid of something)
- Three strikes and you're out. (rules of baseball)
- Better pull the plug on that idea. (forget about it; kill it)

- He's going down for the third time. (a drowning man)
- I'll get you, my little pretty! (get rid of)

embarrass/embarrassed
- I was mortified!
- She turned red down to her toes.
- He turned red plumb down into his shirt collar.
- He turned as red as a gobbler's snout.
- She really rubbed your nose in it!
- I wanted to dig a hole and crawl in!
- I could have gone through the floor.
- I wanted to disappear right there and then.
- I could have died down dead right on the spot!

emotions (or lack of)
- She's as cold as ice.
- He's as cold as stone.
- It hurts my heart.
- She's tightly wound. (very emotional; nervous)
- She's high strung. (emotional)
- He's wired. (highly emotional)

empty
- There's nary a drop left!
- That has a hollow ring to it. (empty, insincere words)
- My head is empty. (out of ideas)
- There's nary a one in that box.

encouragement
- All will be well.
- This too shall pass.
- Keep your chin up.

- If the good Lord put an idea in your head, He will help you get it done.
- Tomorrow is another day.
- You can do it!
- Remember the little engine. I think I can. I think I can!
- You can do anything if you put your mind to it.
- Rome wasn't built in a day. Don't give up!
- Keep trying. You're bound to get it right eventually.

end/ending
- Elvis has left the building.
- You haven't heard the end of this.
- We don't get fairy tale endings in this life.
- All good things must come to an end.
- That's all she wrote!

endurance
- They won't last any longer than Pat stayed in the Army.
- He'll give out before he gets started.
- He'll hold his own.

enemies
- Do not strive to make enemies, to keep them, or befriend them.
- Smile a lot. It aggravates your enemies and drive them crazy trying to figure out what you've been up to.
- Keep your friends close and your enemies closer.
- Deliberately make an enemy of no man.
- Always give your enemies an opportunity to save face.

enough
- I've had about enough of you!
- Enough is enough!
- I can never get enough of you!
- Enough is enough and too much is nasty.

entire
- I can't believe I ate the whole thing!
- What in 'tar nation are you talkin' about?
- He was in the middle of the whole shebang.
- He's got the whole world in His hands.

envy
- She is green with envy. (jealous)
- The green-eyed monster is on the loose.

equality
- What's good for the goose is good for the gander.
- All men are created equal except for the ones who come out with a silver spoon in their mouth. (wealthy)

escape
- I gave him the slip. (snuck away from)
- He's off the hook! (has been released)
- I'm saved by the bell! (rescued just in time)
- He's flown the coop. (ran away)
- Beam me up, Scotty. (transport me to safety)
- He got off Scot free! (didn't have to pay)
- I turned in my walking papers. (get away from – as in a bad relationship or job)

evening
- I sat thinking in the gloaming.
- Lightning bugs come out long about dusky dark.

- I watch for the first stars to shine at twilight.
- I love to sit on the porch at evening time.
- My favorite time is the eve of the day.
- It's sitting on the edge of dark.
- It is evensong. (the time just before dark when the night creatures begin to be heard, i.e. – whip-oor-wills, frogs, crickets, etc.)
- I'm waiting for the moon ball to rise.

exact/exactly
- It went plime blank like he said it would.
- It turned out pine blank like you predicted.
- Nobody can be exact all the time.
- 'Xactly what do you mean by that? (explain yourself)
- Now that's just plain speakin'. (be exact and say what you mean)
- I don't have the zact change to pay for the pop machine. (precise)

exaggerate/exaggeration
- He dressed that story up a little.
- The more it's told, the bigger it gets!
- That's a fish tale if I ever heard one.
- That's making a mountain out of a mole hill.
- What a whopper!
- You don't have to use a sledgehammer to crack a nut.
- Don't make such a big deal out of it!
- He ain't just whistling Dixie.
- Don't make a mountain out of a mole hill!

excess
- Too much of anything is nasty.
- Too much of a good thing is just too much.

- You could take what she wastes and bake a cake!

excited
- You've got ants in your pants!
- Hot ziggety!
- Golly bum!
- I'm beside myself.
- I'm shaking like a leaf!
- I can't hardly live and stand it!
- You'd be gaga over a grandbaby!
- She went nuts when she heard the news!
- He is gung ho and ready to go

excuse/excuses
- But me no buts.
- I couldn't help myself.
- The devil made me do it.
- A poor excuse is better than none at ll!

executives
- Policy comes from higher ups.
- The uppity ups run the place.
- He's just a stuffed shirt.
- He's a fat cat.
- The suits are coming.
- high falutin' bunch
- The gray suits will be here.
- He's upper crust.
- The muckity mucks are making an inspection of the factory today.
- He's a big cheese.
- The hoity toities are visiting today.
- He's a big fish in a little pond.

- He thinks he's a big shot, but he's not.
- He is bringing in the big bucks.

exhausted/exhaustion
- I am worn out.
- I'm worn to a frazzle.
- You wear me out.
- That tired me out.
- I'm all done in.
- I'm pooped.

expensive
- That price is out of this world.
- That cost a fortune.
- He had to shell out a lot of money to pay for that!
- It costs a king's ransom.
- That will cost an arm and a leg.
- That will cost you a pretty penny.
- That's highway robbery!
- That place is very posh.
- You'll pay through the nose for that.

experienced
- He was a man of the world.
- He has been a Jack of all trades.
- She wrote the book on that subject.
- He's street smart.
- He's world wise.

expose/exposed
- She was caught with her hand in the cookie jar.
- He was caught with his pants down.

- It will all come out in the wash.
- She blew the lid off of that story.
- He gave the low down on the whole event.
- She kept digging until she got to the bottom of things.
- She was caught red handed.
- His cover was blown.
- Can you shed a little light on this situation?

eyes
- Her eyes sparkled like diamonds. (in love)
- His eyes sparkled like stars in a midnight sky. (happy)
- I was a goner from the first time I laid eyes on him. (love at first sight)
- Keep your eyes open. (be observant)
- Her eyes flashed like lightning. (anger)
- A storm was brewing in his eyes. (anger)
- Her eyes twinkled with mischief. (sneaky)
- His eyes spoke volumes. (emotions showed in his eyes)
- Keep your eyes peeled. (be watchful)
- You're a sight for sore eyes! (someone that hasn't been seen in a while)
- He has snake eyes. (not trustworthy)
- You stop that eye rolling right now! (said to a child who is giving an insolent look)
- He rolled snake eyes. (rolled two on the dice)
- His eyes were bottomless pools. (thoughtful)
- Her eyes were placid pools. (peaceful)
- He's as blind as a bat. (can't see either physically and/or emotionally)

- Don't roll your eyes at me! (sign of contempt; disgust)
- Don't roll your eyeballs at me like that! (same as above)
- His eyes rolled back in his head. (shock; near death)
- She couldn't hit the broad side of a barn. (can't see well)
- He wears Coke bottles for glasses. (thick glasses)
- Look at four-eyes. (insult to someone who wears glasses)
- She has eyes in the back of her head. (watchful and catches misbehavior)
- He's cross-eyed. (physical condition – lazy eye)
- His eyes are sigoggledy. (crossed)
- Her eyes were like two puddles of mud. (dull)
- Her eyes are like tires. (surprised)
- My eyes were bigger than my stomach. (not as hungry as I thought)
- His eyes were as big as saucers. (surprised)
- She's got the pink eye. (infection in the eyes)
- We see eye to eye. (have similar beliefs/values; agree)
- I've got the big eye. (can't sleep)
- He has a single eye until he gets it finished. (focused on the task)
- His eyeballs rolled back in his head when he saw her standing there. (shock; surprise)
- He has eagle eyes. (good vision; aware of everything)
- I saw her cutting her eyes at me. (giving me angry or dirty looks)

- Don't be rolling your eyeballs all over him! (looking lustfully at his physique)
- He'll look at you with the snake eye. (mean)
- He's looking at me with the stink eye. (mean)
- You'd better keep an eye on him. (watch carefully)
- Keep an eye out for one of those for me. (watch for)
- That's a poke in the eye! (something unpleasant)

F

face
- It's time to face the music. (be accountable for something)
- He has a face only a mother could love. (ugly)
- We sat down face to face. (talked directly)
- You have to face your demons. (confront fears or problems)
- Let's put the best face on it. (try to discover an optimistic outcome)
- I composed my face. (tried not to show emotion)

fact
- Now, that's a fact! (exclamation of truth)
- Is that a fact? (asked in amazement after hearing something surprising)
- When it comes right down to it, here are the facts.
- The bottom line is this…
- Fact is stranger than fiction.
- You need to get your facts straight. (be accurate)

factory
- He works at the Ford plant.

- We worked like a factory assembly line. (organized)
- We cranked the work out like a factory. (a lot of work done)

fad (popular sayings)
- Cool, man! I want to go, too!
- Groovy! It will be a fun party.
- Out of sight! (amazing)
- Awesome! (amazing)
- That's the bee's knees!
- Looky, looky! Here comes Cookie!
- It's all the rage!

failure
- The only total failure is not to try at all.
- That project tanked. (went under)
- The business went belly up. (died)
- That was a bust. (unsuccessful)
- If at first you don't succeed, try, try again. (don't give up)
- No man is a failure that has friends.
- He's a failure at everything he goes at. (unsuccessfully tries to do a variety of things)
- That was a flop. (didn't work)

fair
- Whoever said that life is fair either hadn't lived very long or was a liar.
- I'm feeling fair today. (pretty well)
- I'm fair to middlin'. (doing okay)
- All is fair in love and war. (do whatever it takes to win)
- He won fair and square. (honestly)

family
- Are you kin to me?
- We are blood kin.
- You are one of my kinfolk.
- We are from the Hamlin clan.
- You are of my blood.
- We are close relation.
- I have plenty of cousins.
- I am your own flesh and blood. (son or daughter)

familiar
- Your face looks familiar. (like someone I know)
- He doesn't know me any better than Adam's cat! (knows nothing about me)
- It's hard to get inside someone's head who keeps their doors all locked and their windows closed. (relationship intimacy)
- They have some familiar ground. (things in common)
- We're heading back over familiar ground. (repeating a conversation; reviewing something)

farewells
- Good-bye.
- See you later, gator.
- Ya'll come.
- Ya'll come back.
- Drop in again.
- See you later, alligator. (Response: After while crocodile!)
- Lord bless you.

- Tell your folks howdy from us.
- Come back when you can set a spell.
- Remember me to your family.
- Mention me to your folks.
- Catch you on the flip side.
- See you next time.
- I'll see you on the other side.
- The Lord watch between me and thee.
- Don't wait so long to come back next time.

fast
- He's faster than a race horse on the home stretch!
- He's faster than a speeding bullet.
- She's a fast woman. (loose morals)
- He'll be there at the drop of a hat.
- I'll be there at the drop of a dime!
- Faster than you can say done!
- I'll be back faster than a wink.
- He is always Johnny on the spot.
- I'll be there in a New York minute!
- It's time for me to high tail it out of here! (leave quickly)
- He's faster than greased lighting.
- I'll be back faster than lightning can strike.
- He'll be back in the blink of an eye.

fat
- He's a fat cat. (important person)
- We're living off the fat of the land. (self-sufficient)
- You fat head! (stubborn)
- She really packed it on. (gained weight)

- She's as plump as a partridge. (round shape)
- He's sure putting on since the last time I saw him. (gained weight
- She's still carrying her baby weight. (after a pregnancy)
- It's only baby fat. (pre-teen)
- A fat barn, a fat wallet, or a fat wife, never did a good man any harm.
- I might be fat, but you're ugly! I can lose weight, but what are you going to do?
- She's fat and purty. (applies to good milk cows and/or well fed wives, as a compliment to the husband and the wife)

fate
- The die is cast.
- You can't control fate.
- The fickle finger of fate has found you.
- There's no turning back now.
- This was meant to be.
- At this point, it's inevitable.
- This is my destiny

fear (see also **scared**)
- He turned white as a ghost.
- She is spineless. (a coward in the face of fear)
- She was so scared, she wet her pants!
- He is a gutless wonder. (doesn't take action because of fear)
- You're the biggest scaredy cat I've ever seen!

- He was so scared, he turned every color of the rainbow.
- He was as white as a sheet.
- He's such a chicken, he crows every morning.
- You're afraid of your own shadow.
- She jumps at her own shadow.
- She jumped out of her shoes.
- His hair stood straight up.
- He was so scared, he stuttered.
- That makes my liver quiver!
- Her hair turned white overnight. (physical change resulting from extreme fear)

feather
- There's a feather in your cap. (successful event)
- Birds of a feather flock together. (people with similarities find each other)
- He's feathering his nest. (using his position for his own advantage)
- The feathers will fly! (someone will be in trouble)
- Her feathers were ruffled. (offended)
- She's feathering her nest. (getting ready for the arrival of a baby)

feces (bathroom necessities)
- I have to do Number Two.
- I have to go doo doo.
- I need to hockey.
- I need to take a dump.
- I had to drop a load.
- I've got to get something serious off my mind.
- Do you need to pooh? (to a small child)

- I have to squat. (woodland reference to using the bathroom outdoors)

feed
- Put on your feedbag! (let's eat)
- Don't try to feed me that cock and bull story. (don't expect me to believe a lie)
- You'll have to spoon feed it to them. (convince someone by small steps; make it easy)
- He feeds off of the other boys. (misbehaves when the others are misbehaving)
- It's time to tie on the old feed bag. (time to eat)
- Don't try to feed me a line. (tell me a lie and expect me to believe it)

feel/feelings
- You've hurt my feelings. (upset me emotionally)
- How do you feel about it? (gut instinct)
- Feelings get in the way. (interfere with logical decisions)
- I feel finer than frog hairs. (very good)
- I'm feelin' froggy. (young; energetic)
- If I look as bad as I feel, then I must look pretty awful.
- He's all touchy feely. (likes to hug; make physical contact)
- I feel your pain. (sympathize)
- I'm feeling you. (understand)
- You cut me to the quick! (hurt me deeply)
- I feel like crap warmed over.
- I feel like death warmed over.

- Sometimes it doesn't matter how you feel. You just have to get up off your seat and do what has to be done.

feet/foot
- He has feet of clay. (is human and will fail)
- He looks like he has boat paddles for feet.
- You could use those shoes for skis!
- Sasquatch has nothing on him!
- Has anyone seen a paddle foot? (policeman)
- Where is a flatfoot when you need one? (policeman)
- That's okay. I walk on the bottom. You walk on the top. (a comment said after someone has stepped on your foot.)
- You need to put your best foot forward. (make a good impression)
- You've got to put your foot down! (use authority)
- Her feet look like houseboats.
- Give him a chance. He'll find his feet. (get situated)
- It's time to get your feet wet. (try something new)
- You're a regular Big Foot. (big and clumsy)
- He has foot and mouth disease. (says inappropriate things)
- Get your foot out of your mouth. (said something insulting, but not intentionally)
- Give me a foot up. (help me)
- I hope I can get a foot in the door. (be given a chance)
- Her dad will foot the bill for the wedding. (pay for)
- We are on friendly footing. (good relationship)

- I need some help to get back on solid footing. (financial need)

fell
- She took a tumble.
- He's fell off. (lost weight)
- He fell head over heels for her. (fell in love)
- He fell off the wagon. (started drinking again.)
- He querled in the snow.
- She had a bad spill.

feller
- He's a good feller. (good man)
- That's her feller. (sweetheart)
- He's a yeller feller. (coward)

feminine
- She's a girlie girl.
- She sets the standard for girlie.
- She's a virtuous woman.
- She's all fluff.
- She's all sugar and spice.
- She's a fru fru kind of girl.
- She's all laces and pearls.
- She's a southern belle.
- She's the belle of the ball.

fence/fencing
- Let there be no fences between us.
- Good fences make good neighbors.
- Stop straddling the fence!
- He's trying to fence a hot watch. (sell a stolen item)

- I'll tell you a secret if you'll keep it between you, me, and the fence post.
- Don't fence me in. (try to limit me)
- They're fencing. (dueling with words)

fetch
- Here boy! Fetch! (retrieve)
- Fetch me a glass of water, please. (bring to me)
- She is fetching in that outfit. (very attractive)
- That ought to fetch a hefty price. (bring in; sell for a lot)

fiddle
- He's as fit as a fiddle. (physically fit)
- Why are you fiddling around? (delaying)
- Nero fiddled while Rome burned. (ignored the needs of others; oblivious)
- You better not fiddle around with that girl. (flirting with no intention of developing a serious relationship)
- Well fiddle-dee-dee! (so what?)
- You're going to fiddle fart around until someone gets that job instead of you! (delay)

fight
- Your momma brought you into this world, but I can take you out!
- She flogged him.
- They were out on the playground tearing up Jack.
- He cut a rusty! (got into a fight)
- Put up your dukes!
- I kicked his hind end.
- You'll pack a whoopin' when I catch up with you, if I ever hear tell you've been up to your meanness again!

- He couldn't fight his way out of a paper bag!
- Them there's fighting words!
- Who started this fracas?
- I'll knock you into next week.
- He whomped the tar out of that big bully.
- She hit me so hard I thought it was the Fourth of July.
- I'll knock your block off.
- I cannot live with you under the same roof!
- He threw the fight. (lost on purpose)
- I'll hit you so hard, your momma will feel it.
- I'll sting you like a hornet!
- Billy Bob whomped the tar out of him!
- They had a throw down.
- We've had words.
- We've passed words between us.
- If you want a shiner, keep it up.
- I can lick you with one hand tied behind my back.
- I can whip you with one hand tied behind my back.
- You're asking for it!
- You're begging for a fight!
- You can't let your momma fight your battles for you all of your life.
- I fight my own battles.
- It's an uphill fight.
- He's a crime fighter.
- It's on like Donkey Kong. (ready to fight)
- Don't be bustin' my chops unlest you're ready to get busted.

- Don't be bustin' my things unless you want me to take them out of your hide.

figure – female
- She's a brick house.
- She is well endowed.
- She is curvacious.
- She has all the right stuff in all the right places.
- She has a waspish waist.
- She's built like a Coke bottle.
- She's built like a sack full of door knobs and all of them different sizes
- She's got some junk in her trunk. (big bottom)
- She's a buxom lass.

figure - male
- He has a six pack.
- He's built to last.
- He is a fine figure.
- He cuts a fine figure.
- He is easy on the eyes.
- He's the Alpha Male.
- He is well endowed.
- He's rock solid.
- His legs are like tree trunks.
- He has arms like canons.
- He sure is purdy.

finality
- It ain't over 'til the fat lady sings.
- It's finished when I say it's finished.
- You had your chance and you blew it.
- It's all been said and done.

- It's time for you to get over yourself.
- All good things must come to an end.
- Its all over but the crying.

fine
- She sets a fine table. (nice; beautiful)
- He is mighty fine. (looks good)
- I'm feeling fine. (very good; happy)
- I'm finer than a frog hair split three ways. (doing extremely well)
- Everything is kopasetic. (fine; alright; okay)

fire
- Truth will stand when the world is on fire. (end of the world)
- He got out of there like a house on fire. (quickly)
- There's fire in the hole. (danger)
- He's not firing on all cylinders. (not bright)
- He's got a fire in his belly. (wants something passionately)
- He can preach like his coat tail is on fire. (emotionally)
- Where there's smoke, there's fire.
- If it's still smoking, remember there was a fire.

fish
- That's a big fish tale if I ever heard one. (tall tale)
- You should've seen the one that got away! (bragging about fish size)
- Give a man a fish and you feed him for a day. Teach him how to fish and he'll be happy feeding himself for the rest of his life!

- Something smells fishy, if you ask me. (something's amiss; questionable; suspicious)
- He better keep his mouth shut before he turns up fish bait. (dead)
- There are other fish in the sea. (choices for romantic interests after a break up)
- He's a little fish in a big pond. (insignificant)
- Even a fish wouldn't get in trouble if he'd learn to keep his mouth shut!
- That's like a fish in a pickle dish! (totally useless; makes no sense)

fit
- They are a good fit. (good match)
- It fits like a glove. (perfect fit)
- It's not a fit day for man nor beast. (bad weather)
- He's fit as a fiddle. (healthy)
- She threw a conniption fit. (tantrum)
- He had a hissy fit. (tantrum)
- You need to try to fit in. (get along with others)
- He has fits. (epilepsy)
- He was fit to be tied. (angry)
- She's a good fit. (right for a job)
- You are looking fine and fit. (healthy)

flash
- I'll be there in a flash. (quickly)
- He flashed by me on his way out. (passed quickly)
- Here's a flash… (idea)
- News flash… (interject something into a conversation that was unknown to the other parties involved)
- It's going to storm. I just saw a flash. (lightning)

- Don't flash that thing in my face. (take a photo with a flash)
- He just flashed her. (exposed himself)

flat
- Illinois is flat as a pancake. (flat landscape)
- That cat was squished flatter than a flitter. (run over)
- He can flat out run! (very fast)
- That flattened his tires! (took the arrogance out of him)
- She's as flat as a ten year old boy! (undeveloped bosom)
- That's as flat as a pole cat in the middle of the road!

flattery
- He could charm the buttons off a rattlesnake.
- She's only blowing smoke.
- Butter wouldn't melt in her mouth.
- He's a silver tongued devil.
- He's a smooth talking son of a gun.
- Flattery will get you nowhere.
- Flattery will get you everything.
- Beware of false flatterers.

flatulate
- I heard somebody let a toot.
- He's a tooter.
- Whoever smelt it dealt it!
- I can't help but poot.
- Granny's a pooter.
- He let a stink bomb.
- Who let one?
- I passed gas.

- Who cut the cheese?
- He passed wind.
- I let a stinker.
- Who blew one out?

flexible
- He was as flexible as a cat.
- She is as flexible as a rubber band.
- You are looser than a long necked goose!
- He's as bendable as warm taffy.
- She's as flexible as a Gumby doll.

flirting
- He's going out slue footing.
- Watch her bat those eyelashes!
- She is nothing but a common flirt.
- He is guilty of many dalliances.
- Honey wouldn't melt in her mouth.
- She was swishing around in her skirts.
- She's casting sheep's eyes at him!
- He's mooning over her.
- Butter wouldn't melt in his mouth.
- She's playing hard to get.
- She's trying to turn his head!
- She was holding court. (surrounded by male suitors)
- She was throwing herself around right in his face!
- Just look at her swiveling those hips from one side to the other! (walking in a provocative manner)

float
- Whatever floats your boat. (an indifferent response to someone's plans or news.)

- That boat won't float. (bad idea)
- That girl would float with a cement coat on! (big bosoms)

flood
- It's coming a tide!
- The rivers will be running out of their banks.
- She had a flood of emotions. (overwhelmed)
- Do you have a sanitary pad I could borrow before I flood? (feminine accident)

flowers
- I'm going to pick some fresh blooms for the table.
- I love to smell the blossoms.
- Send me flowers while I live. They'll do me no good in the grave.
- I love every little bud in my garden.

fly/flies
- There's a fly in the ointment. (something has been spoiled)
- I wish I could be a fly on the wall. (spy)
- Fly the flag high. (patriotic)
- Time flies when you are having fun. (passes quickly)
- I'll have to fly by the seat of my pants. (do it, even though I'm unprepared)
- Are you ready to fly? (start something new)
- It's time for that little birdie to fly the nest. (leave home)

focus
- Don't spread yourself too thin.
- Stay focused. (remember your objective)
- I can't focus. (too many things on my mind)
- Everything seems out of focus. (confused)

fog/foggy
- He's in a fog. (uninformed; unaware)
- I'm foggy headed. (not awake; confused)
- When the fog clears, we'll see the truth. (something unclear will become clear later)
- I haven't the foggiest. (not a clue)
- I haven't the foggiest notion. (don't understand)
- I haven't the foggiest idea. (don't know)

food
- This is good grub!
- I'm just about out of vittles.
- I need to stock up on staples the next time I go to trade. (basic supplies like flour, coffee, salt)
- These victuals will last a long time.
- Where do you want the groceries?
- That is tougher than hard tack. (almost rock-like)
- That's sourer than whang.
- That would break your teeth out on the way down.
- This fried chicken is finger lickin' good!
- This cake is absolutely scrumptious!
- Talk about good eats!
- This homemade pie is scrumdidlyitious!
- The spaghetti is might tasty!
- Now, that's quite a Duke's mixture! (a combination of food eaten together like biscuits and sausage crumbled into gravy)

fool/fooling
- I'm nobody's fool! (single; independent; intelligent)
- A fool and his money are soon parted.

- Fool me one, shame on you. Fool me twice, shame on me.
- She's a fool for him. (infatuated)
- It's better to be thought of as a fool than to open your mouth and remove all doubt.
- No fooling? (honestly?)
- I was only fooling. (teasing)
- Do not send me on a fool's errand again! (request for something impossible)
- We were only fooling around. (playing)
- Quit fooling around and get busy. (wasting time)
- She fooled him! (deceived)
- I feel foolish. (should have known something but didn't)

follow/followers
- Follow your dreams.
- If the blind follow the blind, they shall both end up in a ditch.
- Follow your heart.
- You'd follow anybody who acted as if they knew what they were doing.
- There she goes with her little tag-alongs.
- He has his posse with him.
- There are her Velcro children.

force/forced
- They roped me into it.
- It will take brute force to get that job done. (military might)
- He held a gun to my head.

- No one was holding a gun to your head. (You didn't have to do it!)
- The devil made me do it.
- You can't make me do anything I don't want to do! I'm bigger than you! (or I am older than you)
- She was forced. (raped)

forget/forgetful
- I disremember what we decided.
- Forgive and forget.
- It flew right out of my head.
- I was going to say something, but it is gone with the wind.
- It jumped right out of my head.
- I can think of everything else under the sun except what I wanted to tell you!
- It was on the tip of my tongue!
- I can't think of it a bit more than nothing.
- Well, I had it, but it is gone.
- It's right on the edge of my mind.
- I'm drawing a blank.
- It skipped my mind.
- My thinker is on the blink.
- My mind has gone blank.
- I reckon Old Timers has taken hold.
- I'd lose my head if it wasn't attached.
- I forget what I was going to say. Must have been a lie.
- I've gotten so absent minded, I forget what I forgot.
- I can't think of it a bit more than the Man in the moon.

forgiveness
- Forgive and forget.
- Let bygones be bygones.
- That photo is very forgiving. (makes the person look better than they do in real life)
- If we repent, God is faithful and just to forgive our sins.
- Once we repent, our sins are cast into the sea of God's forgetfulness as far as the east is from the west.
- Let it go!

fork
- You've come to the fork in the road. (time to choose one direction or the other)
- Fork it over! (Give it to me!)
- I bet he had to fork out a lot of money for that car. (pay a lot)

fortune/fortune hunter
- That must have cost a fortune! (expensive)
- There is a fine line between fortune and misfortune. (You can lose it all in an instant.)
- She is a gold digger. (looking to become wealthy by marrying a wealthy man)
- She's looking for a sugar daddy. (looking for a man who will spend lots of money on her)
- He's looking for a sugar momma. (looking for a woman who will spend lots of money on him)
- He's a leach. (sucking all the money out of someone that he possibly can)

foxfire
- Did you see the foxfire at the edge of the woods? (an unexplained glow; swamp gas)

- You're believing in foxfire. (something that's not real; no substance)

freckled
- He's a pided little thing.
- That horse is mottled.
- She's as speckled as a pup!
- His nose is smottled.
- She has a blotchy complexion.
- You're as speckled as a bird egg!
- I can hear my freckles popping out in the sun.

free/freedom
- Advice is free and usually worthless.
- I'm as free as a bird. (can come and go as I please)
- I'm giving you a free hand. (putting you in charge)
- It's yours, no strings attached. (no obligations)
- He's as free as a turtle out of its shell.
- I'm as free as a bird on the wing. (free to come and go as I please)
- You're free, white, and 21. It's nobody's business what you do.
- Freedom ends at the end of your nose. (Your freedom is limited to your freedom to choose for yourself.)
- Your freedom ends where another's begins. (You do not have the right to infringe upon someone else's freedom.)
- Some have more freedom than others. (privilege; bias)
- The cost of freedom is measured in blood. (sacrifice of lives in battle)
- He's an unbridled spirit. (wild and free; untamed)

- She's always been a free spirit. (impulsive)

fresh
- You're as fresh as the morning in spring.
- Don't get fresh with me! (flirting; inappropriate comments)
- I feel fresh as a daisy!

fret
- Don't fret. All will be well. (don't worry)
- The baby is fretful. (fussy)
- This is a fractious child. (fretful, cries a lot)
- I don't have a fret in the world. (worry)

friend/friendly
- He's about as friendly as a rattlesnake.
- He's my little buddy. (refers to a younger friend)
- A friend to all is a friend to none.
- I have a new pal.
- We are kindred spirits. (feel the same about important things; have commonalities)
- We were bosom buddies in high school. (confidant; closest friends)
- She's my bestie.
- A friend in need is a friend indeed.
- She's my new B F F.
- They are my posse. (group of friends that stick together)
- Keep your friends close but your enemies closer.

frightened
- He looked like a deer in headlights!
- I was shaking down to my shoes!
- It nearly scared me to death!

- It gave me the shivers.
- They ran in the house screaming bloody murder.
- The whole thing gave me goose bumps.
- It gave me goose flesh.
- He had a white knuckle grip.
- You gave me such a fright!
- My hair stood up all over!
- The hair on the back of my neck stood straight up.
- It made the hairs stand up on the back of my head.
- It gave me the heebie jeebies.
- I just about died down dead it scared me so bad!
- You scared the Willies out of me!
- I nearly peed my pants!
- You nearly gave me a heart attack.

frog
- Quit sitting there courting like two frogs on a log.
- Don't just sit there like two frogs a courtin'.
- I'm feeling froggy. (really good)
- There's a frog in my throat. (hoarse/laryngitis)
- You can't tell how far a frog can jump just by looking at its legs. (you can't tell everything by looking at the outside)
- You have to kiss a lot of toads before you find your handsome prince.

frugal
- She is downright stingy.
- Some people get all they can and can all they get.
- He's a real tight wad.
- He's as tight as Dick's hat band!
- He's tight as a drum!

- Only the grim reaper could separate him from his money!
- She's so tight her shoes squeak!
- He's so tight he squeaks when he walks.
- He'd lie to his own mother if it would save him a dime.
- She's a real penny pincher.

fruit
- He's a fruit. (homosexual)
- She's fruity. (silly)
- Who made you the fruit inspector? (critical)
- You can tell a tree by its fruit. (good or bad deeds)

frustrated/frustration
- I'm at the end of my rope.
- I'm at the end of my tether.
- I'm all bumfuzzled.
- Give me a break!
- I'm fed up!
- I'm flusterpated.
- I got side tracked.
- I am at my wits' end.
- I'm at the end of my wits.
- You're driving me up the wall!
- I've about had enough of this!
- I'd had just about all I can stand!
- I can't take much more of this.
- I just can't hack it any more.
- My patience has flown out the window!
- I've had all I can stands and I can't stands no more.
- This whole mess has just about done me in.

- You are trying to push my buttons.
- He is pestering the life out of me.

full
- I'm as full as a tick.
- I'm as full as a big dog tick.
- I'm ready to pop!
- There isn't room for a good breath in there.
- Standing room only!
- I have foundered myself on this meal!
- I'm a blivit (a five pound football full of ten pounds of air.)I couldn't eat another bite.
- I'm as full as a horse.
- You're full of it. (not to be believed)
- I'm as full as a tick with no air holes in it.
- I'm plumb full!
- He's full of baloney! (braggadocios)
- Her head is chogged full of stories.

fun/funny
- That's about as funny as a three legged man in a butt kicking contest. (sarcastic way of saying not funny.
- That was about as funny as a barrel of monkeys.
- We've been out gallivanting around and having a big time. (a happy outing)
- He's funny in the head. (mentally challenged)
- She's kind of funny. (peculiar or quare personality)
- Sounds a little funny to me. (doubtful, questionable)
- That goes down funny. (I don't like it.)
- He's a card.

- We'll have a ball!
- It will be a blast.
- He's a character.
- He's a regular Bozo the Clown.
- She's a hoot.
- He's a jolly old soul.
- He's a mess.
- He's a real trickster.
- That's a real knee slapper!
- He's a real joker.
- She'll make you wet your britches.
- He'll make you laugh your buns off.
- You crack me up!
- We are having a fun time.
- We are having a big time.

funeral
- He's laid out at the funeral home. (dead)
- I'm going to a wake.
- My uncle's farewell service is tomorrow.
- She has to go to the visitation.
- I have to go to a viewing.

funk/funky
- She has been in a funk. (depressed state)
- That milk is funky. (spoiled)
- I smell something funky. (spoiled or rotting)
- Funky! (cool; good; a compliment)

G

geese/goose
- Trying to get that bunch of girls to cooperate was like trying to herd geese.
- They were squawking like a gaggle of geese.
- You've cooked your goose with me. (caused me to lose respect and will never give you another chance)
- What's good for the goose is good for the gander. (behavior in one gender should be equally acceptable in the other)
- He goosed me! (tickled me in the ribs by surprise)
- I have goose flesh. (chill bumps)
- A goose just walked over my grave. (sudden chill)
- That scary movie gives me goose bumps! (frightened)
- You've led me on a wild goose chase! (deliberately sent someone in the wrong direction or looking for something that couldn't be found)
- Don't kill the goose that lays the golden egg. (recognize your benefactors)
- She believes that all her geese are swans. (has an unrealistically high opinion of herself)
- She's getting married soon. It's time to pluck the goose! (goose feathers were used to stuff a mattress and pillows for a newlywed couple)
- I didn't need that a bit more than a goose! (bought something totally frivolous)

generous/generosity
- He whips out his money awfully fast.
- He'd give you the shirt right off his back.

- She is a big hearted woman.
- She's got a heart of gold.
- He would give you the last dime he had in his pocket.
- She's so big hearted, she'd give you her husband if you asked for him!
- Dig deep! (Give as much as you can.)

gentle
- She was as gentle as a dove.
- He was as gentle as a lamb.
- She was as gentle as a newborn baby calf.
- I had to gentle her down. (calm down a fretful person or animal such as a horse)
- Gentle words take away wrath.

get
- My get up and go has got up and went. (exhausted)
- If you can't get it at Cas Walkers, it can't be got. (unavailable for purchase)
- That's better than anything you can get at Cas Walkers. (homemade; very expensive)
- It's time to get out of Dodge. (leave town)
- Get thee behind me Satan. (Don't tempt me.)
- You get as good as you give.

giggle
- They giggled like a gaggle of geese.
- Stop snickering!
- Your giggle box is turned on!
- They sniggered at the new girl's accent.

gimmit
- It is time to get your little gimmit in the bed. (self)
- Get your gimmit over here! (body)

girl
- Hey, toots!
- She's my little tootsie!
- She is still a woman child.
- She's my little heifer.
- Come here lass.
- She's a bonnie lassie.
- She's my gal.
- She's barely a half pint.
- I've known her since she was a tad pole.
- She's a good little young 'un.
- She's still a baby.
- Hey, baby girl.
- That girl is jail bait! (under 16)
- She's a she-devil!
- She's knee high to a grass hopper.
- That girl of his is a doozie. (Can mean either girlfriend or daughter.

ghost
- I saw a haint!
- She looks like she just saw a ghost!
- Ain't no such thing as ghosts, haints, or boogers!
- Don't be telling those haint stories around me!
- A specter stood at the end of his bed.
- I just saw a spook!
- Ain't no ghost but the Holy Ghost!

give/giver
- She can give as good as she gets.
- You can't out-give God.
- Give 'til it hurts. (sacrificial giving)

- Whatever you give away will find its way back to you.
- Never give up.(persevere)
- Don't give in. (quit)
- I give you my heart. (declaring love)
- You stop that crying right now or I'll give you something to cry about!
- Don't give me a hard time.
- You can't give what ain't yours to give.
- You can't give what you ain't got.
- You're an Indian giver. (take back a gift)
- I'd give my right arm for a good cold drink of water right about now. (can substitute any body part in this saying)
- She's a giver. (performs acts of kindness for others)

gizzard
- That tickles my gizzard!
- I laughed so hard my gizzard flew out!
- That water will cool your gizzard.
- Well, that little bit of news is stuck in my craw. (gizzard)

glop
- I love ice cream. Glop it on! (give me a lot)
- He just glopped the paint on the wall. (did it in a very careless manner)
- She glopped glue on the wall paper. (used too much)

glove
- There's an iron fist in that velvet glove. (a person appears genteel, but rules sternly)
- We fit like hand in glove. (a good match)

- She dropped that glove on purpose! (a ploy to gain male attention)

go/going
- I've got to go! (bathroom break needed)
- That idea will go down like a lead balloon. (fail)
- He's going for broke. (gambling/taking a risk)
- I'm going out on a limb for you. (taking a chance that puts me at risk)
- Time to skedaddle. (leave)
- He is going to his doom. (making a bad choice)
- He's going to meet his maker. (going to die)
- He always goes the extra mile. (does more than required)

goat
- You really got my goat! (played a trick on me)
- He's an old goat! (elderly man who makes sexual advances toward young women)
- He's eats like a goat! (will eat anything)
- Only the Lord can separate the sheep from the goats. (know a person's true motives)

gold
- All that glitters is not gold. (don't be deceived by appearance)
- She's worth her weight in gold. (very important; good)
- I wouldn't do that for all the gold in Fort Knox! (can apply to anything – i.e. go out with him; take that job; buy that house, etc.)
- He acts like he's been dipped in 24karat gold. (conceited)
- She acts like she poops gold bars! (conceited)

good/goodness
- That's mighty good eating! (compliment)
- That's mighty good of you. (kind; generous)
- Good grief! (frustration)
- Goodness gracious! (expression of surprise)
- He's a low down good for nothing! (worthless)

goose
- You're running around like an addled goose – don't know what you're doing!
- What a silly goose! (said about someone who has done something ridiculous or absurd.

gossip
- Her tongue is loose on both ends.
- Don't tie a knot with your tongue that you can't untie with your teeth.
- Tongues are wagging. (People are gossiping.)
- Don't tell him if you don't want it spread all around.
- I want details. Don't leave anything out.
- She's been running her mouth again.
- That tale is no more than a detailed lie.
- He's packing tales again.
- That girl will tell everything she knows and you don't even have to ask.
- What goes in her ears tumbles right out of her mouth.
- She's always throwing off on someone.
- He did a real hatchet job on her reputation!
- She's a regular gossip hound.
- Her tongue is so long it's tied in the middle and flaps at both ends.

- I hear tell the old man next door is cheating on his wife.
- He has a big nose!
- I heard it through the grapevine.
- Gossip spreads like wildfire with little chance of putting it out before damage is done.
- That's nothing but rubbing salt in the wound. (deliberately repeating hurtful gossip to someone)
- You'd better keep your nose out of other people's business before someone slams a door on it.
- You couldn't burp in Virginia without the news of it being in Kentucky before you got home.
- They are burning up the telephone wires.
- Don't believe everything you hear.
- That's old dishwater! Throw it out the back door and forget about it.
- She really knows how to dish the dirt.
- Which face is she wearing today?
- You've got a snake's tongue.
- Mind your own bee's wax.
- You could pass gas on the Virginia side of the mountain and the stink would be back in Kentucky before you got home!
- He talks out of both sides of his mouth.
- I got it straight from the horse's mouth!
- A little birdie told me.
- Tattler, prattler, nothing but a rattler.
- It's the talk of the town.
- Give me the low down.
- What's the scoop?

- Heard any recent scoopage?
- Who gossips with you will gossip about you.
- She's a regular old blabber mouth.
- She spreads it all over creation.
- That girl will tell everything she knows and then some!

grandfather
- Pappaw
- Pap
- Grand-pap
- Grandpa
- Grand-paw
- Grandpappy
- Grand Dad
- Granddaddy
- Gramps
- Grampa
- Grampaw

grandmother
- Granny
- Nanny
- Nanna
- Nay-nay
- Mammaw
- Mumma
- Mummaw
- Grandmaw
- Big Momma
- Grandma
- Grandmama

- Grand Ma Ma
- Grandmom

grass
- The grass is always greener on the other side.
- She's greener than grass. (naïve)
- This is a grass roots movement. (ordinary people in charge)
- She's a grass widow. (her husband is away for work much of the time)

grave
- The situation is grave. (very serious)
- Ain't no grave, gonna hold my body down. (reference to the resurrection)
- You dig your grave with your teeth. (what you say will come back to haunt you)
- He's got one foot on the grave and one on a banana peel! (near death)
- Someone just stepped on my grave. (said when a sudden chill happens for no apparent reason)

green
- Her face turned as green as grass. (sick at her stomach; nauseated; motion sickness)
- He was as green as the leaves in springtime.
- He's a green horn. (inexperienced; without knowledge)
- She has a green thumb.
- She was as green as a frog after she ate that hotdog. (nauseasted; upset stomach)
- He's looking for greener pastures. (better situation)
- The grass is greener on the other side. (someone else's situation looks better)

- The grass always looks greener in someone else's field. (someone else's situation looks better or easier)
- He was greener than grass. (naïve)
- I'm feeling a little green. (nauseated; inexperienced)
- I see a green eyed monster in her. (jealousy)

greetings
- Greetings and salutations!
- Howdy!
- Come right in and sit a spell.
- Hey there! What do you say?
- Hey there! What do you know?
- It's me again Margaret.
- Good to see you.
- Just barge right in and make yourself at home.
- Come on in and make yourself t' home.

grief
- She was overcome with grief. (sorrow because of a loss/death)
- Good grief! (frustration)

grin/grinning (also see **smile**)
- Get that silly grin off your face!
- Look at that possum grin!
- She's got something up her sleeve – watch her grin!
- He's grinning like a possum.
- She's grinning from ear to ear.
- He's grinning like a mule eating saw briars.
- He's grinning like the cat that ate the canary.
- She's grinning like the Cheshire Cat.

ground
- We've run aground. (had an accident)

- She ground him into dust. (broke his will; belittled him; ruined him)
- She worships the ground he walks on. (is enamored with)
- He's well grounded. (stable; has been taught right from wrong)
- His words fell on fallow ground. (took root and grew)
- My feet are itching. I reckon I'll soon be walking on new ground. (a superstition commonly noted)
- This is new ground for me. (new experience)
- He's turning up the ground. (plowing the earth for planting)
- The house shook when he hit the ground! (exaggeration about someone falling or being knocked down in a fight)

groundhog
- Did you see that whistle pig beside of the road?
- Yonder comes granny with a snicker and a grin. Yonder comes granny with a snicker and a grin. Whistle pig gravy all over her chin! (same with groundhog in place of whistle pig)
- My life is one big Groundhog Day! (repetitious)
- You've no more use than a groundhog on February 2. (not very useful)
- Jumpin' green groundhogs! (expression of surprise)
- He hides out in his groundhog hole. (reclusive person)
- Don't come nosin' around here like some little fat groundhog lookin' for a new den. (said to a man

trying to find a woman to take care of him or take him in)

group
- Y'all are welcome to come and stay with us. (family)
- That's a mess of people over there. (crowd)
- Y'uns come over for dinner Sunday. (A group of individuals connected by birth, situation, or circumstance.)
- We're hoping for a big crowd come Sunday.

growing
- He is growing like a bad weed!
- Our family is spreading out like a kudzu vine.
- Did someone put fertilizer in his shoes?
- She is growing like a corn stalk.
- He is shooting straight up!
- They must be feeding that boy fertilizer.
- She's growing like a honeysuckle vine around a fence post.
- We're going to have to set a brick on top of your head to slow you down from growing so fast.
- He's as tall as a tree.

grudges
- They'll die with it or get over it – one or the other.
- Holding a grudge is like drinking poison and expecting your enemy to die.
- She carried it to her grave.
- I wouldn't watch them eat a bail of hay!

guilt
- He looks like a mule eating saw briars.
- She looks like the cat that swallowed the canary.
- He's got that hang dog look.

- He took the fall for that accident. (took the blame)
- She left with her tail between her legs. (ashamed)
- He drug himself out of here. (embarrassed)
- He hung his head in shame. (confronted)
- I'll leave you to stew in your own juices. (think about what you've done)
- Guilt is the foundation of any wise mother's discipline!
- He was caught red handed with the stolen merchandise! (discovered with the stolen item(s) in his possession)

guitar
- I believe I'll hit some licks on the guitar. (play)
- He can strum a few chords. (learning)
- He can make those strings talk. (great player)
- She can make those strings sing. (excellent player)

gullible
- You are a sucker.
- You'd believe anything!
- You fall for everything.
- If you can be taken once, you can be taken twice.

gum
- He's gumming it. (toothless)
- She's chewing chawing gum.
- Professionals should never chew gum on the job.
- Chewing gum in public is a sure sign of a low class woman. (considered unladylike)
- A woman chewing gum in public looks cheap.
- You've made a gummy mess!

- She looks like a heifer chewing her cud. (chewing gum)

gun
- Are you packin'? (Carrying a concealed weapon.)
- Guns don't kill people. People kill people.
- She's gunning for you. (looking for you)
- If you take all the guns away from the honest people, the only ones left who'll have them are the crooks.
- He's a son of a gun if I've ever seen one. (good or bad character)
- Well, I'll be a son of a gun! (surprised at an outcome)
- She's a little gun shy. (had a bad experience and doesn't want to repeat it)
- He has big guns! (muscles)
- He's a big gun. (someone important)
- I'll be riding shotgun. (traveling companion)
- Treat all guns as if they are loaded. (gun safety)

gypsies
- My hoe is missing. Looks like the gypsies have been through. (an expression for something missing or stolen.)
- You children are acting like a band of gypsies! (boisterous; ill mannered))
- Those gypsies would steal you blind. (Traveling bands of gypsies were noted for stealing from an area as they passed through.)
- That band of gypsies will wipe you out. (steal from you)
- I've been gypped. (cheated in a business deal)
- If you don't behave, the gypsies will come in the middle of the night and take you away. (This scare

tactic was based on the notion that gypsies often stole young children and sold them to the highest bidder)
- I'm staying away from that Gyp joint. (a place where you are sure to be cheated or overcharged; sold shoddy merchandise

H

habit
- You're a bad habit. (relationship with someone who is not good for you)
- You're a hard habit to break. (a bad relationship that needs to end)
- We learned his habits. (figured out his daily routine)
- Nuns don't have to wear habits any more. (garb of a nun)
- I need to kick the habit. (quit smoking)
- He dropped by on Sunday afternoon as was his want. (routine; habit)

haint
- They say there's a haint in that house. (ghost)
- I haint seen him all day long. (haven't)
- I'll haint you for the rest of your days if you marry him. (haunt)
- The school is hainted. (haunted)
- I hain't got time for your foolishness. (don't have)
- You look like a haint! (ghost; sickly; frightened)
- I look like a 'fore daylight haint. (unprepared for a visitor)

hair/hairy
- My hair is sticking up like a chicken's behind

- This is an official bad hair day! (unruly hair
- Your hair is as bushy as a squirrel's tail
- Her hair is the color of a brand new penny.
- Your hair shines like glass.
- I'd ruther have my hair turn gray than turn loose!
- His hair is as black as a raven's wing.
- Her hair is sticking up like a cactus
- Bushy head, get out of bed! (fix your hair)
- She uses so much hair spray, if you tried to hug her, you'd be apt to poke your eye out!
- His hair is like a sheep dog.
- Your hair looks like you've stuck your finger in a light socket.
- Her hair is as soft as silk.
- Your hair looks like a rat's nest!
- Her hair is as long as a monkey's tail.
- His hair was as white as snow.
- Your hair looks like Velcro.
- His hair is jet black.
- He crawled out of bed with his hair all foggy headed.
- Let me retten your hair. (Comb)
- I'm rettening the tangles out of my hair. (Combing)
- I haven't seen hide nor hair of him in days.
- He's as hairy as an ape.
- He's so hairy, you could braid his back!
- He's so hairy, his chest looks like a door mat.
- Her legs are so hairy, they are ready to be declared a national forest.
- He's as wooly as a lamb.

- He's harrier than a cave man.
- His moustache is as prickly as a porcupine.

hand/hands/handy
- Many hands make light work.
- Idle hands are the devils' playthings.
- Can you lend me a hand? (help)
- He's a good hand to fix things. (good at fixing things)
- I've washed my hands of it. (walked away from a bad situation and letting someone else work it out)
- He's a hired hand. (employee)
- They all gave her a hand. (clapping hands for a show of approval)
- On the other hand… (opposite perspective)
- Keep your hand to the plow. (choose a steady course; be faithful in your tasks)
- That's as handy as pockets on a shirt.
- That's as handy as a shirt full of pockets.
- That's as handy as a button on a barn door.
- She's a real hand to quilt. (very good at it)

handle
- Can you handle this? (deal with successfully)
- What's your handle? (name; CB road name)
- I'm trying to get a handle on this situation. (get control of; understand)
- I need to get rid of these love handles. (fat roll above the hips that hangs over the waste)
- A vacuum cleaner handle will fit your hand and dishrags and dust rags work for a man just like they do for a woman.

handsome
- Now there is a good looking guy!
- He is nothing to her but eye candy.
- They make a very handsome couple.
- Well hello, handsome!

hang/hung
- Give him enough rope and he'll hang himself. (expose his real motives)
- She hung him out to dry. (told him off)
- Why are you still hanging around? (loitering)
- Would you like to hang out together? (spend time together)

happy
- She was so happy it was all over her face.
- This ought to tickle your fancy!
- I am so happy I could sprout wings and fly.
- He was as happy as a wind-up toy.
- She was on cloud nine!
- I'm jumping for joy!
- I'm as pleased as punch.
- Her smile was like a crescent moon.
- I'm so happy I could cry.
- He's grinning from ear to ear.
- Her feet won't touch the ground.
- She's as happy as a baby with a new toy.
- Her face was as bright as the sun.
- I'm kicking high!
- Getting those flowers really made my day!
- He's happy as a lark.
- I'm as pleased as punch!

- They were as happy as two frogs on a log!
- They were as happy as two little newborn squirrels.
- They were as happy as two peas in a pod.
- She was filled to overflowing with joy.
- He was as happy as a cricket on a hearthstone.
- He was as happy as a hog with a slop bucket.

happy expressions
- Hot diggity dog!
- Boy, oh boy, oh boy!
- Yeee-haaaa!
- You betcha!
- Wooo-hooo!
- Waaaa-haaaa!
- Oh, boy!
- Shazaaaaam!
- Golly!
- Yipppeeeee!
- Gee whillakers!
- I can't believe this could happen to me!

hard/hardship
- He had a hard way to go.
- She had a hard raising.
- He was brought up rough and hard.
- Her face was so hard, if she smiled, it would probably break!
- He's a hard hearted man. (unfeeling; cruel)
- He's so skinny a hard wind could blow him away! (poor; undernourished)
- He's a hard nut to crack.

hat
- He wears many hats. (has many jobs; fills many roles)
- I'm changing hats. (changing jobs; changing roles)
- That's old hat. (old news)
- He's putting on his top hat. (getting dressed up)
- Please pass the hat. (taking up an offering of money)
- His head is too big for his hat. (inflated ego)

hateful
- He's as hateful as an old sore eared bear. (surly)
- She's the hatefulest thing I ever met! (unpleasant)
- The idea is hateful to me. (undesirable)
- That is a hateful use of time. (waste)

hay
- Make hay while the sun shines. (work while you can; take advantage of favorable circumstances)
- Everything went hay wire. (awry; not part of the plan; unexpected interference)

head
- Use your noggin ! (think)
- That's thinking with the old noodle. (brain)
- What's floating around in your think tank?
- He is a pure old hard head! (stubborn)
- What a numb skull!
- Use that melon for something besides a place to set your hat!
- She thinks she's the big giant head. (boss)
- He took a lick on the old bean.
- I hung my head. (sad; ashamed)
- He lost his head. (temper)

- He's head over heels for her. (in love)
- She walks around with her head in the clouds. (daydreaming)
- Head for the hills! (get away as quickly as possible)
- I can't make heads nor tails of what he's talking about.
- He wants your head on a spike! (wants you humiliated)
- My head is on the chopping block. (I'm accountable)
- The Lord only made a few perfect heads. The rest he had to put hair on!
- She is head over heels for him. (in love)
- He is a headstrong boy. (stubborn)
- It will all come to a head soon. (trouble is coming)
- You're headed down the wrong path. (bad choice)
- I'm speaking off the top of my head. (impromptu)
- Let's put our heads together and see what we can come up with. (ideas)
- Heads - I win. Tails – you lose. (said to someone gullible before a coin toss)

health/healthy
- I am fair to middling.
- He has a strong constitution.
- She is stout.
- He is hale and hardy.
- I feel finer than a horse's tail!
- I feel like a million bucks.
- I'm finer than frog hairs.
- I'm fine and dandy.
- I'm fit as a fiddle!

- He is tough as nails.
- He's wiry, but he's stout. (thin but strong)
- I'm finer than frog hairs split four ways.
- Good health is better than wealth.
- People wreck their health to get wealth, then spend their wealth trying to get back their health.
- He's in the pink. (usually refers to someone who has recovered from an illness)

help
- God, holp me.
- Lord, holp me.
- Help is on the way.
- He's not much help.
- I could use a little help over here.
- Help yourself! (usually refers to food or drink as in you are welcome to serve yourself)
- Well, help my time! (phrase to emphasize surprise; frustration)

heard/hearing
- I never heard the beat! (amazement)
- I never heard the like! (shock)
- I never heard tell of such a thing! (surprise)
- He's got ears that hear like a coon dog. (excellent hearing; eavesdrops things not meant for other ears)
- It was so quiet, you could hear a pin drop. (silent)
- He is stone deaf. (can't hear)
- I hear tell you're doing well. (heard through gossip)
- She hears what she wants to. (selective hearing)

heart/heartache
- The old ticker is about worn out.

- My pump is working overtime.
- Your treasure is where your heart is.
- Home is where heart is.
- That movie melted my heart! (sentimental)
- She's as cold as ice, with a heart to match.
- He's hard hearted. (mean)
- She's a good hearted soul. (kind)
- Her heart is as fragile as a vase.
- Her heart broke like a baseball through a glass window.
- She's soft hearted. (compassionate)
- She's got a heart of pure gold. (good person)
- Her heart is the biggest thing about her. (loving; accepting of others)
- He has a broken heart. (romantic split; the result of a terrible loss; disappointment)
- He's broken hearted. (same as above)
- He's cold hearted. (cruel)
- What the heart thinks, the mouth speaks.
- He has a heart of steel. (unemotional)
- Faint heart never won fair maiden. (don't be afraid to pursue someone you are interested in romantically)
- He's faint hearted. (given up hope; coward)
- He doesn't have a heart. He has a thumping gizzard. (cruel; unfeeling)
- My heart just isn't in it. (don't want to do something)
- He's nothing but a heartache.
- He's black hearted. (emotionally unfeeling)
- Her gratitude was genuinely heartfelt.

- He has a heart of stone. (unmovable)
- She's a heartache waiting to happen.
- Her comments were heartfelt. (genuine)
- My heart is an open wound. (emotionally damaged)
- As a man thinketh in his heart, so shall he be. (thoughts reveal a person's character)
- She's heavy hearted. (sad; depressed)
- That hurts my heart. (physical pain associated with emotional pain)
- She has a servant's heart. (cares for others willingly)

heat/hot
- She was hotter than a pepper sprout! (sexy)
- If you can't stand the heat, get out of the kitchen!
- Things are really heating up between them. (can refer to romance or a disagreement)
- It was hotter than a blazing fire.
- It was hotter than an August noon.
- He's hotter than a firecracker!
- She's hotter than a two dollar bill.
- It's hotter than the hinges on the gates of Hades.
- It's four degrees hotter than Hades.
- It is hotter than blue blazes.
- It was so hot, you could scald a cat in the creek.
- It was hot enough to fry an egg on the sidewalk.
- It was so hot, he was panting like a dog.
- You're hotter than the sun.
- He was sweating like a hooker in church.
- You're like a worm on a hot rock. (can't be still)
- That computer is hot. (stolen)
- The microphone is hot. (too loud)

- This heat is sweltering.
- I don't have hot flashes; I have nuclear meltdowns!

heavy
- That's heavier than a sack of taters.
- That's quite a load.
- That weighs about a ton.
- That's like packing a sack of rocks.

hell
- There'll be no picnics in hell.
- I'll be there, come hell or high water. (in spite of)
- We're all going to hell in a hand basket. (on the wrong moral path)
- It's hell for leather out of here! (get out as fast as possible)
- Hell hath no fury like a woman scorned.
- All hell broke loose when he got home. (argument)
- He'll give you hell over that. (quarrel at you)
- That will be hell for certain. (bad news)
- Hells bells! What are you talking about?
- There'll be no atheists in Hell.

hen
- He better leave that girl alone before she turns him from a rooster into a hen. (castrate)
- That plant is as rare as hen's teeth. (extremely unlikely to find)
- He's hen pecked. (dominated by his wife)

heredity
- He came out of the short end of the gene pool.
- She crawled out of the dregs of humanity.

- They are too close kin to be looking at each other that way.
- He's a dead ringer for his old man.
- Like father, like son.
- The apple doesn't fall too far from the tree.
- He's a mirror image.
- Just call him Junior.

hiccups
- I've got the hicky doos.
- She's got the he-cups, she cups.

hide
- I'll tan your hide! (spank)
- He has a thick hide. (tough character; seasoned)
- You can't run and you can't hide! (no choices)
- You can run, but you can't hide! (troubles have a way of catching up)
- Let's play hoopie hide. (hide and go seek)
- The children are playing hide and go seek. (a game)

high
- I'm high on life. (happy)
- Always take the high road. (integrity)
- He's wearing high water pants. (too short)

hint
- Do you get my drift?
- Do you catch my meaning?
- You can knock him over with a hint and he still doesn't get it.
- I caught wind of something that wasn't clear.
- Let me put a bug in your ear.

hit
- Time to hit the hay. (sleep)
- Time to hit the sack. (go to bed)
- I need to hit the books. (study)
- You've hit the nail right on the head! (got something right)
- Ouch! Don't fump me on the head again!
- He's hit his stride. (found something he's good at)
- Hit's so pretty. (reference to a child, hit instead of it)
- It's hit or miss. (chance)
- He's too lazy to hit a lick at a snake.
- There are only three hits – I hit you, you hit the ground, and the ambulance hits 90!
- She beaned him in the head with a rock.
- That is hitting below the belt! (dirty trick; unscrupulous)

hitch/hitched
- It went off without a hitch. (an event went well without any glitches or complications)
- I've got a hitch in my get along. (a cramp in the hip or leg that cause a limp)
- They are getting hitched in June. (married)
- What's the hitch? (hold up; delay)

hitch hike
- My car is broken. I guess I'll be thumbing it.
- Can you give me a lift?
- I need to catch a ride.
- I have hitchhikers all over my pants! (burrs and seeds)

hoe
- It's a hard row to hoe. (difficult)

- There are other rows to hoe. (more work to be done)

hog
- It's root, hog, or die. (survive as best you can)
- Don't hog all the covers. (take more than your share)
- If you turned a hog loose in here, he'd starve to death. (no food available)
- We always used every inch of a hog from the rooter to the tooter. (completely)
- He's like a big fattening hog. (eats too much, works too little)
- Reckon I could trade a good fattening hog for one of those girls?
- That bath water was hot enough to scald a hog!
- It's whole hog or none.
- Half of what you hear is nothing but hogwash. (not to be believed)
- We used every part of the hog but the squeal.
- Suieeeeee, hog! (way to call the hogs)
- I love that souse meat. (hog brain)
- I don't like hog's head pudding! (truly dislike)
- Don't be a hog. (greedy)
- She's hoggish. (greedy)
- She hogged him all to herself. (demanded his attention)
- He's gone hog wild! (misbehaving)
- I'm in hog heaven! (very happy)

hold
- You've got to know when to hold 'em. (be still)
- Hold on a minute! (wait)
- She's holding out. (a virgin)

- Hold on to your hat! (going to speed up)
- Hold your horses. (wait)
- I have all the love I can hold! (content)
- Hold on to your britches (or bloomers)!

home
- There's no place like home.
- Home is where your heart is.
- Home, sweet home!
- Home is where you hang your hat.
- A man's home is his castle.
- Charity begins at home.
- We're heading down the home stretch. (almost finished)
- Is that the light of home I see?
- Make yourself to home. (welcome; be comfortable)
- He's like a homing pigeon. (always comes home)
- She's home bound. (sick)
- He's homeward bound. (headed home)

homesick
- I hear the hills of home calling me.
- My heart hurts for home.
- I'm pining away for the mountains.
- I'm yearning for home.
- I'm longing for home.

honey
- Feed your man honey – not vinegar. (treat him well)
- You draw more flies with honey than vinegar. (kindness accomplishes more than sarcasm)
- She talks so sweet, honey wouldn't melt in her mouth. (flattering)

- Honey, would you go to the store for me? (honey is an affectionate term used for anyone at any age in a close relationship to the speaker. It can begin or end a sentence.)

honest/honesty
- He's as honest as Old Abe.
- He's as honest as George Washington's cherry tree.
- She's on the level.
- There's no reason to hold back.
- He won, fair and square.
- He got a fair shake.
- He's as honest as the day is long.
- Honest to goodness! (that's the truth)
- Honest to Pete! (really; truly)   *Martha Lewis Asher*
- Honesty is the best policy.
- Honest Abe! (truthfully)

honor/honorable
- Everything is above board.
- It's an honor to meet you.
- He's a man of his word.
- Death before dishonor.
- Upon my honor! (truthfully)
- He is honor bound. (obligated by honor)

hoot
- He's a hoot! (funny)
- I don't give a hoot what you do! (don't care)
- Hoot when you're ready to go. (give me a call)
- It will be a hoot. (good time)

hope
- Hope springs eternal.

- Well, I hope to my never! (disbelief; surprise)
- Somebody hope me! (help)
- Help deferred makes the heart sad.

horse/horses
- I'm so hungry I could eat a horse!
- That's a horse of a different color. (whole different matter)
- Don't look a gift horse in the mouth.
- If wishes were horses, then beggars could ride.
- He's the dark horse in the race. (not expected to win)
- He's a dark horse. (mysterious)
- The best horse doesn't always win the race.
- You can't run a thoroughbred against a jackass and expect them to finish at the same time.
- You can't put a thoroughbred horse in a race with a jackass and expect them to come out neck and neck.
- You can lead a horse to water, but you can't make him drink.
- Wild horses couldn't drag it out of me! (I can keep a secret.)
- I heard it straight from the horse's mouth. (from the original source)

hospitality
- Come on in and set a spell.
- Take your shoes off! Make yourself to home.
- Feel free while you're here.
- Glad to have you!
- We've been looking forward to spending time with you.
- Anything you have need of, just let me know.

- We don't have much, but you are welcome to what we do have.
- We're glad to break bread with you.
- Let your hair down and feel at home.
- I hope you'll feel at home.
- Make yourself at home.

hot
- It's hotter than blue blazes in here!
- It's hot enough to fry an egg on the sidewalk.
- Her fever is so hot, you could fry an egg on her forehead.
- That's hotter than Hades.
- It's so hot it just about burned my goozle out. (hot liquid nearly scalded my throat)
- It's hotter than a popcorn fart!
- It just about burned my guzzler out. (same as above)
- You're not so hot. (an insult to an egotistic person)
- What's hot? (popular; fad)

how
- How come me to have it in the first place was that he left it here by accident. (the reason why)
- He has the know-how. (skills)
- How in the world did that happen?

house/houses
- People who live in glass houses shouldn't throw stones.

hug
- I could have hugged her neck! (appreciative of something that has been done for you; happy to see someone; emotional approval)

- I love you a bushel and a peck and a hug around the neck.
- I hugged myself up tight with a book. (curled up with a book)
- He's nothing but a big old huggy bear. (loveable person)
- That's the huggingest bunch I ever did see. (refers to a group of people or a family who greet each other with hugs – i.e. family reunion; church)
- Hugs! (farewell)
- Hugs and kisses! (closing at the bottom of a letter)
- Hug your momma for me. (give her my greeting)
- Now how did you know I needed a hug? (said to an affectionate child who displays affection through hugs)
- She hugged up her teddy bear and went to sleep. (snuggled)

humanitarian
- She's a do-gooder. (concerned with humanity; environment)
- He's a tree hugger. (environmentalist)

humdinger
- He is a humdinger. (a well liked man)
- Now that's a humdinger. (a big lie)
- That car is a humdinger. (beautiful; desirable)

humorous sayings - general
- I'll pay you back just as soon as I get my rich uncle out of the poor house.
- I finally taught my old mule to work without eating and he up and died on me!
- If wishes came true, even beggars would ride.

- I could stretch a mile if I didn't have to walk back.
- She's as pretty as can be. Lord knows if she could be any prettier, she surely would be.
- Did you get your eyes together last night? How did you get them across your nose.
- You are looking bright eyed and bushy tailed.
- Do they have a back door? Well, where do you think they'd want one? (I want to get out of here in a hurry.)

hunger/hungry
- I'm so hungry my backbone is sucking wind.
- I'm hungry as a bear.
- I'm so hungry, I could eat a horse!
- I'm so hungry I could chew my arm off.
- I'm so hungry, I could eat a house!
- I'm so hungry it isn't going to be safe to be around me until I get something to eat!
- Just knock that cow in the head, wipe its butt, put some steak sauce on it and hand me a fork!
- I'm hungrier than a dog on starvation.
- I'm as hungry as a lion on the prowl.
- You don't wait and eat because you're hungry. You've got to eat to keep from getting hungry.
- My stomach is so empty it's shaking hands with my backbone!

hurry
- Make it snappy!
- Step it up!
- Hurly burly!
- Step on it!
- Get the lead out.

- Pick up the pace.
- Hurry up, slow poke!
- Don't dawdle!
- Whickity whack!
- Get a move on!
- Shake a leg!
- Hop to it!
- Hurry up and wait!
- Get with the program.
- I'll be there in a jiffy.
- Snap the cracker!
- Hurry up and wait!
- Don't slack your heels until you get there.
- I'd better high tail it out of here.

husband
- He is her old man.
- He's the breadwinner.
- He is a hound of a husband.
- He is her covering.
- He leant her his last name.
- He's got the whip hand over her.

hyperactive
- He's in overdrive.
- She's like a worm on a hot rock.
- You're a wiggle worm.
- He couldn't be still if he had to.
- You've got ants in your pants.
- That child has a bad case of the squirmels.
- That child is in hyper drive.

- That child is a whirlybird!
- She goes like a house on fire all the time.

I

ice
- She is as cold as ice. (unaffectionate)
- He has ice in his veins. (unfeeling; not afraid)
- You are treading on thin ice. (in danger of going too far and getting in trouble)
- He is walking on thin ice. (same as above)
- She is skating on thin ice. (same as above)

idea
- I've had a notion.
- I've conceived a thought.
- The light bulb just went off in my head.
- I've got an idea bouncing around in my head.
- Let's run it up the flagpole and see if it flies. (try the idea out)
- I ain't got no idée what I'm doing!

identical
- They are like two peas in a pod.
- They must be twins.
- He's a dead ringer for the President.
- They act like they are joined at the hip.
- They are of one mind.
- There is your dobble ganker! (identical look alike)
- He's your doppelganger! (look alike)
- He's a spitting image of his dad!

- I could swear I'd seen a ghost, he looks so much like his dead father.
- He's a chip off the old block.
- They are one in the same.

ignore
- She blew him off.
- She's giving him the cold shoulder.
- She turned a blind eye to his infidelity.
- So, what am I – chopped liver?
- Pay him no mind.
- Don't pay it a lot of mind.
- Pay no mind to it.
- Pay it no mind.
- He walked right on by me like I wasn't even standing there.
- I'm not talking to the wall!
- (said to someone who is ignoring you)
- My advice to you about him is let whatever he says go in one ear and out the other.
- I might as well talk to a tree stump as to try and talk to you.
- You don't pay any more attention to me talking than that old dog howling at the moon.

ill/illness
- I'm feeling puny.
- I'm out of sorts.
- I'm discomfited.
- I've got the cruising.
- I've got the woes.
- I'm sick as a dog.

- I feel green all over.
- He's got the trots.
- She's got the runs.
- He has the squirts.
- I've got the down and outs.
- I've got the oopie poopies.
- I'm sicker than a hound dog sucking eggs.
- I'm feeling discombobulated.
- I've got a hitch in my get along.
- He has one foot in the grave.
- I'm feeling poorly today.
- I'm sick and tired of being sick and tired.
- He was as sick as a skunk.
- You'll catch your death.
- It's best not to speak ill of the dead. (derogatory remark)
- I heard you've got a catch in your giddy-up.
- My giddy-up got up and went.
- He has one foot in the grave and one on a banana peel.

ill tempered
- She's a grouchy old thing.
- He's always out of sorts.
- She's as ill as a hornet.
- What a hateful gut!
- He's downright hateful!
- She's a hornet.
- I'm steering clear of him while he's in this frame of mind.

illegal
- He's breaking the law right and left.
- That'll take a pay off. (activity known by the law enforcement officers)

illegitimate
- He's the red headed step child.
- His daddy was hiding in the wood pile.
- Her daddy never did step out.
- She's an unclaimed child.
- Her daddy never did come forward.
- She was born on the wrong side of the covers.
- He's the black sheep of the family.
- She was a borrowed child.
- She was a love child.

imitate
- Imitation is the sincerest form of flattery. (to copy someone's behavior or appearance)
- I know you are, but what am I?
- Monkey see, monkey do. (behaves like)
- She imitates her mother. (looks like)

impartial
- I'm keeping my oar out of it.
- I don't give two flips about it.
- I don't give two figs about it.
- Makes no never mind to me.
- I'm indifferent.
- I'll keep my two cents to myself.
- Keep your chickens at your own house.
- It's neither here nor there.
- It's a foot one way and 12 inches the other.

- It's six of one, half a dozen of the other.

important
- I have pressing business to attend to.
- It is pressin' on me to get it done.

inaccurate
- That dog won't hunt!
- Wrrrp! Guess again! (sounding like a buzzer on a game show when an incorrect answer is given)
- You missed that answer by a country mile!
- He missed the boat on that one.

inappropriate
- It just ain't fittin'.
- That won't do.
- I wouldn't let you out of the house dressed like that!

inch
- Give him an inch, and he'll take a mile. (take advantage)
- She won't budge an inch. (won't give in)
- An inch is as good as a mile. (a near miss is still a miss)

include/included/inclusion
- How can I get in on that party?
- You're on the short list.
- Count me in.
- I'll have a slice of that.
- Sign me up.
- I'm on the outside looking in.
- For one time in my life I don't feel like it.

incompetent
- That's the blind leading the blind.
- He doesn't know his head from a hole in the ground.

- He doesn't know his tail form a hole in the ground.
- What he knows on that subject wouldn't fill a thimble.

inconvenience
- I hate to inconvenience you.
- It's no inconvenience.
- It just doesn't suit.
- Can I take a rain check?
- Some other time, maybe.

indecisive
- You need to fish or cut bait! (Make up your mind.)
- You need to pee or get off the pot.
- Are you going to fly it around all day or are you going to land this baby?
- You are wavering minded.
- My mind turns one way and then t'other.
- Her mind is tossed to and fro with every wind that blows. (swayed by everyone else's opinions)

independent
- I can do it myself!
- She's a plucky little thing.
- I can paddle my own canoe!

indifference/indifferent
- I don't give a hoot!
- I could care less.
- No one gives a rat's patootie!
- I have bigger fish to fry.
- I don't give a rat's pee.
- I don't give a rat's behind.
- They don't give a rat's patootie.

- Make me no difference one way or t'other.
- Makes me no never mind.
- Makes no never mind to me.
- I don't give a fig about it.
- It doesn't matter a hill of beans to me.
- I don't give a diddley squat what they think.
- Too bad, too sad!
- I don't give a flip about it.

individuality
- She's turned quare.
- He's mighty peculiar.
- To each his own.
- I'll do my own thing. You do yours.
- She's turned a little quare. (peculiar)
- He marches to his own drummer.
- To thine own self be true.
- "To each his own," said the little woman when she kissed the pig.

infer
- You need to read between the lines.
- I got your drift.
- He's left you sign posts along the way if you'd just read them!
- What else could it mean?
- If you put two and two together, it does not come out to three.

ingredients
- I need to get the fixins to bake a cake.

inherited
- He comes by it naturally.

- It's in the blood.
- It runs in the family.
- She took after her momma's people.
- He's the spittin' image of his daddy.
- The apple doesn't fall far from the tree.
- He looks like he crawled out of his daddy's behind.
- He can't deny that one.
- He come by it honest.
- Considering where he came from, what more could you expect out of him?
- That bunch climbed out of the short end of the gene pool.
- They are a proud bunch.
- That kid was dug right out of his daddy's butt.
- You can spot one of that family a mile away.
- They've all got the same look.
- I'd know you anywhere. You look just like your momma. (can be said about any other relative – i.e. father, sister…)
- They all have music in them.
- I never saw one of that bunch I didn't like.
- The apple doesn't fall far from the tree.

inner peace
- End your day at the mirror and see if you like the one staring back at you.
- He'll be sleeping the rest of the wicked.
- Don't let the sun go down on your wrath.
- Do unto others as you would have them do unto you.

insecure
- She's so insecure, she can hardly stand to face herself in the mirror.
- He doesn't have a drop of confidence.
- She's been beat down to a dog.
- He's afraid to stand up to his own shadow.

insignificant
- My opinion and twenty five cents still won't buy you a cup of coffee.
- I'm not even a dot over an "i".
- Nobody loves me. Everybody hates me. Think I'll eat some worms.
- Nobody loves me; everybody hates me. I think I'll eat some worms.
- No one ever listens to me.
- You are inconsequential to me.
- Don't worry about that rinky dink little restaurant coming in to town. They won't hurt your business.
- He is low man on the totem pole.
- His opinion makes me no never mind.
- I feel like the invisible woman.
- He's only small potatoes.
- He's just a little fish in a big pond.
- He's only small fries.

insomniac
- I couldn't get my eyes together last night.
- I've got the big eye.

instinct
- I have a gut feeling.
- It's a feeling coming from down deep inside.

- Always listen to a mother's intuition.
- Some things you're just born with.
- I reckon I was born with it. (natural ability; a propensity to do something well)

insult
- That's adding insult to injury! (making things worse)
- That's the ultimate insult!
- He wouldn't know an insult if it bit him.
- You can't insult an idiot.
- A good insult is wasted on an idiot.

integrity
- Take the high road.
- If he said it, you can believe it.
- If he's behind it, you can count on it.
- When you leave this earth, all you have is your good name.

intelligent
- He is world wise.
- She's smart.
- He's pretty sharp.
- He's got a library between his ears.
- He is as sharp as a tack.
- She is a brainy one.
- He was a rolling archive.
- The boy was a walking encyclopedia.
- His attic is crammed full.
- He's a brainiac.
- She is cranial.
- I'm so bright my daddy calls me Sunny.
- They all have pointy little heads.

- He is book smart, but doesn't have walking around sense.
- He is well studied.
- She is well versed in her field.
- She has a string of letters after her name.
- She's at the top of her game.

intimidated
- We were daresome to open our mouths if momma told us to be quiet.
- I dared not do it after my husband said, "NO!"
- She's got the whip hand over him.
- You'd best not go against his wishes.
- He's scared of his own shadow.
- She has to ask permission to breathe.

intoxicated
- He's drunker than drunk.
- He's drunk as a skunk.
- He's dog drunk.
- He's blistered.
- She drinks like a fish.
- I'm afraid he's stewed again.
- He's jacked up on Jack Daniels.
- His eyes are patriotic – red, white, and blue.
- She got smashed last night.
- He's half blithered.
- Time to leave the bar. I'm all done in.
- No more drinks. I'm feeling a little tipsy.
- He was bass over ackwards drunk.
- He's three sheets to the wind.
- He's been out warpin' and swarpin'!

introductions (on making a new acquaintance or handshake)
- Glad to know you.
- It's good to meet you.
- I'm pleased as punch to meet you.
- Howdy do. How are you?
- Proud to know you.
- Glad to meet you.
- Proud to meet you.
- My pleasure to meet you.
- Glad to make your acquaintance.

invent
- Necessity is the mother of invention.
- We don't have to invent the wheel again.
- If we put our heads together, I'm sure we could come up with something.

invitations (casual)
- Come on in and set a spell.
- Take your shoes off and rest a while.
- Come on in and chew the fat.
- Stop by sometime.
- You're welcome any time.
- Give me a heads up and come on over.
- Bring your little self over here any time you want.
- We're always glad to see you.
- You're always welcome.
- Come by and swap howdies.
- Come on over. We'll stay up all night and tell lies.
- We'll have a big time whenever you come.
- Come hungry!

- Holler at me and I'll come a running.
- We don't stand on ceremony. You're welcome any time.
- Friends and family are always welcome.

involvement (or lack of)
- Leave me out of it!
- I'll have no truck with that bunch.
- I'm square dab in the middle of it.

irrelevant
- What's that got to do with the price of rice in China?
- What's that got to do with the price of wheat in Russia?
- What's that got to do with anything?
- That's a moot point.
- That's neither here nor there.

itch/itching
- He's itching for a fight. (trying to antagonize)
- I'm itching to see some spring flowers. (wanting very much)
- He's slower than the seven year itch. (a disease)
- He's got the seven year itch. (unsettled/unhappy in marriage)
- She's got an itch and wants him to scratch it. (wants to develop a romantic relationship.

J

jaw
- That girl can sure jaw! (talk a lot)
- I'll punch you right in the jaw!

- He looked at me with that slack jawed expression. (oblivious)
- Stop jacking your jaws and come on! (stop talking)
- She could jaw the ears off an elephant!
- She can jaw your legs off! (talk too much)

jealousy
- There's the green eyed monster!
- She's got her nails sharpened.
- She's got her dander up.
- She's green with envy.
- She watches him like a hawk.

jig/jiggered
- Well, I'll be jiggered! (informal curse word)
- I'll be jiggered if I'll let him get away with that! (determined not to)
- I'm all jiggered out. (tired)
- We will dance a jig. (a type of dance)
- Play a jig on the piano. (music to dance by)
- Use a jig to catch a lot of fish. (a type of manmade bait)
- I'll see you after I finish this jig. (job)

jilted
- I've been jilted. (left for another person)
- She got cold feet at the altar. (wedding)
- He got cold feet right at the last minute. (couldn't commit to a relationship)
- She was left at the altar. (groom didn't show up for the wedding)

job
- That's a job well done.

- I'm trying to do myself out of a job. (done so well, it is almost finished)
- I'm the poorest hand in two counties. (don't know how to do something I've been asked to do)

joking
- He was only teasing. (didn't really mean it)
- I was only fooling. (trying to play a joke)
- Just kidding! (not serious)
- I was just funning you. (playing a trick)
- He was deviling her. (deliberately annoying in jest)
- We were cutting up.
- He is a big cut up. (jokester)
- I was just pranking with you. (teasing)
- He was just pulling your leg. (teasing)
- Are you joshing?

judge/judged
- You can't judge a book by its cover.
- You can't judge a person by their family.
- You can't judge a man by one mistake.
- You have been judged and found wanting. (inadequate)
- The jury is still out. (a decision hasn't been made yet in a trial)

jumping
- That boy jumps like a kangaroo. (talent for jumping)
- He jumps like a politician on Election Day. (nervous reaction)
- He jumped like a scared rabbit. (skiddish, frightful)
- She jumps around like a jack rabbit. (hyperactive; very busy)

- She jumped like a frog. (long distance; nervous reaction)
- She jumps right in the middle of mischief at every opportunity. (gets involved in)
- I nearly jumped out of my skin. (startled reaction)

justice
- He got what he deserved.
- In the end, he'll get what he deserves.
- The way she's treated others will come right back to her.
- You got what was coming to you.
- You'll get your just desert.
- She'll have to ride the horse she saddled.
- You can't take the law into your own hands.
- He brought it on himself.
- What goes over the devil's back has to come back under his belly.
- He needs to get a good dose of his own medicine!
- You need a taste of your own medicine.
- You even have to give the devil justice.
- Whenever I can, I try to give the benefit of the doubt.
- What goes around comes around.
- What goes over the ducks back comes back under his belly.
- What goes over the devils back will pass under his belly.
- His little dittlers will one day come home to roost.
- Payback is rough.
- What's done in darkness will come to light.

- You don't get away with anything – you just put it off.
- He planted a rotten crop and he can expect a rotten harvest.
- He will get his due one way or another.
- She'll get her just desert.
- You've done me wrong and the same wrong will come knocking on your door before all is said and done.
- People don't really get by with anything. They just think they do until it turns back up on their doorstep.
- Sometimes you get and sometimes you get got.
- I can give back as good as I get.
- You've made your bed. Now lay in it!
- You may dance now, but you'll have to pay the fiddler.
- You might like the song, but you'll have to pay the piper.
- If you keep fooling around, you'll have a new blister in the same place you popped the last one!
- If you get burned, don't complain when you have to sit on the blister!
- If you burn a blister, you will have to sit on it.
- It will all come out in the wash.
- You will reap what you sew.
- You've sewn a rotten crop and you'll reap a rotten harvest. As a man sews, so shall he reap.
- You brought it all on yourself!
- I ken what you mean. (understand)

kick/kicking
- He kicked the bucket. (died)
- She kicked the habit. (stopped a habit)
- He was dragged in kicking and screaming. (protesting)
- Never kick a cow chip. (unwise decision)
- Never kick a man while he's down. (Don't take advantage of someone having a hard time.)
- Now ain't that a kick in the teeth? (disappointment)

kill
- They were wiped out.
- He was blown away.
- I'll take you down.
- You better be ready to meet your Maker.
- Kill them with kindness.
- You kill me! (make me laugh; frustrate me)
- You can't kill a dead horse. (pointless)
- There are more ways to kill a hog than choking it on butter.
- There are more ways than one to skin a cat.

kin
- She is my next of kin. (closest living family member; the one responsible for me)
- We are kith and kin. (close family)
- Blood makes us kin but choice makes us friends. (related and friends, also)
- They are my kin folk. (relatives)
- Yes, we're kin, but don't hold that against me. (refers to a discovery of a relative known by a new acquaintance)

- We're bound to be kin to each other. You look just like my family. (similar facial or physical characteristics)

kind/kindness
- Remember the golden rule: Do unto others as you would have them do unto you.
- It don't hurt nobody to be nice.
- You are one of a kind. (unique)
- I've seen your kind before. (someone of poor character)
- You can pay in kind. (payment with something besides money)
- He's a kind hearted soul. (treats others well)
- Thank you for your kindness. (help; assistance in time of need)

kiss
- Give me a smooch.
- How about a little sugar?
- Pucker up baby, 'cause here I come!
- Give me a little peck on the cheek.
- You can kiss my grits! (leave me alone)
- She gave him the kiss off. (got rid of him)

L

lady
- She's my lady. (girlfriend)
- She's my old lady. (mom; wife)
- She is a well bred young lady.
- Act like a lady.
- Remember you're a lady.

laid/lay
- He's laid out at the funeral home. (dead)
- Lay your head right down here and rest.
- All she does is lay around all day watching soap operas.
- He lays in the bed half of the day.

lamb
- He's as gentle as a lamb.
- Here we go like lambs to the starts.
- They are being led astray, like lambs to the slaughter.

land
- He owns a big bounder of land.
- This is a lovely boundary of land.
- That is a handsome acreage.
- We own a small plot of land.
- He owns a big parcel of land up on the mountain.
- I'd rather for him to be plowing up the red clay of Georgia than to have a million dollars and to do like he's done.

late/later
- I'll be there atter while.
- Better late than never.
- He's always a day late and a dollar short.
- I'm paying for news, not history! (a late newspaper)
- That ship has sailed! (opportunity lost)
- You missed the boat on that one! (missed a good deal)
- Too little, too late!
- I got behind every slow moving thing coming and going on the highway!

- We were about to give you up! (stop expecting you to come)
- He said he'd stop in at a while. (after while)
- He'll be late for his own funeral.

laugh/laughter
- I nearly laughed my head off.
- Laughter is good medicine.
- I laughed so hard I nearly wet my britches(or pants).
- A merry heart doeth good like a medicine.
- He who laughs last laughs last.
- We're not laughing at you. We're laughing with you!
- It's better to laugh than cry.
- Sometimes it's either laugh or cry, so you might as well laugh.
- We all need to learn to laugh at ourselves.
- Laugh and the world laughs with you. Cry and you cry alone.
- He laughs like a hyena.
- She laughs like a hen caught on an electric fence.
- His laughter rolled like thunder.
- I laughed until I cried.
- I laughed until tears rolled down my face.
- I laughed until I couldn't laugh any more.
- He laughed just like Santy Claus.
- I laughed so hard, I nearly peed my pants!
- You will laugh your socks off
- His laugh is like a dying seal.
- She doesn't have enough sense to know that people are laughing at her.

law/lawless/lawyers/
- The law is made for those who make them more than those who are subject to them.
- Keep lawyers and skunks at bay.
- Keep skunks and lawyers at a distance.
- He's an ambulance chaser.
- He's a schiester.
- They are a law unto themselves. (don't follow regular social standards)
- It is the law of the jungle… kill or be killed; eat what doesn't eat you!
- They are a lawless bunch! (don't have any regard for the law or what is socially acceptable; unruly; trouble makers)
- The law will get you for that. (reprimand for someone breaking the law)

lazy
- He's sorrier than cyarn.
- She's lazier than cyarn.
- That boy is plain sorry.
- He's too lazy to breathe if it took an effort.
- He wouldn't hit a lick if his life depended on it.
- He wouldn't strike a lick a snake if it was about to bite him.
- He's too sorry to breathe if it took any effort on his part.
- He's a couch potato.
- She's a house cat.
- If he saw a rattlesnake coming straight for him, he'd be too lazy to get out of the way.

- He wouldn't work in a pie factory!
- She's as lazy as the day is long.
- He's too lazy to step over poop.
- She loves to wallow the bed.
- He just wallows around all day and doesn't hit a lick at anything.
- He's too sorry to throw a rock at a snake.
- He's too lazy to strike a lick at a snake.
- He's too lazy to step over a pile of poop in his path.
- The first day you go to work, the rest of your life is ruined – do don't ever start.
- She's nothing but a sleepy head.
- He's a dead head.
- He's a dead beat.
- She is not very workified.
- He won't get up and out no matter who begs him.
- He can't crawl out of bed before 10:00 a.m.

leave/leaving
- Make like a tree and leaf.
- Don't leave mad – just leave.
- Go jump in the lake.
- Here's your hat and cane.
- Here's your hat and there's the door.
- Don't let the door hit you on the way out.
- Don't let the door hit you where the Good Lord split you.
- Why don't we make like a bakery truck and haul buns out of here?
- Why don't you make like a banana and split?
- It's time for me to take my leave. (depart)

- You leave – you take the horse you rode in on.
- I hate to leave good company, but I've got to go.
- Don't let the doorknob hit you in the butt on the way out.
- See you on the flip side.
- See you on facebook.
- See you in my dreams.
- He skipped out a few minutes ago.
- Don't wait so long to come the next time.
- Tell your folks howdy for me.
- Until tomorrow…
- See you soon.
- I'll take my leave now.
- I bid you farewell.
- Come again.

leg/legs
- He has legs like tree stumps.
- I need a leg up. (help)
- She's a leggy girl. (long legs)
- He's like granddaddy long legs. (great dancer)

lend/lender
- Can I borry a cup of sugar?
- Never lend relatives or friends money. Just call it a gift and be done with it.
- Never a borrower or a lender be.
- Can you lend me your life for a day or two? (said to someone who is extremely blessed)

liar
- He talks out of both sides of his mouth.
- She is two faced.

lie

- You're a barefaced liar!
- He speaks with a forked tongue.
- He wouldn't know the truth if it slapped him in the face.
- If you tell one lie, you'll have to tell another to prop the first one up!
- He can't keep his stories straight.
- What he tells depends on who he's talking to.
- She changes her tune a lot!
- Liar, liar! Pants on fire!
- That is a base slander!
- That's a big windy you're telling.
- You made that up!
- I can see the devil in your eyes.
- You lie like a dog!
- That's a golly whopper!
- That's poppycock!
- She's spinning a yarn.
- He just told a big windy!
- You lie like a rug!
- She's lying through her teeth!
- Something stinks in Denmark.
- You're telling a fairy tale!
- That's a fib if I ever head one!
- That's bull!
- That's a tall story!
- You're shining me!
- You're just jerking my chain.
- He lies when it's not even worth the trouble.

- To lie is a habit and a bad one at that.
- There's no use trying to squirm your way out of it!
- It was just a little white lie. I didn't think it would hurt anything.
- He'd lie to the devil if he thought he could get away with it.
- You wouldn't know the truth if it bit you in the hiney.
- Some people would walk a mile to tell a lie before they'd stand still and tell the truth.
- Now that's a pile of cow plop if I've ever heard it!
- That's the biggest crock of bull I've ever heard.
- He lies so much he doesn't even know when he's telling the truth.
- If you tell a little lie, you'll have to tell a bigger one to prop that one up.
- If you lie, you'll get caught in it.
- That is a bold face lie.
- That's a lie, if I ever heard one.
- That's not true! It is purely made up.
- He talks with a serpent's tongue.
- She has a tongue like a snake.
- Her tongue is unhinged on both ends.
- Your nose is going to start sprouting like Pinocchio.

life
- Life is like a vapor. (gone quickly)
- Life is a fleeting thing.
- Life passes like a shadow. (evasive)
- He's the life of the party. (center of attention)
- I've had the time of my life. (a good experience)
- Life is like a box of chocolates. (variety)

- Life is like a bowl of cherries. (You get the pits with the fruit.)
- Life is like a rosie bush. You have to take the thorns to get the beauty.
- Life is sweet and sour. Don't forget to remember the one when you're tasting the other.
- Life is what you make it.
- Life goes on. (In spite of disappointments, life continues.)
- In this life, you've got to play the hand you're dealt. (Make the best of your circumstances.)

light
- Walk in the light.
- I'm holding you in the light.
- Shine your light in the darkness. (show a better way)
- Let your light shine. (be a good example)
- She made light of feelings for her. (disregarded)
- He made light of that crippled child. (made fun)

like
- How does that suit your fancy?
- When it comes to work, you don't have to like it. You just have to do it!
- Some like it hot.
- I think the world of her (or him). (affectionate connection; friendship; respect)
- I don't care if you like it or not!
- What's like got to do with it? (some things are necessary)
- Like you care! (don't pretend you do when you don't)

lions
- He'll toss you to the lions. (won't care what happens to you)
- She'll feed you to the lions. (betray your trust)
- He does the lion's share of the work. (most)
- When the lion roars, the jungle listens. (When the person in charge speaks, pay attention.)

little
- You little pip squeak! (very small and/or very irritating person)
- She's little, but she's feisty.
- I know about a thimble full about that subject.
- A dime is littler than a nickel, but a dime is worth more!
- Fare thee well, my little love! (good bye to a sweetheart)
- He was the runt of the litter. (smallest; sickliest)
- Mighty oaks from little acorns grow.

location
- Over yonder is where I want to build my house.
- I come from over hyonder.
- Over yanner is a sycamore tree.
- I plan on living here abouts the rest of my life.
- I believe I'll put my garden there abouts.
- What are you doing in my neck of the woods?
- She lives out in the sticks.
- I've been looking at a piece of land up in the holler.
- She was sitting catty cornered to me.
- The drug store is kitty corner to the bank.
- We like to travel off the beaten path.

- He lives out in the boonies.
- Come hither. (come here)
- I live at the head of the holler. (end of the road between the mountains)
- I'd like to live nigher to my folks than I do. (closer)
- That boy is scattered hither and yon.
- You can't get there from here.
- If you go any further in, you'll be on your way out.
- Here I sit, in the middle of nowhere.

lonesome
- She has neither chick nor child to keep her company.
- I'm so lonesome I could cry.
- Here I sit, beside myself and no one in between.
- I'm lonesome blue. (sad)

long/longing
- How I long for a day in the sunshine!
- I'm hankering to see my brother.

look/looking/looks
- Get a load of this picture.
- I'll take a gander at the newspaper.
- He was straining his neck to get a look at her.
- He was craning his neck to see.
- He was stretching his neck to get a better look.
- I'll take a peek at that new book.
- If looks could kill… (contemptuous facial expression directed at a specific person)
- I'll give it the once over.
- She's giving you a dirty look.
- I'll give it a glance. (look briefly.)
- If I look as bad as I feel, I'm in trouble.

- He's looking for a needle in a haystack. (something that is going to be very difficult to find)
- Dang! Look at that!
- I didn't like the way she cut her eyes at me.

loose
- He is a loose cannon. (unpredictable)
- Little Miss Loosey Goosey (sexually promiscuous)
- She has loose lips. (gossip)

lose/loser
- Don't lose your head. (think clearly)
- You're apt to lose your shirt on that deal. (fail)

lost
- I once was lost but now I'm found.
- He's a lost ball in high weeds.
- He's a lost dog in high weeds. (confused)
- You've lost your mind! (ridiculous idea)
- Have you lost your mind? (refers to something outrageous someone is going to do)
- I've lost my edge.
- She's lost her sparkle.
- She's lost her place in line. (social status diminished)
- It's better to have loved and lost than never to have loved at all.

lost things
- If it was a snake, it would have bitten you!
- I'm going to tie it around your neck.
- If your head wasn't attached to your shoulders, you'd lose it.
- I guess it grew legs, got up and walked away.

- If anyone sees a mind running around, please save it for me. I've lost mine.

loud
- They nearly brought down the house.
- That's enough to bust your eardrums.
- That's so loud it makes my liver quiver!
- You'll be stone deaf if you don't turn that down. (refers to listening to music that is far too loud)
- That is loud enough to wake the dead.
- She always wears loud clothes. (very bright; colorful)

love
- She's the butter on my biscuit.
- He's looking for love in all the wrong places.
- He's mooning around over her.
- There's nothing worse than unrequited love. (unreturned)
- I love you more than a fat kid loves cake!
- I love you more than a cold icy drink on a hot summer day!
- Hell hath no fury like a woman scorned. (rejected)
- He's love sick.
- He's been enchanted. (fallen in love)
- She's plumb foolish over him.
- The end of marriage is not the end of love.
- Even death cannot separate us from the one we love.
- Love can be as cruel as the grave.
- He's the peanut to my butter.
- She's the peanut butter to my jelly.
- He's plumb twitterpated.
- The course of true love never did run smooth.

- She's over the moon for him.
- They are eat up with it.
- He's the cookie to my milk.
- She's the apple of my eye.
- He's my answered prayer.
- She's the icing on my cake.
- Love makes the world go 'round.
- My love for you is as wide as the ocean.
- Love is like lemonade – sweet and sour all mixed up together.
- I've got my heart in my pocket.
- He holds my heart in his hand.
- She completes me.
- He found his lost love. (reunited with a love from his youth)
- He's the love of my life.
- They're a perfect match.
- She's the key to my door.
- He holds the key to my heart.
- She has more love in her little finger than most people have in their whole body.
- I'm looking for my split apart.
- She said she loved the dirt on her first husband's grave better than she loved any other man she ever married or ever laid her eyes on.
- They're a match made in heaven.
- You're the missing piece of my puzzle.
- They are eat up with it.
- They are twitterpated.
- They are over the moon.

- They are over the moon.
- She's gaga over him.
- I love you better than a new pair of shoes.
- I love you better than a cushaw's neck.
- She's in her room, pining away over him.
- I love you a bushel and a peck, a bushel and a peck and a hug around the neck.
- I love you better than flowers love sunshine.
- Love is a hurtin' thing.
- Love will make a better man out of you.
- Love will turn you inside out.
- All is fair in love and war.
- I love you more…
- Great hate and great love are next of kin.
- There's a fine line between love and hate.

luck/lucky
- That's just beginner's luck.
- Lucky in cards, unlucky in love.
- It's the luck of the draw. (purely chance)
- Better lucky than good.
- I wish some of your luck would rub off on me.
- If it weren't for bad luck, I'd have no luck at all.
- There's no such thing as luck.
- You make your own luck.

M

mad (also see **anger**)
- She was as mad as an old wet hen. (anger)

- I'm so mad I could smoke a pickle.
- I'm so mad I could chew nails.
- I'm so mad I could whip the devil.
- I'm so mad I could spit nails.
- She was so mad she nearly had a cow!
- He was so mad he 'bout had a calf!
- He was so mad, he would have fought a buzz saw.
- Why don't you scratch your mad spot and get over it?
- Why don't you scratch your mad spot and get glad?
- He was as mad as a hornet.
- He's as mad as a March hare. (insane)
- She is mad about her new boyfriend. (infatuated)
- He is mad for UK. (a big fan)
- I'm as mad as thunder! (very angry)
- She's mad as fire.
- He is mad about his new video game. (really likes)
- Don't go to bed mad. You never know who might not wake up.
- She's madder than a hornet's nest!
- You make me so mad I could spit!
- You make my blood boil!

man/men
- He's a good feller.
- Men never grow up.
- Men have a very short attention span.
- If you want to keep a man, you'd better tie him up good and proper.
- Someone's got a fella. (sweetheart)
- He is a handsome fellow.
- Be a man! (quit whining)

- Man up! (Stop being a wimp.)
- Old man so and so (old man followed by a last name)
- Her old man is too lazy to hit a lick at a snake. (husband)
- Beware of the man whom children shun and dogs despise.
- Every man Jack among us will be there. (absolutely everyone)
- He's a one trick pony.
- One man's trash is another man's treasure.
- One man's loss is another man's gain.
- One man's meat is another man's poison.
- You can't hold a man who doesn't want to be held.
- He's a one man band. (plays many instruments or does something all by himself)
- You've got to teach your man to be a man. (instruct children as they grow up how to behave)
- A man crying is not a sign of weakness.
- He's the Alpha male. (dominant male; leader)

manners
- I don't know where my manners are! (please forgive me for not following socially acceptable hospitality or protocol)
- He has no more manners than if he'd been raised in a barn.
- His manners are peculiar. (the way he acts is strange; unfamiliar)
- What manner of fabric is this? (what kind)

mantle
- Put that picture on the fireboard. (over the fireplace)

- He passed his mantle on to his son. (responsibilities)

marriage
- They're getting hitched.
- They've tied the knot.
- It's time for those two to jump the broomstick.
- They two have become twain.
- They make the perfect couple.
- They've put on the old ball and chain.
- They are shackled for life.
- We will do whatever my lady wife desires.
- They've thrown in together.
- They took up housekeeping together.
- They took their vows.
- They took the plunge.
- He's off the market.
- Marry in haste, repent in leisure.
- They've said their ever afters.
- Marry a mountain girl and you'll be marrying the whole mountain.
- She better get busy before she ends up an old maid. (needs to find a husband)
- Marry a woman, marry her family.
- A son is a son 'til he takes a wife, but a daughter's a daughter for the rest of her life.
- She will dance in the hog trough. (refers to a younger child marrying before an older one)

masculine
- He's a real man's man.
- He's a John Wayne kind of guy.
- He's a root 'em up, shoot 'em up kind of guy.

- I like the set of his jaw.
- He's got rugged written all over him.
- Give me a he man, not a girlie man. (feminine acting)
- I like to see a man look like a man. (strong masculine build; attire)
- The measure of a man is the way he takes care of his family.

match
- He's met his match. (equal in business or authority)
- They're a good match. (romantic couple)
- They are a match made in heaven. (well suited)

maybe
- They might would if you'd ask.
- Could be.
- It's a possibility.
- Maybe yes, and maybe no. I'll let you know when I make up my mind.
- Maybe I will and maybe I won't - ain't nobody's business but my own.
- You better do what I say and I don't mean maybe!

mean
- She's as mean as a rattle snake.
- He's as mean as Old Scratch. (the devil)
- Don't corner anything meaner than you!
- Meanness don't just happen overnight.
- She is meaner than the devil riding straddle of a rattlesnake (or rattlesnake).
- Some kids are so mean, you could pinch their heads off and not even feel guilty.
- He's meaner than a mad dog.

- He's meaner than a striped snake!
- That old woman's as mean as the devil.
- He's as mean as a rabid wolf.
- He'd put a Rottweiler to shame.
- He's meaner than a junk yard dog.
- He's meaner than a red bellied frog.
- She's cantankerous.
- He's plain ornery.
- Some children are so mean, you just want to snap their heads off!
- Some kids are so mean, they could be the poster child for why some animals eat their young!
- Some kids are so mean, you could pinch their heads off and it would be an improvement!

meanwhile
- In the in between, she read a book.
- Whilst you kept me waiting, I baked some bread.

measurements
- This needs a smidge more sugar.
- I'd like to have a peck of peaches.
- You need a dab of cinnamon in this oatmeal.
- I picked a bushel of green beans last night.
- Add about a pinch of sugar to your cornbread batter.
- I'll have a drop of milk with my supper.
- Give me a tetch of cream in my coffee.
- I'll take a drap of water if you don't mind.
- Pull it in a notch.
- I need a dash of salt on these fried eggs.
- Give me just a hair more room.
- I'll take a dallop of butter.

- I need a swish of pop.
- Would you like a spot of tea?
- Add a a sprinkle of pepper.
- This needs just a touch of color.
- You could give me a mite more gravy on my potatoes.
- I'll not have nary a one. (none)
- Put in just a shade more pepper.

memory
- She's got a memory like an elephant. (long)
- I've got a memory like a sieve. (has holes in it)
- My memory is about as long as a gnat's butt.
- I think I'll take a stroll down Memory Lane. (think about the past or do an activity that refreshes memories – i.e. look at a photo album)
- My memory is like Swiss cheese – full of holes.

menopause
- Please excuse me while I have a mental pause.
- She's going through the change.
- She's in her change of life.
- I'm having a nuclear meltdown.
- Steam is coming out of my head.
- No wonder you shouldn't have a baby over 50. You'd forget where you left it.
- My thinking is scrambled and my nerves are akimbo.

menstrual cycle
- She started her period.
- It's that time of the month.
- She's on the rag.

- Aunt Fanny has come for her monthly visit.
- Aunt Flo will be stopping by any time now.
- It's a woman's curse.
- I'm two weeks late.
- She's having a visit from Mother Nature.
- She has her monthly visitor.
- She missed her monthly visitor.
- My monthly guest checked in last night.

mentally challenged
- He's not all there.
- You're higher than boat gas.
- He was born that way.
- His momma dropped him on his head.
- She's off her rocker.
- He's off his nut.
- He's as mad as a March hare.
- She's not all there.

mess/messy
- What a gaum you've made!
- This is a gome if I ever saw one!
- Your room looks like a pig's sty!
- You look slouchy today.
- Your room looks like a cyclone's been through.
- This house looks like a heard of pigs has been through.
- This kitchen looks like a pack of wolves were here for dinner.
- It looks like a bird's leg in an oatmeal box!
- Your room looks like a rat's nest.
- His room was a jungle!

- This house looks like a tornado has hit it.
- What a gummy mess you've made!
- I've got tar gaum all over my britches. (sticky stuff)

middle
- I am caught betwixt and between.
- I'm in the midst of canning tomatoes.

might/mighty
- I wish I may, wish I might, have the wish I wish tonight.
- Even little acorns into mighty oak trees grow.
- I'm mighty glad to see you. (very glad)
- You are looking mighty fine. (especially good)
- That boy is mighty tall. (extremely tall)
- (Mighty can be inserted in any phrase as an adjective to emphasize a noun.)

milk/milking cows
- I don't like Blue John. (spoiled milk)
- It's milking time.
- It's time to strip the cows.
- Time to hunt the cows and take care of business.
- Don't buy the cow if the milk is free!
- He's milking that broken leg for all it's worth. (gathering sympathy for the injury; letting others take care of him)
- You have milked me dry. (taken all I've got; got nothing more to give)

mind
- That is just mind boggling! (Hard to believe or hard to comprehend.)
- You better mind your mamma!

- A mind is a terrible thing to waste.
- Do you mind? (Excuse you!)
- Do you mind if I sit next to you? (permission)
- What's on your mind? (What are you thinking?)
- I'll give you a piece of my mind. (opinion)
- You need to take your mind off of things. (stop worrying)
- You know what that puts me in mind of? (reminds me of)
- That just blows my mind! (Shocking.)
- It has plagued my mind. (troubled thoughts)
- Mind your manner. (behave well)
- Mind your Ps and Qs. (behave well)
- An idle mind is the devil's playground.
- Have you made up your mind? (come to a decision)
- I don't know what mind I was in, but it wasn't my right one!
- I'm about to lose my mind!
- You'd think a man would know what's on a woman's mind.
- I'm going out of my mind with worry.
- Don't mind me. (ignore me)
- It crossed my mind that I shouldn't go on this trip. (had a thought)
- Out of sight, out of mind. (People tend to forget about things that are not right in front of them.)

mirror
- Have you seen yourself in the looking glass?
- Before you judge someone else, spend a few minutes in the mirror.

- Are you at peace with the one in the mirror?
- Mirror, mirror on the wall
    Tell me, tell me, tell me do
    Is that really me
    Looking back at you?
- Mirror, mirror on the wall
    Ain't you got no sense
    a'tall?

misbehaving
- He is acting up.
- She is acting out.
- Stop fooling around.

mischief
- No more of your shananigans!
- Keep your clothes clean.
- Stay out of trouble.
- Those children act like Apache Indians on a drunk!
- Stop acting like you've just been let out of a cage!
- Someone's up to mischief. (children acting sneaky)
- They are cutting monkey shines.
- They've been raising Cain!

misery
- Misery loves company.
- She's a pure old misery guts! (always unhappy)
- She draws misery like a magnet.
- The world loves misery.
- I'm in a pure misery. (sick; unhappy; distressed)

misfit
- He's like a fish out of water.
- Now that's a fish in a pickle dish!
- That's like a bird's leg in an oatmeal box.

- She's a square peg trying to fit in a round hole.
- I feel like I'm on the outside looking in.
- No matter how hard I try, I just don't fit.

mistake/mistaken
- You've driven your ducks to a dry pond.
- You'll have to lick that calf again.
- You'll have to chew your backer over.
- You've stuck your foot in it now!
- You jumped from the frying pan into the fire.
- I guess you found out the grass is not greener on the other side of the fence after all.
- If I'd only known then what I know now…
- Son, you don't know your sh_ _ from shinola!
- You are sadly mistaken.
- You might think you know what you are talking about, but you've been reading the wrong directions.

mistrust
- That's hog wash! (untrue)
- I smell a rat! (something's amiss)
- Something stinks in Denmark. (something's not right)
- I wouldn't trust him any further than I could pick him up and throw him!

misunderstanding
- They are at crossed purposes.
- That might be what you think you heard, but that's not what I said!
- They got their wires crossed.
- They've crossed swords.

mixture
- Now there's a Duke's mixture. (mixing food like gravy, biscuits, eggs, and sausage, all together on the plate)
- That dog is a Heinz 57. (mixed breed of unknown origin)
- There's a dupe's mixture for you. (someone trying to be deceitful and telling untruths to be convincing)
- This meal is a hodgepodge of leftovers. (mixture of foods)
- This is a hodge podge. (a little of this, a little of that)

money
- A fool and his money are soon parted.
- Money is the root of all evil.
- The love of money is the root of all evil.
- He was throwing money around like it was going out of style. (spending freely and making a show of it)
- Money doesn't grow on trees. (hard to come by)
- Don't let that money burn a hole in your pocket. (Don't spend your money too quickly.)
- Money talks! (Money has great influence.)
- Dig deep into your pocketbook! (give generously)
- The fastest way to double your money is fold it in half and stick it back in your wallet!
- It is easier to spend another man's money than it is your own.
- I'm saving my money for a rainy day! (in case of emergency)
- She carries her money in her own First National Savings and Loan. (money stuffed in her bra – bank

name is substituted for the local bank in the area or the person's name)
- He stays close to his money. (saves it)

monkey
- What's this monkey business? (mischief)
- He cut a monkey shine. (acted terribly in public)
- Monkey see, monkey do. (imitate)
- You'll not make a monkey out of me! (deceive)
- He's a powder monkey. (works with explosives in the coal mining industry)

monsters
- The Jabberwocky will get you if you don't watch out.
- Watch out for the Booger Man. (devil)
- The Boogey Man will get you if you lie. (devil)
- Be good or the Boo Hag will get you. (witch)
- The Windego is on the prowl. (a wind riding creature that comes with storms)
- I heard a Wampus screaming on the ridge. (unidentified creature)
- The Banshee is passing by. (death)
- I believe I heard Sasquatch in the woods. Something was running and breaking timbers as it went. (Big Foot)
- She looks like the bride of Frankenstein. (ugly)

moody
- She's hormonal.
- She's hit puberty.
- You never know if he's going to rain or shine.
- You never know what to expect from her.
- She must be menopausal.

- There's too much estrogen in this house! (too many women and not enough men living in the house)

moon
- She can see the man in the moon. (big imagination)
- Stop mooning over her! (sulking; pining for someone romantically)
- The moon is made of green cheese.
- The moon is made of Swiss cheese.
- The moon-ball is bright tonight.
- You'd better stay home on the dark of the moon. (new)
- Children misbehave on the light of the moon. (full)
- He just shot you the moon. (dropped his pants and exposed his behind toward you)
- You aren't paying a bit more attention to me than the man in the moon! (inattentive)

morality
- He walks the straight and narrow. (a very moral person)
- He's not worth a plug nickel.
- She lives at the foot of the cross. (a very religious person)
- He has trouble keeping his wings under his shirt.
- She's of a good moral character.
- It may be a popular thing to do, but is it moral? Is it right?

mort
- There's been a mort of people passing on lately. It's not come in threes, but by sixes. (a lot - refers to the superstition that death comes in threes)
- I was mortified! (humiliated)

mountain
- I've got one more mountain to climb. (near death)
- I'm living on the dark side of the mountain. (near death)
- I'll move mountains, if I have to! (determined to get something accomplished)
- I long for the mountains. (homesick)
- The mountains are in my blood. (really love the mountains)
- There's highland blood in my veins. (love for the mountains; may refer to Scottish heritage)

mouth
- Big mouth! (said to someone who has told a secret)
- She's mouthing something, but I can't tell what it is. (whispering to a person hard of hearing)
- He's only mouthing the words to that song. (lip sinking)
- He has a potty mouth. (uses foul language)
- She's a loudmouth! (always spouting off about something and wanting to draw attention to herself; the volume of her voice)
- She works her mouth more than anything else.
- She can't keep her mouth closed. (tells secrets)
- It slid right out of my mouth before I could stop it. (unintentionally told a secret)
- Get your mouth off of me! (stop talking about me; criticizing)
- What's in the heart comes out the mouth.
- He's mouthing off again. (criticizing something; complaining about something)

- She's always running her mouth about something. (pontificating)
- You've got to hold your mouth right. (said to someone having a difficult time repairing or making something)
- I must have held my mouth right. (said by someone when good fortune comes to them or they were able to accomplish something others were not able to do)

move
- You need to let the spirit move you. (respond to spiritual directives)
- That girl can move! (dance)
- He's sure got the moves! (good dancer; knows how to charm a woman)
- I'm going to pull up stakes. (relocate)
- Move your feet, lose your seat!

mud
- Here's mud in your eye! (spoken before a toast)
- He's a real stick in the mud. (dull personality)
- He'll drag you through the mud with him. (ruin your reputation)
- She's as ugly as a mud fence. (very unattractive)
- You can't jump in mud holes without getting mud on you! (getting involved in other person's scandals will associate yourself with them)
- They are having a mud-slinging contest. (talking bad about each other.)
- That girl is like trying to look through muddy water. (hard to understand her)
- Don't muddy the waters. (make things worse)
- Don't give him reason to muddy your reputation.

- I don't believe that's mud on your shoes. (refers to having stepped in manure or some other mess – figuratively or literally)
- He's on the move. (looking for; traveling)

muscle
- She's the brains. He's the muscle. (She thinks of ideas, but he does the physical work.)
- Use your muscle to get the job done. (power; strength; political influence)

mule
- You are stamping around like a mule! (angry)
- He's as stubborn as a mule.
- She'll make a pack mule out of you. (make you do all the work)

mush
- I hate eating this mush! (distasteful food)
- This apple is mushy where it fell in the floor. (soft)
- You are talking mushy. (overly affectionate; sappy)
- There's nothing better than a good mush melon. (cantaloupe)
- Mush! (get going; speed up)

mushrooms
- Hickory Chickens (Wild mushrooms that are a delicacy in the mountains, thoroughly washed, soaked in salt water overnight, rinsed, dipped in egg and milk, rolled in meal and flour, salt and pepper and fried)
- I love a good mess of dry land fish in the spring.
- You can find morels growing near where a tree once stood.

- There's nothing tastier than Molly Moochers in the spring!

mystery
- He is a man of mystery.
- He's a man of many faces. (changeable)
- The answer to that is one of life's great mysteries.
- It will take a while to ravel that one out.
- I'm trying to unravel the details around that murder.

N

nag
- That old nag doesn't stand a chance of winning the race. (old horse)
- She is such a nag! (grumbles, complains, quarrels constantly)
- Don't nag at me! (repeat commands to get something done)

naive
- I wasn't born yesterday.
- Do you think I just fell off the cabbage truck?

naked
- You came into this world naked and you'll leave the same.
- He was as naked as a jay bird!
- He was wearing his birthday suit.
- There she stood in nothing but a smile!
- There he stood in all his glory!
- She was wearing naught but her wherewithal!
- He had nary a stitch on!
- She's in the buff.

- There she stood without even a blush to hide her shame.

name
- What's your handle?
- What's your proper name?
- What's your given name?
- Bum. Bum. Here I come. What's your trade? Lemonade. Get to work and get it made. What's your name? Puddintame. Ask me again and I'll tell you the same.

nasty
- That is plumb cyarnified!
- That little old nasty thing! (an insult toward someone)
- That's not fit to wipe your hiney on!
- He looks pretty grungy.
- That is just pure old nastiness.
- That is pure sorriness.
- This place looks like a hog waller!
- Now there is a motley crew.
- They are a smotley crew.
- That is smottled up all over!
- You are raunchy.
- That family is as nasty as a flock of buzzards.
- You're plain nasty. (said to someone who makes sexual overtures)

nature/naturally
- He's a nature boy. (loves the outdoors)
- She's a tree hugger. (environmentalist)

- He's a regular Marlin Perkins. (knowledgeable about woodland facts)
- I like nature. (outdoor things)
- It is not in her nature to be cruel. (personality)
- Naturally, he didn't know what he was talking about. (of course)
- She was naturally curly headed. (inherited trait)
- Singing is second nature to her. (happens easily)

near
- It's just a hop, skip, and a jump away.
- It's the next house over hyonder.
- She's just stepped out for a minute.
- It's close enough that you could throw a rock and hit it.
- You could sling a dead cat and hit it.
- If it had've been a snake, it would have bit you! (said when searching for something and finds it nearby)

necessary/necessities
- There are needful things in this life but most are just wishful.
- It is needful for you to come with me. (important; expedient)
- I wouldn't go with him unless it was pure necessity. (couldn't be avoided)
- I need to find the necessary room. (bathroom)

neck
- He broke his neck to please her. (tried as hard as he could)
- I'll wring your neck if you don't shut that up! (a threat)

- They are necking. (making out; kissing; physical contact)
- He won by a neck. (barely)
- You goose neck looking thing! (long neck; looking from side to side)
- This is a real bottle neck. (traffic jam)
- They are running neck and neck. (the same; tied)

nerves/nervous
- My nerves are worn thin.
- You are getting on my last nerve!
- He was sweating bullets.
- He was as nervous as a wet cat.
- His knees were doing the jitterbug.
- Her knees were knocking.
- She's a bag of nerves.
- She is as fidgety as can be.
- He was as nervous as a wet cat.
- His knees were doing the jitterbug.
- Her knees were knocking.
- She's a bag of nerves.
- She is as fidgety as can be.
- I'm a bundle of nerves.
- I shook like an earthquake
- My palms are sweating.
- She was a nervous wreck.
- Her lip was quivering.
- She's always up tight.
- He's got cold feet.
- I was shaking in my shoes!
- He is really tense.

- She's all wound up.
- She's about to go off the deep end.
- My nerves are shattered.
- You are getting on my last nerve!
- He was as nervous as a mouse in a room full of cats.
- She was as nervous as a cat in a room full of rocking chairs.
- I'm shakier than a leaf on a fuzzy tree!
- He's strung as tight as a banjer (banjo) string.
- She's so nervous, she could thread a sewing machine and it running wide open!
- He's as nervous as a cat on hot bricks. (fidgety)
- He's as nervous as a coon up a tree with the dogs baying on his heels. (cornered; no way out)
- My nerves are strung out.

new
- That's a ground breaker.
- It's store bought.
- It's brought on.
- It's fouched on.
- It's fotched on.
- I've got a new lease on life.
- He's the new kid on the block.
- We need some new blood. (new ideas, new friends)
- He's a new man. (completely changed for the better; reformed)
- I can't work that new fangled contraption!
- It's brand spanking new.
- There's a new sheriff in town. (someone new in charge.)

- All the new has been worn out of it. (used)

news
- No news is good news!
- That bit of information is not newsworthy. (not worth repeating)
- No news here. Everything is boring – but sometimes boring is a good thing.
- No news on this end.
- I never heard of such a thing! (bad news)
- He carries the news. (delivers newspapers; carries gossip)
- That is old news. (already known)
- That's old dishwater. Throw it out the back door and forget about it. (let go of news that upset you)

nod
- He's in the land of Nod. (asleep)
- He's nodding off. (falling asleep)
- A wink is as good as a nod. (understood)
- He gave me the nod. (permission to proceed)

noise
- You sound like a room full of magpies.
- Who's making that racket?
- You make more noise than a flock of crows!
- You make more noise than a pig eating slop!
- Stop that catterwalling!
- Her voice is like fingernails across a blackboard.
- You sound like a gaggle of geese!
- You sound like a bunch of crows squacking!
- That racket could raise the dead!
- She sounds like a guinea hen squawking.

- You're making more noise than a bunch of bore hogs at breeding time!

none
- That baby wants an apple, but I have nary a one to give her.
- I hain't seen nary any salesmen in these parts for many a moon.

nose/nosey
- It's as plain as the nose on your face.
- Her nose is always out of joint. (always in a bad mood)
- Don't get your nose out of joint. (Don't get upset.)
- Keep your nose in your own business and you'll be better off.
- The nose knows. (sense of smell)
- Don't stick your nose in where it doesn't belong. (Stay out of the affairs of others.)
- She walks around with her nose in the air. (thinks she's superior to others)
- Keep your nose clean! (stay out of trouble)
- You'd better stop noseying around before you get caught!
- You'd cut your nose off to spite your face!
- Blow your nose instead of your own horn and you'll get more out of it.
- Blow your nose instead of your horn and it will do you more good.
- It's no skin off my nose what you do. (doesn't matter to me)
- Why are you noseyin' around? (prowling)

- You can pick your friends. You can pick your nose. But you can't pick your friend's nose!
- Keep your nose to the grindstone and your shoulder to the wheel. (work hard)
- We're not lost. Just follow your nose.
- You are a nosey newsy. (asking questions to create gossip later on)
- You're a nosey little pooch, aren't you?
- Keep your nose out of other people's business.
- Her nose in everybody's business but her own.
- Keep your nose out of what does not belong to you.
- Leave other people's stick alone. (Don't be nosey.)

nothing
- There's nothing worse than unwanted company who has decided to move in!
- All of that hard work has been for naught.
- She has neither chic nor child.
- Nothing ventured, nothing gained.
- If you are willing to do nothing, you can expect to get nothing.
- Nothing newsy going on here.
- I didn't say cruisin'. (a response to "What did you say?" when a child is mumbling under their breath.)
- Nothing plus nothing equals nothing.
- Nothing is going to get done if you don't get busy doing something!

numerous
- There's too many to count.
- I've told you umpteen times to pick up your clothes!
- I've told you forty-leven times to cut it out!

- I've been there more times than I care to count.
- If I've told you once, I've told you a thousand times!
- They outnumbered us ten to one.
- She's got more dishes than Carter's got liver pills. (Carter's Little Liver pills were tiny and many came in one bottle.)
- He had more descendants than the sand on the beach.

oar
- He put in his oar. (had an idea)
- Keep your oar out of this! (mind your own business)

obedience
- Do as I say, not as I do.
- Do as you are told.
- It behooves you to do as you are told.
- Things will turn out better for you if you do as you are told.

object (unidentified)
- Have you seen my new gizmo?
- Hand me that thingamajiggy over there.
- Put the doomafloppy on the inside of the screw.
- I dropped the thingamabob that holds this together.
- I put that whirlyjig out in the yard.
- He said my car needs a new thingamajig.
- That whirlyjigger doesn't look right over there.
- I need a new whatchamacallit for my computer.

oblivion
- The tornado tore that house to smithereens. (fragments)
- I blow you to smithereens. (do irreparable damage)

obsessed
- Those boys are are gun crazy. (this can apply to being obsessed with anything – knives, horses, basketball, cars, etc.)
- Football, football! That's all he ever thinks about. (can apply to a person, activity, or goal)
- He eats, drinks, and sleeps basketball. (can apply to any sport or activity)

obscenities
- I will not listen to that black guard.
- You need to wash your mouth out.
- He has diarrhea of the mouth. She has a potty mouth.

obvious
- He was standing in the river and dying of thirst.
- You can't see the forest for the trees.
- It's as plain as the nose on your face.
- It's written all over your face.
- He was standing there as big as Pete!
- Duh! Big red truck! (hard to miss a big red truck so your answer should be obvious)
- No one wants to talk about the big white elephant in the room. (the thing everyone knows, but no one wants to deal with)

occasionally
- I take it by spells, working on a quilt when I get time.
- Sometimes maybe, I might go fishing.
- From time to time I go sit by the river and think.

- I only see him once in a blue moon.

occupation
- If you aren't careful, you'll be a Jack of all trades and the master of none.
- Do what makes you happy.
- It don't matter what you do, as long as it is honest and brings home a check.

odd
- He is very queer,
- She is quare.
- He is turned funny.

offense/offended
- He put me off.
- I take offense to that!
- You couldn't offend him if you tried!
- He doesn't have enough sense to be offended.

ointment
- You need to rub some of that saive on your sore.

old (also see **age**)
- She's older than dirt.
- I'm too old of a pony for you to try to put a saddle on and ride.
- That's an old fangled contraption. (antique machine)
- She has old fangled ways. (old fashioned; conservative)
- I'm old and hard to offend.
- He's older than Methuselah.
- It's as old as the hills.
- He was around when God was a boy.

- There was an old geezer who lived down the road. (old man who made perverted comments to young women; obnoxious old man)
- There's snow on the roof, but fire in the furnace.
- She's long in the tooth.

open
- He can open doors for you. (give a good recommendation; call in favors to help you get a job)
- Will you prize this jar open for me? (get a lid off)

opinion/opinionated
- I'm outspoken.
- I speak my mind.
- I say what I think.
- That's just plain talk.
- Opinions are like rear ends. Everybody's got one.
- Opinions are like noses. We all have one.
- I don't think anyone pulled your chain. (No one asked for your opinion.)
- He's of a mind to disagree.
- He has a mind of his own. (has his own opinion)
- I've half a mind to tell him no! (don't think so)
- I didn't ask you to put your two cents in! (didn't ask for your opinion)
- Now I've put my two cents in. (gave my opinion)
- Some opinions are best left to yourself.
- Not everybody wants your opinion.
- When a woman speaks her opinion, that does not especially mean that she wants a man to speak his.
- She thinks her opinion is the final word.
- He thinks his opinion is the only one that matters.

- She thinks her opinion is dipped in 24 karat.

opportunity
- The moment passed.
- You don't know if you like something until you try it. (Take advantage of new opportunities.)
- When God closes a door, he opens a window.
- If you keep doing what you're doing, you'll keep getting what you've got.
- If you want something new, you've got to do something new to get it.
- You never know until you try.
- You need to make hay while the sun shines!
- His retirement is an open door for you.
- If you want to get something new out, you've got to put something new in.
- Strike while the iron is hot.

optimistic sayings
- Every cloud has a silver lining.
- It's always darkest before dawn.
- You must have rain to make a rainbow.
- Make hay while the sun shines.
- If life hands you lemons, make lemonade.
- There's always light at the end of the tunnel.

orator
- Words just roll off his tongue.
- He's a silver tongued devil.
- He knows how to hook his words together just right.

other
- Not that one, hand me t'other one.

ought
- I ought to go to bed earlier.(should)

- You oughtn't to have said that. (shouldn't have)
- If you have ought against your brother, you need to make it right. (resolve conflicts; drop grudges)
- I ought not to stay up so late! (shouldn't)

outgoing personality
- He never sees a stranger.
- She'd talk to a stump.
- He must be running for office.
- He's bound to be a politician or a politician's son.

over
- I'm over you. (no longer romantically interested)
- They've got me over a barrel. (no choice)
- The only way you'll leave this house is over my dead body! (not going to happen)
- I got it over the counter. (bought it at the store)
- She's over the hill. (old)
- They are over the moon for each other. (in love)
- Your behavior is over the top! (totally unacceptable)
- When he talks about technology, it is all over my head. (I don't understand)

overbearing
- Give him an inch and he'll take a mile.
- She's a steamroller.
- Do yourself a favor. Hide and stay out of his way.
- She's too pushy.
- Give Jimmer and inch and he'll take a mile!

overcome/overcoming
- They couldn't have stood it without the Lord. (overcoming grief)

- He has a lot to overcome. (refers to someone who has endured great difficulties in life.
- We shall overcome. (prevail)
- She was struck with rheumatism in her legs and back. (debilitating condition)

overweight/obese
- He's as broad as the day is long.
- I look like the Michelin tire man.
- He looks like marshmallow man.
- She looks as stuffed as a sausage and tied in the middle
- She's so fat, when she dropped her napkin and bent over to pick it up, they threw a table cloth over her and served four more people.
- I'm not fat. I'm just big boned.
- I'm not fat, I'm just too short for my weight.
- You're as big around as a jelly roll.
- He's as big around as he is tall!
- She's curvaceous.
- He's a regular little rolly polly.
- She's a chunky monkey.
- He's carrying a wide load.
- She's full figured.
- She's a well rounded girl.
- He's full bodied.
- She's well rounded.
- He's as big as a house.
- She's as big as an elephant.
- He's as big as a boulder!
- Fatty, fatty, two by four,

- can't get through the kitchen door.
- It ain't over 'til the fat lady sings.
- He'd weigh in with a good fattening hog.
- She's good and healthy.
- He's fleshy.
- She's stout.
- She's so fat, when she stepped on the scales, it screamed!
- She's pleasingly plump.
- He's a little on the pudgy side.
- He's so fat he'd have to go outside to change his mind.
- She's so fat, if she sat down on a quarter, she could squeeze a booger out of George Washington's nose.
- She's so fat, if she sat on a dollar bill, it would give change.
- If you don't stop gaining weight, they are going to have to give you your own zip code.
- He's so fat, I got lost going around him.
- She's so fat you have to hug the back and then the front.
- He's a portly gentleman.
- He's so fat his eyes look like pennies on a pumpkin.
- She looks impregnated.

ox

- That boy is as strong as an ox!
- He's as big as an ox.
- I may be as big as an ox, but that doesn't mean I'm as dumb as one.
- She's as broad as an ox.

P

pain
- It felt like a hundred needles sticking in my back.
- The pain in her side doubled her up.
- It hurt like the dickens.
- It hurt like there was no tomorrow.
- It hurt like the devil.
- The pain was like a knife blade twisting in me.
- It hurt so bad, I nearly cried.
- It hurt so bad, it took my breath away.
- It hurt so bad, I saw stars.
- It burned like liquid fire.
- It hurt so bad, I broke out in a sweat.
- I'm in a misery.

pajamas
- I want to put my PJs on and go to bed!
- My night shirt is in the washer.
- I love this flannel night gown.
- I forgot to pack my night clothes.

pale
- She looks like one of the children of the corn.
- You're as pale as death.
- You're white as a sheet.
- He looks like he's never seen daylight.

parents
- You cannot let the parents run the show. (set the precedents in a school)
- Parents are afraid to parent.

- Some people ought not ever become parents.

party
- That was some shin dig they had the other night!
- What a bru ha that was!
- Were you invited to the frollickin'?
- It was a real lollapalooza!
- We are going to have a do!
- We'll have a big spread.
- We'll have to have a big throw down for his big 4 0!

pass
- If you keep growing, you'll pass me up. (get taller)
- Pass the hat. (take a collection for something)
- If he's not careful, he'll pass over the roses and land in a cow pile. (pick the wrong girl)
- We were just passing the time of day. (pleasant conversation)
- He always tries to pass the buck. (make someone else responsible for a mistake)
- It passes muster. (meets requirements)
- He made a pass at me. (a flirtatious gesture; inappropriate invitation)
- I think I'll pass. (decline an invitation)
- I passed with flying colors. (a test; a trial handled successfully)

passive/nonpassive
- He'll just lay there and take it like a door mat.
- She's nothing but big talk, little action.
- He's a teakettle without the steam.
- Her face was a stone wall.
- I'm nobody's door mat.

- Makes no difference to me.
- Whichever way is best.
- I'll take the eenies or the meenies.
- Whatever you decide.
- She's like an old dishrag.
- All the fight has been whipped out of him.
- She's plumb quit caring about anything.
- He's such a wimp.

past
- Back in the day we listened to radio instead of TV.
- Back in my day girls didn't call boys on the telephone.
- Some time ago he bought that land from his brother.
- In my distant remembrance he never came to visit before.

patience
- Hold your taters!
- Don't get your britches in a wad!
- Don't get your drawers in a bunch!
- Just hold on a minute.
- I've been waiting forever and a day.
- Tomorrow never comes.
- Don't get your panties all twisted up.
- Hold your horses!
- A watch pot never boils.
- Good things come to those who wait.
- I prayed and asked the Lord for patience and He sent you into my life.
- My patience with that boy has worn thin.

- Don't grow weary in well doing.
- Rome wasn't built in a day.
- Patience is a virtue.
- I prayed for patience and God gave me children.
- Don't ask for patience when you pray. Life will provide ample opportunity for you to develop it anyway!

pay
- I'll make sure you pay for that! (justice)
- Pay on the nail. (immediately)
- Pay on the barrel head. (when you get the merchandise)
- A workman is worthy of his hire. (pay)
- Pay back is rough. (revenge)
- Pay it back. (get even; reciprocity)
- Pay it forward. (If someone has shown you a kindness, you should show kindness to someone in the future.)
- You will pay for your raising. (However you behave as a child will come back to you in the way your child behaves.)

peacock
- They keep pea fowls on their lawn.
- He's strutting around like a peacock.

penny
- A penny saved is a penny earned.
- It shines like a new penny.
- Find a penny, pick it up, all the day you'll have good luck!
  Find a penny, let it lay, bad luck will follow you all the day.

- A penny for your thoughts. (What are you thinking?)
- Now that's a pretty penny! (expensive)
- He's like a bad penny – he keeps showing up.

permission
- Have at it!
- We got the green light.
- We got the go ahead.
- It's better to go ahead and do something then apologize than to ask permission and get turned down.
- I don't need your permission, but I would like to have your blessing.
- You are a grown man/woman. You don't need my permission.

persevere
- You just have to soldier through it. (ignore personal discomfort and complete a task)
- Tie a knot and hang on. (Don't give up.)
- Hang in there. (Keep trying.)
- Do or die trying. (Quitting is not an option.)
- Be like a duck and let the rain roll of your back and keep going.
- Get over it. (Ignore your difficulties in a task.)
- Keep your hand to the plow and don't look back.
- Winners never quit and quitters never win.

personality
- We don't have the same taste. (don't have the same likes and dislikes)
- She's turned quare. (odd personality)
- He has an odd turn. (odd personality)

- He's turned like his daddy. (similar personalities)
- She's downright peculiar. (socially challenged; odd mannerisms)
- She is a hateful gut! (unpleasant)
- He is a sourpuss. (grumpy; negative)
- She's the orneriest thing I ever saw. (mean)
- She is cantankerous. (hard to please)
- He's an ornery old cuss. (unpleasant; willful)
- What a prune puss! (dour expression)
- She's a pickle puss. (sour; unhappy; negative)
- She draws people like bees to a honeycomb. (pleasing personality to which others are attracted)
- She always sees the glass as half full instead of half empty. (optimistic)
- He's a willful child. (stubborn; independent)
- She's always been momma's little helper. (domesticated; enjoys homemaking skills)
- Looks aren't everything when you have a personality like that! (personality is important)
- She can win people over in a heartbeat. (likeable)

pessimistic
- She's a real Debbie Downer.
- Aren't you a little ray of sunshine! (sarcasm)
- Aren't you a little dew drop! (sarcasm)
- He always sees the glass as half empty. (negative)

pest
- He's always under foot. (in the way)
- He's worse than my shadow. (can't get away from him)

- He's stuck to me like Velcro. (won't give me any space)
- She's the peskiest child I ever saw.
- He's a thorn in my side.
- She gets under my skin.
- He's a pain in the neck.

piano
- He can really tickle the ivory! (play the piano well)
- He can make that baby talk! (beautiful, moving music)

pick/picky
- Pick on someone your own size. (said to bullies)
- He's the pick of the litter! (best in the bunch)
- He's picking in high cotton. (easy work)
- Be careful how you pick your friends.
- You can pick your friends. You can pick your nose. But you can't pick your friend's nose!
- He is a picky eater. (finicky)
- My oldest brother was daddy's pick. (favorite child)
- She's too picky. (finds many faults in others)
- She'd be married already if she wasn't so picky. (thinks that no man is good enough for her)

picture
- Take a picture! It lasts longer. (said to someone staring)
- A picture is worth a thousand words.
- A picture paints a thousand words.
- She's as pretty as a picture.
- Picture this… (imagine)

- Picture me gone! (said when breaking a romantic relationship)

pie
- He needs a piece of humble pie. (needs his ego deflated)
- That's as American as apple pie.
- I don't believe in that pie in the sky when I die attitude. (refers to a person who talks all the time about heaven without dealing with day to day reality)

pig/pigs
- If you wallow with pigs, expect to get dirty. (The company you keep affects you.)
- He's buying a pig in a poke. (doesn't know what he's getting)
- You can't make a silk purse out of a sow's ear. (It's hard to change the uncouth.)
- He eats like a pig. (poor table manners)
- "To each his own," said the little woman as she kissed the pig. (There's no accounting for individual taste.)
- Mind your momma, little pig, or trouble will come your way.
- It would be like putting lipstick on a pig. (superficial changes)
- Put a ribbon around a pig's neck and it's still a pig. (You can't hide the truth.)
- This place looks like a pig's sty. (messy; disheveled

pill
- He's a pill! (funny)
- She's a pill. (hard to be around)
- Take a chill pill. (calm down)

- Can't you take a pill for that? (stop acting silly)
- That's a bitter pill to swallow. (refers to having to accept something very unpleasant)

pinch
- If we talked in church, momma would pinch the dickens out of us. (hard pinch)
- If you don't stop that, I'll pinch the fire out of you. (pinch hard)
- He pinched the daylights out of me. (deliberately hard pinch)
- If you don't be quiet, I'm going to pinch your head off. (shut up)
- He tweaked the girls. (pinch their butts)

pity
- More's the pity. (unfortunately)
- For pity's sake! (term of frustration)
- I pity the woman who ends up with him. (sorry for whomever he marries)
- I don't want your pity. (Don't feel sorry for me.)
- The poor little thing! (can be said about anyone for which the speaker feels pity)

place
- Do you have a sense of place? (know where you belong)
- I need to clean up around the place. (house; property)
- Remember your place. (Behave according to your situation in life.)
- You'll come to a little place about half a mile down the river. (spot of land)
- Keep your place. (Live up to what is expected of you.)

- I'm just trying to find my place in this world. (searching for a place to fit in; find a niche)
- Your place or mine? (Where shall we meet?)
- Come on over to my place. (where I live)

plain
- I'm plain spoken. (speak what I think honestly)
- I'm plain. (homely)
- It's as plain as the nose on your face. (obvious)
- We are plain folk. (live simply)
- When you're plain you're plain and there's no help for it. (If you are considered homely, do the best you can with yourself and don't worry about it.)

plan
- Here's the 411. (information about a person or event)
- He doesn't have a lick of forethought before he gets into something. (acts without thinking)
- You cannot plan for every little thing that might go wrong.
- I have a plan. (idea)
- He flies by the seat of his pants. (no planning before performing a task or making a public appearance or speech)
- He's winging it. (acting or speaking without previous planning)
- If we put our heads together, we can come up with a plan. (group effort to solve a problem)
- Any plan is better than no plan at all.
- If plan "A" fails, move on to plan "B."
- Do you have a back-up plan? (an alternate plan of action in case the first one fails)

- The best laid plans of mice and men often go astray. (One cannot predict what might go wrong.)
- Plan every day as if you'll live forever, but live every day as if it were your last.
- Do you have a floor plan for this castle in the air you're building? (Do you have a plan of how you are going to make your hopes/dreams come to pass?)
- Do you have a plan? (What shall we do?)

play/playing
- She's play acting. (pretending)
- He plays by ear. (plays a musical instrument according to the sound, not according to formal lessons)
- He's playing for keeps. (serious outcome)
- He loves his play-diddles. (toys)
- She's playing for time. (stalling)
- We played hooky today. (skipped school or work)
- I played right into his hand! (reacted exactly how he anticipated that I would)
- She's playing possum. (pretending to be asleep)
- I won't play second fiddle to anyone! (I want to be first choice)
- He's playing the field. (dating lots of girls)
- Don't play the fool. (behave foolishly)
- If you play with fire, you are bound to get burned. (get what you deserve)

pleasant
- He was in good form.
- It was a pleasant afternoon. (agreeable)

- The weather promises to be pleasant. (clear; comfortable)

please/pleased/pleasure
- Pass the salt, if you'd please. (polite request)
- Please pass the pepper. (polite request)
- He pleases me a great deal. (I like him very much, romantically speaking.)
- Women are hard to please. (satisfy)
- You can please some of the people all of the time. You can please some of the others part of the time. But if you spend your whole life trying to please everyone else, you'll please yourself none of the time.
- You can please some of the people all of the time. You can please some of the people none of the time. But most of the people can be pleased at least part of the time.
- I'm pleased as punch to meet you. (delighted)
- It is a pleasure to meet you. (greeting)
- It would be my pleasure. (in response to an agreement to do something)
- It pleasured me to hear her sing again. (made me happy)

policeman
- The law will be watching for him.
- Where's a police officer when you need one?
- Someone call the cops!
- This speed trap is monitored by a local yokel.
- He's a bad copper.
- He's the flatfoot on the night beat.
- Look out, because here comes the fuzz.

politics
- It's a regular idiocracy! (idiots holding political office)
- With most politicians, it's a matter of ignorance and apathy... don't know, and don't care.
- The sheriff has him in his hip pocket. (has control over)
- He's bought and paid for. (someone who won an election where allegations of vote buying were present)
- I changed horses in mid stream. (changed the side I was voting for)
- He thinks he's the Great White Hope.
- I bet on the wrong horse. (voted for the loser)
- He's a fence sitter! (won't take one side or the other on an issue)
- I have no dogs in this fight. (don't care how the election turns out)
- He's waiting to see which way the wind blows. (once public opinion is determined, he will support the most popular outcome)
- One hand washes the other. (political favor)
- You scratch my back; I'll scratch yours. (political favor)
- The candidates are having a ballyhoo down at the train depot. (debate; argument; big social event)

poor (finances)
- He's as poor as a church mouse.
- She's as poor as Job's turkey.
- We can barely keep the wolf from the door.
- He's as poor as a black snake.

- I'm so broke, if I needed to buy something, I'd have to get it on my good looks.
- We were as poor as snakes.
- His salary is so low, he can barely keep body and soul together.
- There's no shame in being poor, but it's a disgrace to be nasty.
- It's root hog, or die poor.
- Times were hard and things were bad. (usually refers to the depression)
- I've got holes in my pockets. (no money)
- I don't have two pennies to rub together.
- He may be a big shot now, but I knew him when he didn't have a pot to pee in. (before he became successful)
- Things will be different when my rich uncle gets out of the poor house.
- She only had two and now there's only one left. (dollars; cents; ideas)
- They are so poor, they don't have a pot to pee in. (too poor to own a chamber pot)
- You can't get blood out of a turnip. (too poor to pay debts)
- We can barely make ends meet.
- We're on a shoestring budget. (little cash)
- When poverty comes in at the door, love flies out the window. (Financial problems put tremendous strain on a relationship.)
- We have to pinch a penny hard enough to make it squeal. (extremely thrifty)

poor (inadequate performance of a task)
- That was a slip shod way of doing things.
- Poorly done!
- That was about half baked. (incomplete)
- I'm so poor, I couldn't afford to buy a thing. They'd have to give it to me on my good looks.
- They're as poor as a whip-oor-wills.

possibility/possibilities
- Let's run it up the flag pole and see if it will fly.
- If I had my druthers…
- You never can tell.
- Lord willin'…
- Depends on which way the wind blows, I reckon.
- It will all work out one way or t'other.
- Life is like a bowl of cherries – you get the good with the bad.
- You can eat a dozen apples that are perfect, but sooner or later, you are bound to get one with a worm.

position (see also **location**)
- My car is square dab in the middle of the yard!
- She's betwixt and between. (in the middle)
- He's from up the creek.
- She's from down the creek.
- We grew up on the creek.
- He's at the head of the line. (in front literally or figuratively)
- I'll be the cow's tail. (come last; follow at the end of the line; finish last)
- He's the head honcho. (in charge)

- He's low man on the totem pole. (an underling; new hire)

pot
- A watch pot never boils.
- He's taking pot shots at me. (needlessly insulting comments)
- He doesn't have a pot to pee in.
- There's a lid for every pot. (a mate)
- He has a pot gut. (large belly)
- She's a crack pot. (crazy)
- Put your money in the pot. (collection)
- Are you putting any money in the pot? (money set aside for someone who wins a bet)
- Now that's the pot calling the kettle black! (accusing someone of a fault or guilt that is the same as the accuser's own)

potatoes
- That's only small potatoes. (inexpensive; insignificant)
- She uses Arsh potatoes to make her best mashed potatoes.
- Sweet taters are my favorite.
- Are we having spuds for supper?
- He's a meat and potatoes kind of man.
- Time to dig some taters out of the tater hole. (get what is needed from available resources)

pouting
- He's puffed up like a big adder.
- She's puffed up like a bull frog.
- He's sitting there all puffed up like a big toad!

- If you pooch that lip out any further, you're liable to step on it.
- This kind of behavior will get you absolutely nothing.
- Pout all you want. The world is not going to stop spinning.

power/powerless
- She's powerless over herself when he's around.
- He's as powerless as a broken stick.
- He's got the power; she's got the brains.
- Winners never quit and quitters never win.
- He's sitting in the cat bird's seat.

pray/prayer
- Pray for me. (farewell; leave taking)
- Stand with me in prayer. (prayer of agreement about a specific thing)
- Prayer changes things.
- My prayers seem to have a broken wing. (no answers evident)
- My prayers feel like they are bouncing off the ceiling. (don't feel like God is hearing them)
- I'm a prayer worrier – pray awhile, worry awhile. (battle between faith and circumstances)
- Pray until you can't pray any more, then stand and see the salvation of the Lord.

precaution
- Better safe than sorry.
- An ounce of prevention is worth a pound of cure.
- Have you taken precautions? (birth control)
- You can't be too careful.
- Measure twice, cut once.

precision
- I went over it with a fine toothed comb.
- You'd better check every jot and tittle.
- This car runs like clockwork.
- This is a well oiled machine. (actual machine; political machine

predict/predictions
- She's got the seventh sight.(a gift of knowing the future or the hidden)
- You just hide and watch and see if it doesn't turn out that way.
- You don't have to be a psychic to predict the obvious.

preferences
- If I had my druthers, I wouldn't go at all!
- I don't care for them much. (not a favorite)
- I don't much care for that dress you're wearing. (don't like)
- If I had my druthers, I'd druther not. (prefer not to do something)
- I'd like to go fishin'. Does that suit you? (Do you mind if I go fishing?; Do you want to go fishing with me?)
- If it suits me, it suits. (If I like something that's all that matters to me.; I don't need anyone else's approval.)
- That's not my cup of tea. (don't like)
- It's not my bag. (lack of interest)
- Question: Do you want to go to the movies? Response: I don't care to. (actually means okay; sure; yes)

pregnant
- She's got biscuits in the oven.
- She's got buns in the oven.
- Is she impregnated?
- She's expecting.
- She's with child.
- She's in the family way.
- She's showing.
- She's knocked up.
- Have you heard who's preggo?
- When's she due?
- She swallowed a watermelon seed.
- She's got biscuits baking.
- Their cake is rising rapidly.
- She's getting big.
- She swallowed a basketball/

prepare/prepared
- I'm ready to roll!
- I'm fixing to go to the store.
- I'm aiming to see him in a few minutes.
- Muster up.
- Steady yourself.
- All hands on deck.
- I'm ready to haul out of here. (ready to leave)
- Ready? Set? Go!
- One for the money, two for the show, three to get ready, and four to go. (often said at the beginning of an outing of any sort at the time of departure)
- He's building up a head of steam.

- I'm girding myself up to see him face to face. (getting ready)

pretend/pretender
- She's the best pretender I've ever seen. (acts exactly how she thinks the person she's with would want her to act)
- Don't pretend you didn't hear me! (ignore)
- I can pretend with the best of them. (act completely out of character if the occasion calls for it; insincere)
- Let's pretend this didn't happen. (keep it secret)

pretty
- She's as pretty as a picture.
- She's as pretty as a butterfly.
- She's quite a looker!
- Your face is as fresh as a morning in spring.
- He's as lovely as a summer morning.
- She's a baby doll.
- She's as pretty as can be. If she could be any prettier, she surely would be.
- Pretty is as pretty does.
- Pretty is on the outside, but ugly is skin deep.
- She's as pretty as a spotted calf.
- She's as pretty as a speckled pup.
- She's as pretty as a baby doll.
- Pretty wings make pretty birds.
- Pretty actions make pretty girls.
- You're as pretty as a magazine cover.
- You're as pretty as a catalogue cover.
- She's pretty ugly and pretty apt to stay that way.
- It takes pretty to know pretty.

- Better clever than pretty.
- Aren't you a pretty sight? (can be spoken to a child who has gotten very grimy as a sarcastic remark; or to someone who hasn't been seen in a while; or to someone who is very dressed up)

pride/proud
- Pride goeth before a fall!
- Pride doesn't pay.
- Pride has a heavy payback.
- She takes pride in her work. (tries to do her best always)
- Everyone thinks their own crow is the blackest.
- Every momma crow thinks her baby is the blackest.
- Every momma cow knows her own calf.
- She thinks she's above the rest of us.
- He thinks he's above his raisin'.
- She walks around with her head held high.
- I'm as proud as a peacock! (happy about good news)
- He's so proud, he's strutting peacock feathers. (making a great display of joy – as in the birth of a first child)
- Don't get on your pompous horse with me.

proceed
- We've got the green light.
- We've gotten the go ahead.
- Full steam ahead!
- Raise anchor!
- What are you waiting for? Get started!
- Get a move on!

procrastinate
- You'd better quit dragging your feet!
- Quit fiddling around.
- Quit fiddle-farting around.
- Don't put off until tomorrow what you can do today.

profit
- What does it profit a man if he gain the whole world, but lose his soul?
- He's making a killing on that deal!
- He's made a mint off of his idea.
- She's making money hand over fist.

progress
- We're making headway.
- I've got more done today than I had yesterday.
- We're getting there.
- Almost done!
- If we keep at it at this rate, we'll be done in no time.

promises
- Promises! Promises! That's all I ever hear! (promises not kept)
- Promises don't fly. (don't usually get fulfilled)
- He promised her the moon, but fell far short. (wasn't able to live up to his word)
- Promises are best kept in your pocket and not handed out freely. (Don't make them if you can't keep them.)
- You will starve to death on promises. (can't depend on them)

prostitute
- She's a bad woman.
- She's from the red light district.
- She takes her love to town.

- She's a hooch.
- She's a hoochy momma.
- She acts like a ho.
- She's a street walker.
- She gives out treats, but they are not free.
- She's loose.

protrude/protruding
- Her belly was all pooched out.
- Her lip was stuck out as far as she could stick it.

pull
- Don't yank my chain! (deliberately try to irritate)
- He's only yanking your leg. (trying to play a trick on you)
- He's pulling your leg. (teasing)

punctual
- He's always on the dot.
- You can set your clock by her arrival.
- He's Johnny on the spot.
- She arrived right on the nose.

punish/punishment
- That was no more than a slap on the wrist.
- Let the punishment fit the crime.
- He will punish her for choosing the other man over him.

purse
- I left my pocketbook in the car!
- Why is she always sackin' that big purse around?
- I've got my saddle bag and ready to go!
- It's all in the handbag. (I have whatever you need.)

- Why are you pursing your lips? (pouting)
- I'd like to know what all she carries in that big old sack.

pursue
- You've got to go after what you want.
- It is man's place to pursue who he wants and woman's place to reject who she doesn't want.
- Pursue your dreams.

Q

quarrel
- I'm staying out of it.
- I have no dog in this fight.
- I have no horse in this race.
- Don't scotch about it… just do it!
- It's better to live on the rooftop than with a brawling woman.
- That woman is all the time Scotchin' around about something. (quarreling; grumbling)
- They had a big falling out. (disagreement)
- I never saw such a quarrelsome bunch.
- She's more trouble than a month of Sundays.
- I have a bone to pick with you.
- He is a cantankerous old thing. (quarrelsome)
- I have a little crow to pick with you.
- My dog's bigger than your dog.
- You're more trouble than you're worth.
- She lit into me for all she was worth!

- I'll have you know… (used at the beginning of any important statement in a quarrel)
- They are at crossed purposes.
- They've had a falling out.
- They are on the outs.
- I'm going to give him an ear full!
- I'm gonna let you have it with both barrels!
- When they go at each other, it's Katie bar the door!
- It's only a lover's quarrel. 'Twill soon be mended.

queen
- I'd like to be Queen for a day!
- She thinks she's the queen in her own little fairy tale! (thinks more highly of herself than she ought)
- She's the queen bee around here. (dominant female)

questions/questionable
- That's nothing but bull!
- What you talkin' about, Vern?
- Which a way did you say?
- How come you can't go with me?
- Why for did you say that?
- What in all are you bringing to the picnic?
- Who in the tar nation do you think you are?
- Who told you that you are the ruler of the universe? And you were dumb enough to believe them!
- Who died and left you boss?
- Who died and made you King Bo Bo?
- Do you reckon we could go for a walk tomorrow?
- What's new with you, Scooby Doo?
- Well, what do you know about that? (surprising news)
- Sure enough? (Really? Honestly?)

- I have some questions to put to him. (ask)
- What's up with that? (please explain)
- That's hogwash.
- That's a load of bull hockey!
- That's a crock!
- What a load of hooey.
- That's blarney.
- If you believe that, I'd like to sell you some swamp land.
- Surely you don't expect me to believe that.
- Do I look like I was born yesterday?
- That's doubtful, isn't it?

quick
- I'll be there quick as a wink.
- He's quicker than Jack Robinson.
- I'll be there quick as a flash.
- I'll be there in the whip of a stitch. (refers to a sewing stitch)
- I need to make a quick buck. (fast money)
- There's a quick fix for your problem. (easy solution)
- He's quick on the draw. (gets ahead of trouble)

quiet
- She's as quiet as a mouse.
- She's tongue tied.
- Cat got your tongue?
- I'll keep quiet about it. (Keep a secret.)

quit
- Throw in the towel.
- Cut it out!
- Stop it!

- Cease and desist.
- Cut the crap out!
- Drop the ball.
- Let the matter drop. (stop pursuing something)
- Quittin' time! Quittin time! (end of a work day)
- It's time to call it quits. (romantic break up; divorce; give up on an idea, situation, or business)
- It's time to throw in the sponge.
- Quitters never win and winners never quit!

R

rag

- Those children look like a raggle taggle band of gypsies! (not well taken care of)
- Now there's a rag, tag, and bobby bunch! (rough looking)
- She's on the rag. (menstrual cycle)
- He's a rags to riches story. (went from poverty to wealth)
- Don't rag me about it! (aggravate; nag)
- They keep ragging me about my girlfriend. (teasing)
- Put on your glad rags. (dress up/party clothes)
- I can't wear that old rag to go out in public. (old garment)
- That newspaper is nothing but a rag. (carries gossip and inflammatory stories that are half truths)

rain

- It's raining cats and dogs
- It's coming down like down like cats and dogs!

- It's like driving through a car wash. (can't see the road)
- It's coming down in buckets full. (very heavy)
- It's a real gully washer out there. (cloudburst)
- It's raining. It's pouring! The old man is snoring.
- Only three "Ss" melt in the rain – salt, sugar, and can you guess the other one?

ramble/rambling
- You do ramble on! (talk a lot about disconnected things)
- His speech was all over the map! (jumped around; changed topics; did not stick to a main theme.
- His lecture was all over the place!
- She's a rambling rose. (can't be content in one place)
- She goes off on tangents. (rambling conversation)

rare
- That is rarer than hen's teeth. (unheard of)
- That's a rare find. (unusual)
- Girls like her are few and far between. (a prize)
- Some days are diamonds. (very, very good)

ready
- I'm rarin' to go. (excited)
- Get ready, Freddy, cause here I come!
- I've got my game face on. (psyched up; prepared)
- I'm ready with my A game.
- Bring it on!
- I'm chompin' at the bits to start my new job. (anticipating)

rebuke
- It just isn't done! (a rebuke to someone wanting to do something socially unacceptable)
- You ought to be ashamed of yourself!
- Your daddy would roll over in his grave if he could see you acting like this! (talking like this might be substituted; treating people like this, thinking like this; etc.)
- No gentleman (or lady) would behave in such a way!
- I am ashamed of you!
- I am disappointed in you!
- I would never have believed you were capable of such a thing!

recently
- Here lately, I've thought about taking a vacation.
- For the last little while I've had that person on my mind.

reciprocate
- You scratch my back, I'll scratch yours.
- Do unto others as you would have them do unto you.
- She fixed his little red wagon, just like he fixed hers.
- The things you do will come back to bite you in the butt.

recovering (from an illness)
- He's on the mend.
- I'm improving.
- I'm better than I ort to be. (survived a serious illness or accident)
- I believe I'll live.
- I'm getting my strength back. (improving)
- She's getting better.

- I'm better than I was yesterday, and the day before.
- I'll live until I die.
- I reckon my time wasn't up. (near death experience)

reckon
- I reckon I might go out with him. (thinking about)
- There is a day of reckoning. (to give an accounting for)
- Do you reckon it will rain? (suppose)

red
- Her lips are as red as cherries.
- Her mouth was red as a ripe strawberry.
- His hair was as red as a carrot.
- I caught you, red handed. (in the act)
- His face was as red as a pickled beat. (embarrassed; sunburnt)
- He turned red from the top of his hid to the tip of his toes. (embarrassment)
- She went red all of a sudden. (anger; humiliation)
- I'm redding up the house. (cleaning; making right)
- Your face is as red as a mad bull. (angry)
- Your face is as red as a turkey's gobbler. (too much sun)

redd/redden
- I need to redd up the house. (clean; straighten up)
- Will you help me redden up the kitchen? (do the dishes)

refresh/refreshed
- I've got my second wind.
- Let me catch my breath.
- I'll perk right back up in a minute.

- I'm as good as new.

refuse/refusal
- I don't think so!
- You can't make me!
- You don't own me!
- You're not the boss of me!
- I wouldn't do that for love nor money.
- You couldn't pay me enough to do it.
- Wild horses couldn't get it out of me.
- I wouldn't have you if you were the last man on earth!
- I respectfully decline your proposal. (marriage; business)
- I wouldn't touch that with a ten foot pole.
- Never darken my door again!
- If I never see you in forever and a day, that will be too soon!
- You're welcome back when Hell freezes over.
- There is no way in this world you are going to convince me!

regret/remorse
- I will regret it until my dying day. (remorse)
- I have no regrets. (wouldn't do anything differently)
- He shows no remorse. (not sorry for a bad deed)

relationships
- He drove a wedge between us. (a third party affected a relationship in a negative way)
- We need to mend some fences. (restore a past relationship)

- It's time to bury the hatchet. (forgive and put the past behind)
- It's time to forgive and forget, then move on.
- I'm moving on with my life. (leaving a bad relationship behind)
- They need to smoke the peace pipe. (make amends)
- We parted on good terms. (amicably)
- We went our separate ways. (let go of the relationship)
- We drifted apart. (had less and less in common over time)
- He's on the rebound. (getting over a broken heart)
- She got the short end of the stick when she married him. (bad choice)
- She drew the short straw when she got stuck with him.
- He got the short end of that deal when he married her.
- They are thick as thieves. (very friendly)
- They are in cahoots together. (working together on a scheme)
- It's better to be an old man's darling than a young man's fool.
- You don't have to love a husband, but you do need to respect him.
- He's robbing the cradle. (dating someone much younger)

relative/related (family)
- We are kin.
- We are blood.
- We are blood kin.

- He's my own flesh and blood. (my child)
- We're cut from the same cloth. (alike)
- We're of the same clan. (family)
- We spring from the same tree. (same family tree)
- We come from the same bloodline. (lineage)
- We have the same lineage. (ancestors)
- We have a common bond. (family in common)
- We have the same pedigree. (family lineage)

reliable/unreliable
- They don't reckon much on me. (doesn't depend on)
- You can depend upon it. (reliable)
- Count me in. (committed)
- Don't count me out. (give me another chance)
- You can count on me. (dependable)
- You can't depend on him. (unreliable)
- Don't put your hopes in that basket. (Don't depend upon certain future outcomes.)
- I'll believe it when I see it. (doubtful result)

relieved
- Thank God and Greyhound they're finally gone! (refers to people decades ago coming to visit and leaving on the Greyhound bus.)
- That's a load off my mind.
- Whew! I'm glad that's over.

remember
- Do you recollect the time we went to Chicago?
- I hope the good Lord will bring me to your remembrance from time to time. (think of me)
- Remember me. (said in parting)

- I can't remember what I forgot! (forgetful)
- I knew so much, I had to start forgetting it to remember something new. (age related forgetfulness)
- Every once in a while something from my childhood will spring to mind. (memory)
- Remember me to your folks. (send my greetings)

repair
- It's been Jimmy rigged. (made a mess of)
- All it needs is a little duck tape. (simple repair)
- If he can't fix it, it can't be fixed! (great repairman)

repeat
- You will have to lick that calf over again.
- I've been down that road before.
- You've got to get back on the horse that bucked you.
- Try, try again.
- If I live to be a thousand, I'll not do that again!
- Same old, same old.
- If you fall off a horse, the best cure is to climb right back on and ride.

reprimand
- I knew I'd had it. (expected a reprimand)
- I knew I was in for it.
- You're just like your daddy (mother; brother; any relative)!
- I brought you into this world and I can take you out!
- You know better!

repulsive
- Gross me out!
- He makes my skin crawl.

- Seeing a dead animal in the road gives me the heebie jeebies!
- She makes me want to poke my eyes out with a fork and stick my fingers in my ears!

reputation (general)
- She has a good name. (good reputation)
- Everybody gives him a good name. (speak well of him)
- I've always given that store a good name. (recommendation)
- That is one pure and honorable human being.
- A man's good name is the most important thing he'll ever own and the hardest thing he'll ever keep.
- Never cause anyone to lose face. (don't destroy someone else's reputation)
- A good name is easy to lose and hard to ever get back.
- She's a woman of good repute. (good reputation)
- Your name will be mud. (do something unpopular)
- You're rotten to the core! (bad reputation)
- She's/he's a dandy. (a very good person)

reputation – female (bad)
- She's loose. (promiscuous)
- She's free with her favors. (sexual conduct)
- She's from the red light district. (prostitute)
- She can't keep her skirt down.
- She's a heartache waiting to happen.
- She's a feisty one.
- She is hot to trot. (promiscuous)
- She's ripped her britches out. (promiscuous)

- Her pants are on fire. (promiscuous)
- She's just plain sorry.
- She doesn't know the word NO.
- She's not fit to wipe your tail on.
- She's got a bad name.
- She's burned her reputation.
- She's a strumpet.
- She crawled out of the dregs of humanity.

reputation – male (bad)
- He's a man of ill repute.
- He's a player.
- He's a good for nothing biscuit eater.
- He's lower than a snake's belly.
- He's lower than a snake's belly in a wagon rut.
- If you see THAT ONE coming down the road, you'd better turn and go the other way.
- He's a first class jerk.
- He's a piece of filth.
- If it stinks bad enough, you know what it is… or in his case, WHO it is.
- He's just waiting for a roll in the hay.
- He's a scallywag.
- He's low down.
- There comes trouble.
- He visits the red light district.
- There comes trouble with a capital T.
- He can't keep his pants up.
- He can't keep his pants zipped.
- He is trouble on the hunt.
- He's a scoundrel.

- He's a rake!
- He's a knave!

rescue/rescued
- He sure pulled your fat out of the fire! (got you out of trouble)
- She threw me a rope. (helped me out)
- He threw me a line. (gave me a reason to go on)
- She pulled some strings for me. (made arrangements; called in favors)
- I couldn't have made it without you. You're a life saver. (said to someone who gave help in time of need)

resemble
- There is no semblance whatsoever between them.
- That dress puts me in mind of one I saw in a catalogue.

rest/resting
- I need to go sit down before I fall down.
- I need to set a spell. (rest from work)
- I'm not sleeping, I'm just resting my eyes. (eyes closed)
- I'm recharging my batteries. (going to take a nap)
- Just give me a few minutes and I'll be raring to go again!
- Take your rest. (said to someone near death when the person releases them to depart)
- Rest in peace. (spoken of the dead; to the dying)
- You can rest assured that whatever you do in darkness will be brought to light. (depend upon it)

restless
- I've got the squirmles.

- I can't be still!
- You are like a cat on a hot tin roof.
- You act like a worm on a hot rock.
- You act like you've got ants in your pants!

reveal
- She really showed herself. (let the true personality come out)
- It will all come out in the wash. (truth will become evident)
- The truth has a way of rising to the top. (reference to cream rising to the top)
- The truth has a way of coming out.
- Be sure your sins will find you out! (you'll get caught eventually)
- An eye for an eye and a tooth for a tooth. (exact payback)
- All will be revealed in due time. (Some things must be kept secret for a season.)

revenge
- "Vengeance is mine," saith the Lord.
- Revenge is sweet.
- The best revenge is to live well.
- I'll get you back if it's the last thing I ever do!
- Revenge is never as sweet accomplished as it is in thought.
- An eye for an eye and a tooth for a tooth. (exact payback)

reverse
- That's inside out and backwards!
- That is wrong side outwards.

- That is wrong sundowners. (backwards)
- He goes about things bass backwards.
- He does everything backwards.
- He tries to do things tail backwards.

rhythm
- He's got rhythm! (plays the drums well; instinctive musical inclination)
- I love to hear the rhythm of the rain on a tin roof.

rich (also see **wealth**)
- He has more money than Fort Knox.
- She's as rich as a chocolate bar.
- He's an old money bags.
- She wants to find her a sugar daddy. (a man who will spoil her with money and expensive gifts)
- He's so rich; he doesn't even know how much he's worth.
- That feller has so much money; he doesn't even have to tie his own shoes if he doesn't want to.
- He has so much money in his wallet; he needs two belts to hold his pants up.
- The rich get richer and the poor get poorer.

ride/rides
- Can you carry me to town?
- How about a lift?
- Are you going my way?
- You've got to quit straddling the fence. (riding both sides of a situation)
- You can't ride a dead pony. (let go of the past
- My boss rides my back all the time. (picks on; criticizes)

ridicule
- Why were you poking fun at him?
- Watch your mouth when you talk about my kin.
- She's always making light of somebody.
- That woman is a monkey on his back.
- She never sees the good in her man.
- You don't have to throw down on people all the time.

rimy
- Her eyes are rimy. (hazy)

ring
- Give me a ring. (phone call)
- That has a ring of truth. (sounds likely)
- He really rings my bell. (find him attractive)
- Give me a dingle. (ring on the telephone)
- I'll give you a jingle. (telephone call)
- He has a ring through his nose. (dominated by a female)
- She has rings on her fingers and rings on her toes. (wears an abundance of jewelry; too much jewelry)
- Did you see that rock? (diamond in an engagement ring)
- Let me get my sunglasses. That ring is blinding me. (huge diamond)
- I'll ring your jaws if you don't shut up. (hit)
- I'll ring your neck if you tell on me. (whip you)
- My ears are ringing and the room is spinning. (feel faint)
- Ring in the New Year! (let it begin)
- I'll see you in the ring. (boxing ring; fight)

road
- I've been down this road before. (repeating the past)
- It's a rocky road ahead. (rough times)
- I've come to the end of the road. (run out of options/resources; facing death)
- It's an uphill road. (difficult)
- It's a long and winding road. (can be done but will take persistence)

rock
- You rock my world. (make me happy)
- I believe rocks grow in my garden. The more I clear, the more I find.

romance
- Good riddance! (said after a break up)
- He is an old flame. (former sweetheart)
- He's got her number on speed dial. (talks to her frequently on the telephone)
- She has a crush on him.
- He sought her out.
- He makes me go weak in the knees. (huge attraction)
- He's head over heels for her.
- She's met her match. (counterpart)
- He's looking for his split apart. (soul mate)
- It's time to fish or cut bait. (commit to a relationship or leave)
- It's time to poop or get off the pot. (commit to a relationship or end it)
- She's smitten with him. (infatuated)
- He's taken with her. (infatuated)
- He singled her out of the herd.

- She's got the fever for him. (desires him)
- They are struck on each other.
- She's been bitten. (has fallen in love)
- You take my breath away.
- He's set his sights on her. (decided he wanted her for his own)
- He left her out in the cold. (broke up)
- Old flames die hard. (hard to forget a first love)
- He's been shot through the heart for her. (wants only her)
- The love bug has bitten him. (has fallen for someone)
- Let him down easy. (be kind when you break up)
- She wrote him a Dear John letter. (break up letter)
- I don't want just any old Tom, Dick, or Harry! (selective)

romantic opportunist
- He's a cad. (dates more than one girl at a time)
- He's a player. (only wants sex from a variety of women)
- She's a gold digger. (only interested in men with money)
- He's a user. (only cares about what he wants)
- He thinks he's a real Romeo. (fancies himself to be suave with the ladies)
- She's looking for a sugar daddy. (wealthy man who will indulge her financially with or without emotional commitment)
- He's looking for a sugar momma. (wealthy woman who will spoil him)

- It's better to be an old man's darling than a young man's fool. (treated better by an older man)
- He's a real Casanova. (charms all the ladies)
- She's a black widow spinning another web. (evil plans for enticing a man)
- He plans to real her in. (play on her emotions and slowly win her confidence or love)
- He's after one thing. (sex only)
- Love 'em and leave 'em. That's his motto. (sex only)

rooster
- He struts around like a bainty rooster. (proud, arrogant)
- He's the only rooster in the hen house. (one man in a family of females; one surrounded by women)
- If he cheats on me again, I'll be turning that rooster into a hen! (castrate)
- Every rooster can crow, but does he know what he's crowing about? (men brag, but they don't always have a right to)

rope/ropes
- I'm at the end of my rope! (completely frustrated; don't know what to do next)
- When you're at the end of your rope, tie a knot and hang on. (Don't give up.)
- She had him roped and branded before he knew what hit him. (married; engaged; in love)
- He's walking a tight rope. (in a dangerous situation; trying not to offend anyone on either side of an argument)

- Know the ropes. (Figure out what you need to do in a specific situation.)

rose/roses
- There's never a rose without a thorn. (good and bad come together)
- She's the rose between two thorns. (a good girl surrounded by bad choices)
- My love is like a red, red rose. (a thing of beauty)
- The roses have left her cheeks. (sick)
- Her life is no bed of roses. (difficult)
- She's looking through rose colored glasses. (looking optimistically and unrealistically)

rotten
- Something is rotten in Denmark. (dishonest)
- I smell something rotten. (deceitful)
- He is rotten to the core. (thoroughly bad)
- One rotten apple doesn't spoil the whole bushel. (Don't discard all because of one bad person; bad experience.)
- He's a low down, rotten, good for nothing, scalliwag! (supreme insult of character)

rough
- He's as rough as a cob. (uncultured)
- Your skin is as rough as a porcupine. (poor complexion)
- She was brought up rough. (poor; hard times)
- He's rough and ready. (prepared to go; prepared to fight)
- It's a rough row to hoe. (difficult)

routine
- One day just runs into the next, same as always.

- It's all in the day to day running of a place.
- Same old, same old.
- Day in and day out, it's always the same old thing.
- I've got my routine down pat. (way of doing things)

rug
- I'm as snug as a bug in a rug. (cozy; warm; comfortable; tucked in bed for the night)
- She can really cut a rug! (dance)

rule
- He rules the roost. (is the boss)
- Here's the rule of thumb… (approximately)
- She has the rule of you. (authority over)
- Live by the golden rule – do unto others as you would have them do unto you.
- He has the whip hand over her. (dominates)
- Rules are made to be broken.
- He rules with an iron fist. (cruel; powerful)
- She rules with a velvet fist. (appears gentle, but is stern or demanding)
- Rule wisely, my son. (Make good choices in life.)
- She was lax on the rules. (didn't adhere to rules; let others break rules)

run
- He's always running off at the mouth. (talks too much)
- How fast can you pump those legs? (running speed)
- I'm run down. (tired)
- You're running around in circles. (not getting anything accomplished)
- She went running lickety-split. (quickly)

- She ran down hill with her legs all akimbo. (awkwardly)
- I've got to run. (leave)
- I've got a run. (a snag in a stocking or hose)
- I've got the runs. (diarrhea)
- It's an uphill run. (difficult situation)
- He tries to run over me and expects me to lie down and take it! (tries to bully me)
- He thinks he's got to run with the pack. (do what his friends do)
- He runs with the herd. (does what everyone else does)

S

sack
- He got sacked. (dismissed from a job)
- Time to hit the sack. (go to bed)
- I need a poke of flour. (bag, sack)
- You can put those potatoes in a toe sack. (burlap bag)
- She'd jump in the sack with anybody. (engage in sexual activity)
- Time to jump in the sack. (go to bed)

sad
- There's nothing sadder than a wet cow. (wet with no way to get dry or warm)
- Be careful what you do, or you'll be sucking sorrow soon. (have regrets)
- I'm bummed out. (unhappy)
- It was a grievous thing. (very hurtful)

- He's a regular sad sack. (depressed)

safe
- Better safe than sorry.
- There's no safe way to tell him the news. (expect the recipient to be angry)
- I'm home safe. (a job or task completed in a favorable manner)

sale/salesman/selling
- It was a doozy of a sale!
- The sale price is what the original price should have been!
- The drummer came by the store today. (a wholesale representative who tried to get orders from small stores)
- He's trying to drum up business. (get new customers; make sales)
- If things were selling any cheaper, they'd have to give them away. (a real bargain)
- He's a real wheeler dealer.
- She'd sell her soul for a dollar bill.
- He'd sell his granny if he could do it for a profit.
- He'd sell his mother for the almighty dollar!
- The books were selling like hot cakes.
- I wish I could buy him for what he's worth and sell him for what he thinks he's worth. (refers to someone with an inflated ego)
- Did you buy anything from the pack peddler? (a door to door salesman with a suitcase of goods to sell or samples to show from which to take orders)
- He had a rolling store. (someone who sold good off of a wagon, automobile trunk, or truck)

sale/salesman/selling
- It was a doozy of a sale!
- The sale price is what the original price should have been!
- The drummer came by the store today. (a wholesale representative who tried to get orders from small stores)
- He's trying to drum up business.
- If things were selling any cheaper, they'd have to give them away.
- He's a real wheeler dealer.
- She'd sell her soul for a dollar bill.
- He'd sell his granny if he could do it for a profit.
- He'd sell his mother for the almighty dollar!
- The books were selling like hot cakes.
- I wish I could buy him for what he's worth and sell him for what he thinks he's worth.
- Did you buy anything from the pack peddler? (a door to door salesman with a suitcase of goods to sell or samples to show from which to take orders)
- He had a rolling store. (someone who sold good off of a truck)

sail/sailing
- He set sail down the road. (moving quickly)
- You'd better lower your sails. (Don't make a decision too quickly. Be still and consider carefully.)
- We are heading into a storm. (unavoidable trouble)

salt
- That's like rubbing salt in the wound! (deliberately hurting someone)
- He's the salt of the earth. (a good person)

- That language is a little salty. (inappropriate)
- A little salt goes a long way. (kindness; effort)
- I'm going down to the Salty Dog. (tavern)

sandwich
- Make it a Dagwood. (put everything on it)
- I'll take everything on mine but the dishrag! (Pile on the toppings.)
- I'll take a little bit of everything you've got.
- The bigger, the better.
- If it's edible, pile it on. (condiments)
- He's an ignorance sandwich – ignorance, apathy, ignorance.
- She's sandwiched in between two big guys. (sitting between)
- I'll give you a knuckle sandwich. (hit you in the mouth)

savings
- I've got my egg money to depend on. (side job; small savings account)
- I've put by a little money in case of an emergency. (saved a little cash)
- Do you have much put away in the bank? (savings)
- She's the savingest woman you ever did see. (thrifty)
- I stuck some money back for vacation.
- My piggy bank is starving. (financially broke)

say
- What do you say about that? (What is your opinion?)
- He's always got something to say about everything. (shares his opinion freely)
- I will have my say! (be heard)

- Unless hear say can say who say, leave it at no say! (Don't repeat unfounded gossip.)
- He always has to have the last say! (final word)

scared/scary
- She looks like a Boo Hag.
- I've got the heebie jeebies.
- You scared the living daylights out of me!
- You nearly gave me a heart attack. He just about jumped out of his head.
- He just about jumped out of his head.
- She was as scared as a rabbit out of its hole.
- That gives me the creeps.
- That's kind of Scooby Doo.
- That was a real nail biter!
- That girl is downright spooky! (frightening)
- It was a white knuckle experience. (scary)
- She jumped out of her skin! (frightened)
- My heart dropped like a rock. (severely startled)
- You scared the life out of me!
- I could hardly draw a breath. (too scared to breathe)

scatter/scattered
- Don't scatter promises. (make too many promises to keep)
- Don't scatter pearls before swine. (waste of something precious)
- She is scattered to the four winds. (going in all directions)
- Don't scatter your seed among the rocks and thorns. (don't be wasteful)

- He's got youngins scattered all over the place. (illegitimate children)

school
- That's old school. (a former attitude or way of doing things)
- He's been through the school of hard knocks. (learned difficult life lessons)
- Where did you get your schooling? (education)
- School is cool!
- School's out! School's out! Teacher let the monkeys out!

scoundrel
- He is a rascal!
- He is a good for nothing. He's no account.
- He's a sorry thang.
- That sorry tailed good for nothing!
- He is low down.
- He's a bottom dwelling scum sucker!

scream/screaming
- He was screaming like a little girl!
- She was screaming like a banshee.
- She was screaming like a panther.
- He was screaming like a bob cat.
- She screamed like a Boogy Man.
- She was screaming at the top of her lungs.
- The tires were screaming as he pulled out.

screw
- I don't know how things got so screwed up. (plans went awry)
- He screwed around and missed his chance. (responded to slowly or didn't act quickly enough)

- She put the screws to him. (forced him to do something he didn't want to do)
- She's a little screwy. (mentally unstable)
- He'll put the screws to you! (put pressure on; treat unfairly)

searching
- I've been beating the bushes. (looked everywhere outside)
- I've searched high and low. (looked everywhere inside)
- I've been prowling around for it. (hunting for)
- I was just pilfering for something to eat. (trying to find)
- I've looked clear beyond the county line.
- At this point in my life I'm searching for something. (seeking fulfillment in life)
- Don't leave any stone unturned. (look everywhere until you find what you're seeking)

secret/secrets
- Oops! I guess I let the cat out of the bag. (told something by accident that wasn't supposed to be told)
- Keep it on the QT! (quiet)
- Mum's the word! (I won't tell.)
- I'm taking you into my confidence. (trust you with privileged information)
- It's common knowledge. (no longer a secret)
- They've been meeting on the sly. (secretly)
- Don't air your dirty laundry in public. (tell family secrets)
- Off the record… (unofficially)

- Keep it on the hush.
- Between you, me, and the lamp post…
- Between you, me, and the fence post…
- Between you, me, and the bed post…
- Keep this close to your heart. (protect the secret)
- That was a slip of the tongue. (accidentally told)
- If you are going to tell her, you might as well shout it from the rooftops.
- Keep it under wraps. (guarded secret)
- A secret may be safe among two, but never three. (a secret told is no longer secret)
- Wild horses couldn't drag it out of me. (I won't tell.)
- There's a skeleton in his closet. (a hidden past deed)
- If you shake his family tree, how many monkeys will fall out? (family secrets)
- Two can keep a secret if one of them is dead.
- The best way to keep a secret is to keep it to yourself.
- I got wind of what folks are saying about the job opening.
- I caught wind of what you've been saying about me.

seldom
- Every oncet in a while.(same as above)
- It's been a month of Sundays since I saw you.
- It's been a coon's age since we've been to visit.
- Never in a blue moon would I be seen in that outfit.

sell/selling/sold
- I'm selling out lock stock and barrel. (getting rid of everything in preparation for retirement or a move)
- He's selling out. (giving in to the establishment rather than taking a firm stand on an issue)

- He could sell swamp land in the desert. (persuasive)
- These books are selling like hotcakes. (quickly)
- She sold him down the river. (betrayed)
- Don't sell yourself short. (underestimate)
- Don't sell your soul. (betray your own values)
- He sold his soul to the devil. (went after something he wanted regardless of the cost of his moral or spiritually)

sense
- She doesn't have the sense the good Lord gave a goose!
- He doesn't have enough sense to come in out of the rain.
- There just no sense in that. (not logical)
- He doesn't have walkin' around sense. (not bright)
- She's got good sense. (smart)
- These children have plenty of sense. (smart)
- She has the sixth sense. (psychic)
- She has good nose sense. (strong olfactory senses)
- He has an acute sense of danger. (strong instincts)

sensitive
- He is a sensitive child. (emotional)
- That burn is tetchious. (bad; painful; hurts to touch)
- That bruise is tedgious. (sore)

set
- Set right down and enjoy yourself. (rest; visit)
- She set you up. (betrayed you)
- She'll set that little man on a shelf and tell him what to do, and he'll jump when she tells him to.

sex
- They have known each other in the Biblical sense.
- Making love is only part of a marriage.
- They have done the deed.
- The marriage bed is undefiled.
- Have you had the birds and the bees talk?
- They are baby making or at least using that as an excuse.
- He's got the key to her lock.
- She's tickling his fancy.
- They've become as one.
- She's putting out for him.
- Let's get jiggy.
- I think they are going to hook up. (get together; tryst)
- He's trying to hook up with her. (reach a mutual agreement for sex)
- Did somebody give her a booty call? (a late night call/date just for the sake of sex)
- They are screwing around together.
- They have carnal knowledge of each other.

sexual organs
- Cover you nether regions.
- Stop scratching the land down under.
- Make sure you wash Australia.
- He hit me in my privates!
- He kicked me in the family jewels
- He kicked me in the unmentionables.

shake/shook
- Shake it off. (a coach may say to an athlete who has just had a minor injury)

- Shake it off and go on. (forget about some unpleasant incident and keep moving forward with your life)
- It's time to shake, rattle, and roll. (get in the car and go)
- I shook him off. (romantic break up; deliberately got away from someone who had been following or tailing another person)
- I was shaking from head to foot. (frightened; nervous)
- He shook hands with the devil. (made a deal that will cost him severely from his moral character or integrity)
- My knees were shaking. (nervous)
- I felt the earth shake. (strong emotional response)

shampoo
- I'm lathering up my hair. (washing)
- I'm sudsing up my head. (washing)
- I'm going to shampoo that man out of my life.
- You need a good shampoo. (hair wash)

sheep
- He's a wolf in sheep's clothing. (deceiver)

Sometimes it's hard to tell the sheep from the goats. (deceitful vs. honest people)
- I've been counting sheep. (asleep)
- She's been making sheep eyes at him. (flirting)

shocking
- It blew my mind.
- It is mind boggling.
- I can't wrap my head around it.

shoes
- Have you seen my new brogans?

- I think these blogans are too big for my feet)
- Her shoes are like sled runners. (long and thin)
- His shoes are the size of boat paddles. (big)
- You've got your shoes on the wrong feet! (going about something the wrong way; making a mistake)
- He leaves behind big shoes to fill. (replacement after death)
- If the shoe fits… (if something applies to you…)
- Walk a mile in my shoes. (try my life on for size)
- Put yourself in their shoes. (empathize)

shop
- Shop 'til you drop. (until you're exhausted)
- If they make shopping an Olympic sport, she'd win the gold medal.
- She's shopping around. (single, looking for a boyfriend)
- I'm only window shopping. (looking; wishing – but not buying)
- He's down at the shop. (workplace)

short
- He's a short shanks.
- He's vertically challenged.
- He's short on common sense. (lacks)
- We're running short on milk. (not enough)
- He has short man's syndrome. (defensive)
- He has a Napoleonic complex. (tries to dominate in order to make up for lack of stature)
- Good things come in small packages.

should
- You ought to know. (should)

- I orta go to the grocery store. (should)
- I ort to get up from here and get to work. (should)
- No sense thinking about what you should've done – just get it right the next time. (learn from past mistakes)
- Should've, would've, could've – but didn't!

show
- That just goes to show you! (proves)
- She is showing herself. (trying to draw attention to herself)
- He's putting on a big show. (trying to impress someone)
- It's all show. (insincere)
- He's trying to show me up. (look better than me to impress someone else)
- I'll show you a thing or two! (teach you a lesson)
- That's awfully showy. (refers to apparel that is too bright; too colorful; too many sparkles; too revealing)
- The show must go on! (Regardless of setbacks, engagements must be kept.)

shut up
- Shet your mouth! (shut up)
- Latch the door! (lock)
- Shut it up. (Silence!)
- Put a lid on it. (Keep it quiet; contain something)
- If you don't hush, I'll smack your face.
- Hush now. (said to a fretful child who has been crying)
- Shut your pie hole! (stop talking)
- That's enough! (a warning to stop balk talking)

- Pipe down! (get quiet)
- Keep your yap shut! (be silent)
- Put a cork in it! (stop talking)
- Zip your lips. (stop talking)
- Put a sock in it!
- You better quieten down!
- That's more than enough.
- You'd better shut that mouth before I shut it for you.

shy
- She's bashful.
- He's backwards.
- She's a shrinking violet.
- He's a wall flower.
- The cat's got her tongue.
- She's kind of backerds.
- She always hangs back.

sick/sickly/sickness
- He's a puny young un. (unhealthy)
- That's a poor child. (sickly)
- That child is weakly. (not well)
- I'm down in the gitworks.
- I was down in my gears.
- She's got one foot in the grave and the other on a banana peel.
- She's not sick. She's hippoed. (a hypochondriac)
- That child is weakly.
- Granny has the miseries.
- I'm feeling a little under the weather.
- I'm feeling a little green around the gills.
- I've seen better days.

- He's looking to die. (not expected to recover)
- My grandma is ailin'.
- My grandpa is bad off. (very ill)
- I'm sick to death of your attitude! (fed up)

sight
- "I see," said the blind man to his deaf wife over 500 miles of disconnected telephone wire. "I see clearly."
- Hind sight is 20/20. (reflection is easier than prediction)
- She has the gift of sight. (sixth sense)
- You're a sight for sore eyes! (glad to see you)
- That boy is a sight! (memorable; mischievous)
- I've got my sights on you! (watching)
- She's got her sights set on him. (wants to be in a romantic relationship with him)

sign
- All signs point north. (clear indication)
- Sign your John Hancock. (signature)
- Sign on the dotted line. (receipt; contract)
- It's a sign. (superstitious indication)
- What sign are you? (zodiac)

silence/silent
- He's as silent as the grave.
- I didn't open my mouth.
- She's as silent as the dark.
- If you can't improve the silence, don't talk.
- Hush!
- Be still!

- Silence is the same as consent. (If you don't speak out against something wrong, you might as well be in agreement with it.)
- I'll silence you permanently if you don't keep your mouth shut. (kill)
- Silence is a virtue.
- Silence is golden.
- No comments from the peanut gallery.
- Silence is its own reward.

silly (also see **dumb)**
- You are plumb silly.
- You are so silly, you probably can't tell which sock goes on which foot.
- That's the silliest thing I ever heard.
- That plan is about half baked.
- You're a regular knuckle head.
- He's a dip stick.
- You must be kin to Squirrel Nutkin.
- You're a goof ball.
- What a nut you are!
- He's a doofus.
- You're so silly, your daddy must have dropped you on your head when you were born.
- He runs around all willy nilly.
- He's a namby pamby.

silver
- Every cloud has a silver lining.
- He's got silver in the temples. (middle aged)
- She is a silver haired fox.

- He is a silver tongued devil. (charmer)
- You sold him out for 30 pieces of silver. (betrayed for the price paid to Judas for betraying Jesus)

similarities
- You are as much alike as two bookends.
- I'm happiest among my own kind.
- You are like two peas in a pod.
- She says, "God bless you," before he sneezes.
- They can finish a sentence for each other.
- They speak the same language. (have similar views; understand each other)
- Birds of a feather flock together.
- Two heads are better than one.
- What's good for the goose is good for the gander.
- You're a chip off the old block.
- They're joined at the hip.
- We are kindred spirits.
- She's a chip off the old block, even if she ain't got a stick!
- This is me and mini me.
- It's just me and my shadow who like the same things.
- You're as much alike as two book ends.

simple
- It's as simple as falling off a log.
- It's as easy as one, two, three!
- It's as easy as A, B, C!
- It's as easy as falling off a log.
- It's as easy as apple pie.
- It's as simple as apple pie.
- It's as plain as the nose on your face.

- Couldn't get any easier!

sin/sinner
- Ain't no sin going to enter in! (reference to heaven)
- The more skin, the more sin! (implies that the more scantily clad a person is, the more sin they have embraced in their life)
- That's a pure sin! (something bad)
- It's a sin to waste these leftovers. (should do something useful instead of putting them in the trash)
- He's a rank sinner. (lives sinfully and doesn't care)
- That painting is so bad, it ought to be a sin. (not good)
- You can sin if you want to, but you'll also pay the price. (You are accountable for your own behavior.)

singing
- He sure makes purty songs. (sing well)
- He can sure make music. (sing well)
- She carries a fine tune. (pretty voice)
- He couldn't carry a tune in a bucket. (off key)
- He can sure pack a song. (sing loud)
- She's squawling with the radio. (singing along)
- Stop that caterwalling! (singing too loudly)
- She sounds like a screech owl. (unpleasant sound)
- He has a fine voice. (good)
- She can sing as pretty as a bird's song. (pleasant)
- She has a voice like an angel. (lovely)Sing out! (speak up louder)
- She was lifting her voice to the ceiling.
- Don't worry. He won't sing. (won't serve as an informer for the law)

sissy
- He's a big sissy. (Doesn't enjoy manly activities.)
- He is sissified. (spoiled)
- He is candified. (feminine acting)

sit
- Sit yourself down! (come sit with me and let's visit)
- Sit on it! (keep it to yourself; don't talk about it)
- Sit on your fist and rare back on your thumb. (said to someone when there aren't enough seats available)
- Take your sorry self over there and sit down! (a reprimand to someone misbehaving; time out)

skeptic
- I'm a doubting Thomas.
- Show me, and then I'll believe you.
- Show me the proof and I'll get in line.
- The proof is in the pudding.
- It'll take more than her word to convince me.
- Don't believe what you hear and only half of what you see!

skin
- Your skin is as soft as a baby's bottom.
- Your skin is as soft as a snake's belly.
- Your skin is like peaches and cream. (pretty complexion)
- I'll skin you alive if you don't straighten up! (spank)
- It's no skin off my nose what you do. (makes no difference to me)
- I skinned my knee! (abrasion)

skinny
- That girl is thinner than a piece of paper.

- He's so thin, if he stood sideways and stuck out his tongue, he'd look like a zipper.
- That boy wouldn't weigh 50 pounds soaking wet.
- He's as skinny as a rail.
- She is pole thin.
- He's a scrawny little thing.
- He's a puny little thing.
- You've fell away. (lost weight, usually due to health problems)
- Now there goes a bandy legged looking fella.
- You've got poor. (lost too much weight)
- She's really gone down. (deliberately lost weight)
- He's withered away. (weight loss due to illness)
- She's melted like a snowball. (lost weight quickly)
- He's skinny as a bean pole.
- He looks like a stick figure.
- She's so skinny she has to run around in the shower to get wet!
- He's so skinny he has to tie a knot in his knees to keep from going down the drain when he takes a shower.
- She's so thin a strong wind could blow her away.
- He's so skinny he has to tie a knot in his knees to keep his socks up.
- She is as light as a feather.
- You're so skinny, if you got caught outside in a cloudburst, all you'd have to do is walk under the telephone wire to keep from getting wet.

- You're so skinny you can't drink through a straw without an anchor around your ankle to keep you from falling in.
- She's so skinny, if she swallowed a marble, she'd look pregnant.
- He's so skinny he'd have to wear a life preserver in the bathtub to keep from going down the drain.
- He ain't near big around as the size of a toothpick.
- He is very gaunt.

skunk (also called pole cat)
- You good for nothing, low down, dirty rotten pole cat! (person of low moral character)
- I smell a skunk. (something is not right; suspicion)
- He's a yellow bellied pole cat. (coward)
- Don't try to skunk your way into that job. (scare everyone else off by his presence)
- I reckon I know a skunk when I smell one! (recognize something for what it is)
- You scallywag of a skunk! (low moral character; cheater; liar)
- We skunked you! (beat you without you scoring any points – applies to any game where a score is kept)

slap/slapped
- I've been slapped around more than yesterday's biscuits!
- I'll slap you silly!
- He slapped a lawsuit on us!
- Slap yourself down and have a seat!

slathered
- She slathered a ton of lotion on her face. (too much)

- He slathered on the compliments. (overdone)
- She slathered him with praise. (continually)
- She slathered on the icing to cover the imperfections in her cake. (Attempted to cover or hide the truth.)

sleep/sleepless
- I slept like a baby. (peacefully)
- It's Nappy time. (nap time)
- I need forty winks. (refers to Rip Van Winkle's sleep)
- I can't hold my eyes open. (very sleepy)
- I've got the big eye. (can't go to sleep; not sleepy)
- I didn't sleep a wink! (none)
- Time to hit the hay. (bed time)
- Time to hit the sheets.
- Time to go to Nappersville.
- I need some match stems to prop my eyes open.
- I'm half way to Winkin', Blinkin', and Nod.
- I tossed and turned all night long.
- Time to make like Rip van Winkle and get a good night's sleep. (extended sleep)
- Time to crawl in the hole until morning.
- I've got to get some shut eye.
- Time for bed. We've got to be up at the crack of dawn.
- Better get some sleep. We've got to be up by the crack of day.
- Sleep fast. We'll be up before the roosters.
- Did you sleep well last night? You are looking bright eyed and bushy tailed.
- I wrestled the mattress all night.

- She was sleeping like a dead woman.
- He's passing through this life asleep. (oblivious to what's going on around him)
- This is good sleeping weather. (rainy; cold)
- The good Lord neither slumbers nor sleeps.
- It's time to get some shet eye.
- If you don't get some sleep tonight, you'll be feelin' it in the mornin'.

slick
- That dress is slick as a ribbon. (ironed smoothly)
- He's slick as a ribbon. (a deceiver)
- That is slicker than snot on a doorknob.
- That is slicker than greased owl poop!
- He thinks he's pretty slick. (clever)

slime
- He is as slimy as a slug. (disgusting)
- She is as slimy as a frog's underbelly! (undesirable)
- He is pure slime. (sleezy)

slow
- You're slower than a month of Sundays.
- He's slower than molasses.
- He's as slow as a slug on a rug!
- What are you waiting for? Christmas?
- Would you stop lollygagging around?
- You are slower than Christmas!
- Granny was slow, but she was old!
- Your legs might be fast, but the rest of you is mighty slow.
- Flowers don't run.

- I believe I'll mosey on down the road. (go slowly; walk leisurely)
- Would you please stop piddling around? (poking; taking too long for a task)
- You are plain pokey!
- You're as slow as a snail. (very slow)
- You're as slow as the seven year itch. (a disease that is hard to cure and lasts a long time)

small
- He walks around like a bainty rooster! (small and cocky)
- Her eyes are too teeny for her face.
- I'll take a teensy bit of cream in my coffee.
- That's the teensiest baby I ever saw.
- The new kittens are so cute and tinesy.
- He's the least un in the bunch. (smallest)
- You have a teeny weeny spot of ink on your cheek.

smart
- He's sharp as a tack!
- He will outfox you every time. (cunning)
- She's smart as a whip. (not lazy)
- Smarty pants! (showing off their intelligence to deliberately annoy others)
- He could run circles around his brother. (gets more done)
- She can run rings around anyone else in her class. (quicker to comprehend than others)
- He's on smart cookie! (bright)
- She's a sharp cookie. (clever)

smell
- I smell something rotten! (deceitful)
- Something smells fishy. (not right)
- Something smells in Denmark! (deceitful)
- I smell a rat! (a snitch, a deceiver)

smile
- Show those pearly whites! (toothy smile)
- Get that silly grin off your face!
- Look at that possum grin!
- He's grinning like a possum.
- His mouth turned up at the corners.
- Turn that frown upside down!
- She's grinning from ear to ear.
- He's grinning like a mule eating saw briars.
- He's grinning like the cat that ate the canary.
- She's grinning like the Cheshire Cat.
- She spread her lips from ear to ear.
- A smile is the most attractive thing you'll ever wear.
- She showed up at the door wearing nothing but a smile! (nude)
- Smile often. It makes your enemies wonder what you've been up to.

smooth
- I will try to smooth things over. (diffuse a quarrel)
- Her complexion is as smooth as a baby's bottom.
- He thinks he's pretty smooth. (sophisticated)

snacks
- There are goodies in the bread box.
- I just need a little bite.

- I need something to hold me over.
- I need some nummy nums.
- Where are the yum yums?

snake
- He's an old sneaky snake. (someone lurking about)
- He's a snake in the grass. (deceitful; a betrayer)
- He's lower than a snake's belly in a wagon rut. (bad reputation; poor character)
- He's as dangerous as a copperhead. (danger that you can't see until it's too late)
- He's sneakier than a rattlesnake. (get in unexpected places waiting to strike)

sneeze
- That's nothing to sneeze at. (don't take the opportunity lightly)
- If someone sneezes, the response is: "God bless you," or "Bless you!" (For multiple sneezes, the phrase is repeated for each sneeze in rapid succession.)
- I'm about to blow! (sneeze)
- Ah – choo! (said at the time of a sneeze)
- Ah- chooeeee! (said at the time of a sneeze)

snooze
- You snooze, you lose. (If you hesitate, someone will take and opportunity you are not taking.)
- I think I'll have a little snooze. (nap)

snob/snobbery
- He thinks he's above his raising. (looks down on family and place of birth)
- She's all hoity-toity. (high society)

- Don't be looking down your nose at me! (superior attitude)
- She thinks a fly wouldn't light on her. (above the norm)

snoring
- He snores like a freight train.
- She snores so loud she could wake the dead.
- He snores so loud the dead saints are liable to think it's Gabriel blowing his horn!
- She snores loud enough to suck the paint right off the walls!
- She snores so loud she rattles the timbers.
- He snores so loud he sucks the walls in and out.

snot
- He irritates the snot out of me!
- He's slicker than snot on a doorknob. (not too cool)
- She's such a snot! (a snob; brat)

snug/snuggle
- He's as snuggly as a big old teddy bear.
- He's as snug as a bug in a rug.
- You two look pretty snug! (cuddling)
- This is snuggle down delicious.
- Snuggle down right here next to me. (get comfortable)

soak
- I just want to sponge it in. (soak it up)
- Go soak your head! (said in anger to get rid of someone)
- What you need is a good soak! (hot, long, bubble bath)

sober
- He was sober as a jug.
- He sobered up in a hurry.
- I'm stone sober.
- The car wreck scared him sober.

soft
- Her skin was as soft a silk.
- Her skin is as soft as a baby's bottom.
- It was as soft as a brand new feather bed.
- The bed was so soft, it was like sleeping on a cloud.
- He's just an old softy. (kind)
- She has a soft spot for you. (affection)
- He's gone soft. (out of physical fitness habits; ceased being a hard hearted person)
- A soft answer turneth away wrath. (diffuses anger)

sour
- She's so sour, she looks like she's been sucking a dill pickle.
- He's a regular old sour puss. (unpleasant)
- That's a case of sour grapes. (someone pretends they didn't want something they didn't get, but in reality, they really did)
- That's as sour as whang. (very sour)
- That's as sour as mash. (the fermented makings of moonshine)
- Whew! That lemonade has a real whang to it! (too sour)
- She's so sour, she could curdle cream! (unpleasant)

sow/sewn
- She finger sewed her quilts. (did them by hand)

- All of her clothes were hand sewn. (homemade)
- Sow seeds of kindness along the way.

space
- She's a space cadet. (absent minded)
- He won't give me my space. (leaves me no individual time)
- I need some breathing room. (time on my own)
- They were sitting so close, you couldn't stick a pencil between them!
- I just want my own space. (a place to live of my own)
- He gets in my personal space. (gets too close physically – inside the three foot radius that is considered socially acceptable)
- She invades my space. (comes when unwanted; without invitation)

spank/spanking
- That dress was brand spanking new. (never worn)
- You need a good dose of willer tea. (spanking with a willow switch)
- I'll tan your hide.
- You'll get a thrashing when pa finds out that you got in trouble at school.
- If you did something wrong, Momma would fly into you like a buzz saw! (swift to spank)
- I'll give you a sound thrashing if you ever do that again!
- Your daddy will tan your britches.
- I'll cut me a switch and wear you out!
- You'll get a whoopin' when you get home.
- That's one I'm laying up for you.

- Daddy use to take me out behind the woodshed whenever I needed it.
- There's a difference between beating and instructing.
- Your ma is going to whomp you.
- You'll get a striping for disobeying your teacher.
- Momma will dust your bottom for throwing rocks.
- The teacher will dust your pants for not doing your homework.
- Grandma will dust the seat of your pants for cussing.
- I'll dust your fanny if you do that again!
- Do you need a trip to the woodshed to straighten you out?
- Do I need to cut me a switch.
- I'll wear you out!
- This will hurt me more than it hurts you.
- I'll set your tail on fire!
- I'm going to blister your tail!
- I'll bust your bottom!
- I'm going to bust your tail!
- You are not too big for a spanking!
- You are going to get an attitude adjustment.

speak
- Don't stop at that speak easy. (tavern; house of prostitution)
- Don't speak unless you're spoken to. (Remain silent.)
- I always speak my mind. (blunt)
- Don't speak your voice unless you're asked to. (Keep your opinions to yourself.)

speculate
- Just supposing it was so.

- How some ever it might be…

speed
- One goes fast and one goes slow, but in the end they both reach the same destination.
- He ran as fast as a squirrel on a hot Texas road.
- He's as fast as greased lightning.
- I'll be back, quick as a wink.
- He's faster than the speed of light.
- Move it or lose it.
- Don't slack your heels until you get to the store and straight back!
- I'll be back faster than lightning can strike.
- He was as fast as an arrow.
- You are dragging like an old turtle.
- She's faster than a .38.
- That boy is faster than a panther with a load of buckshot!
- She is slower than a dying snail!
- He's slower than a turtle.
- You're as slow as an eight day clock.
- You're slower than the seven year itch!
- Snap the cracker.
- She's slower than my granny and my granny is 96 years old!
- He's as fast as a squirrel that lost its tail.
- You'd better get in gear!
- He ran like a scalded dog.
- Granny was slow, but she was old!
- He's as slow as a turtle with a bad leg.

spell
- She's having a spell. (temper tantrum)
- He's having a spell. (a bout with a recurring illness)
- I could spell you down any day! (superior intelligence)
- I took a spell of wanting dill pickles every day for a week. (craving)
- Come in and sit a spell. (a little while)
- She's having a sick spell. (minor illness; short duration)
- We're expecting a cold spell. (change in the weather)
- Spell me. (take my place working; let me rest or go to the bathroom)
- He lived for a spell on the other side of the mountain. (a little while)
- She's under his spell. (supernatural influence)
- She won the spell down. (spelling bee)

spill
- She spilled the beans. (told a secret)
- Don't cry over spilt milk. (Don't worry about things you can't undo.)
- His mess slopped over onto me.

splendid
- This is absolutely splendiforous! (wonderful; glorious; splendid)

spoon
- She was born with a silver spoon in her mouth. (wealthy)
- They are spooning. (dating)
- Come get under the covers and spoon with me. (snuggle in behind me, shoulders to shoulders, back to

stomach, knees to knees, like two spoons fit together in a drawer)
- Spoon some honey on my biscuit. (Drizzle a spoon full of honey over my biscuit.)
- You can't talk with a spoon in your mouth! (Say what you mean!)

spot/spotted/spots
- That is a pided pup, if I ever saw one!
- Your face is motley. (dirty spots)I spotted him the other night down the road. (saw)
- He's as spotted as a pided cow. (blotchy)
- A leopard can't change its spots. (We are what we are.)
- I see spots before my eyes. (precursor to a migraine)
- I could spot her a mile away. (locate visually)

spouse
- She's my better half.
- He's my split apart.
- He's my old man.
- She's my old woman.
- How's your Mrs.?

spraddle
- A girl should never sit all spraddled out. (knees apart, sitting inappropriately)
- You can't spraddle the fence. (one leg on one side and one on the other)

sprite
- She is a sprite little thing. (energetic; determined)
- She is a wood sprite. (loves nature)

squander
- Don't squander your youth. (waste)

- We are frittering away our days. (using them foolishly)
- She would squander her last cent! (spend on foolish things)
- Don't squander love.
  (waste; take for granted)
- Don't squander your days. (don't take your life for granted)

squeak/squeaky
- I don't want to hear a squeak out of you! (don't complain, or be absolutely quiet)
- The squeaky wheel gets the oil. (people who are the loudest in their demands often get them)
- Now you are all squeaky clean! (just out of the bath)
- He is squeaky clean. (nothing of reproach in his background)
- I want this house squeaky clean! (thoroughly clean)

squinch
- Don't squinch your eyes up at me!
- Her face was all squinched up.
- His car was squinched from the wreck.
- The sunball makes my eyes squinch up.

squirrel
- You are squirrelly. (crazy)
- There's nothing better than squirrel gravy and dumplings.
- I shot a fairydiddle today. (red squirrel)
- Even a blind squirrel finds a nut every once in a while. (Keep trying and you'll be right some of the time.)

stare/staring
- Take a picture! It lasts longer.
- Take a gander, why don't you?
- What are you looking at?
- I can beat you at a staring contest. (Stare at each other eyeball to eyeball and see who blinks first.)
- She stared at me with a death wish! (hateful look)
- Him staring at me like that ran a shudder down my spine! (frightened; repulsed me)
- Do you want me to take a picture and send it to you?
- Didn't your momma teach you it's not polite to stare?

stature
- I drew myself up. (stood as tall and straight as possible to increase an appearance of size or authority)
- She holds herself well. (poised)
- He holds himself right. (a sense of dignity surrounds him)
- He is as round as he is tall! (portly)

steal
- She will steal you blind.
- He'll snitch it when you are not looking.
- He can swipe it right out from under your nose.
- He has sticky fingers.
- She can lift just about anything she wants if it's small enough.
- The gypsies have been through.
- That child will pilfer anything that's not tied down.
- He got it at the midnight sale.
- He got it by the five finger discount.

- He said it fell off a truck.

steep
- The hill was as steep as a cow's face.
- That mountain is so steep, if it snows, no one will be able to get up it until the spring thaw.
- That price is pretty steep. (too expensive)
- This job looks pretty steep. (difficult)

stiff
- You're a lucky stiff. (lucky guy; man)
- Keep a stiff upper lip. (be brave; don't let emotions show)
- That icing was a stiff as a board.
- He's stiff as a poker. (dead)
- He's a stiff neck if I ever saw one. (thinks himself superior; unwilling to listen or bend)
- He walks like he's had a poker shoved up his back bone. (stiff; arrogant)

still
- Still waters run deep. (quiet people have strong emotions)
- You're still the one! (remain as my love)
- I stood stock still. (afraid to move)
- He kept his moonshine still in his dog lot. (illegal whiskey making operation)

stingy (also see **frugal0**
- He's so stingy he'd steal the quarters right off his mother's eyelids.
- She can squeeze a penny until it squeals.
- He's tighter than Dick's hat band.
- He wouldn't let go of one red cent!

- He's still acquainted with the first nickel he ever made.
- Now there's one that can actually get blood out of a turnip.
- He's tighter than a banjo string.
- She could make a penny squall.
- He stays close to a dollar.

stink
- Somebody smells like a pole cat.
- Shewie! Something's rotten.
- That smells like something died, changed its mind and died again!
- The more you stir, the more it stinks. (stay out of other people's business)
- Shooo! Something smells cyarny! (rotten)
- I smell something fishy. (not true; peculiar stink)
- I smell something funky. (spoiled)
- Go wash that stink off! (go bathe)
- You smell like an outhouse.
- Yuck! It smells like the sewer has backed up.
- She smells like an ashtray.
- You smell like you've been rolling in stink.

stomach/stomach ache
- I've got a tummy ache.
- That boy has a cast iron stomach. (can eat anything)
- My eyes were bigger than my stomach. (took a bigger serving than can be eaten)
- I can't stomach the sight of her. (nauseating)
- I've got a belly ache.
- She turns my stomach. (don't like; anger)

- I've got a pain in the gut!

stole/stolen
- He plucked her right out of my hand. (usually refers to a girl who has eloped at a very early age)
- He has stolen my heart.

stop/stopped
- Cut it out!
- Cease and desist!
- I'm going to nip it in the bud. (stop a problem that is just beginning)
- We need to stem the tide. (stop something)
- Stop before it becomes a habit!
- I'm going to pull the plug on that notion. (stop someone before they act on an idea)
- If you don't stop crossing your eyes like that, they're going to get stuck that way!
- Stop, drop, and roll. (fire safety rule)
- Stop, look, and listen. (safety rule for crossing the street)
- He stopped right then and there! (immediately gave up on something ; broke a bad habit)
- The sound of his voice stopped me right in my tracks. (startled me; caused me to become discomposed)
- The gunshot stopped me dead in my tracks. (couldn't move; startled reaction)
- Cut him off. (block escape route; quit enabling a person to continue in a self destructive manner)

store
- I'm going to the jot 'em down store.
- Time to go to market.
- He is a storehouse of knowledge. (knowledgeable)

- Her house looks like a dry-good store. (crowded with stuff)
- Her closet looks like a clothing store.
- He's a drummer. (A wholesale representative who went around and took up orders from small stores.)
- He's a pack peddler. (Door to door salesman with his wares in a suitcase.)
- Time to spend my egg money. (Money saved away for something special.)
- I'll wait for the rolling store. (A truck that came periodically carrying dry goods.)

storm
- There's a storm brewing. (trouble on the way)
- We'd better hunker down before the storm gets here. (get prepared)

story telling
- He can sure crank them out!
- He can call up the shivers! (tell scary stories well)
- Let me tell you a good one on my grandpap. (a story)
- She can spin a good yarn.
- That's a tall tale and a half.
- She's always telling some big rigamarole! (long story; complicated)

straight pin
- I need some stick pins to put up this hem.

strain
- I think I've strained my brain. (been concentrating on a difficult task for an extended amount of time)
- I strained my ears. (tried to overhear)
- She puts a strain on his checkbook. (spends too much)

stranger
- He meant no more to me than a stranger off the street. (indifferent)
- We are strangers and kin. (related, but nothing in common)
- Truth is stranger than fiction.
- He's a rank stranger to me. (not a clue who he is)
- He was stranger than a three legged bandicoot!
- We are only strangers until first we meet.

stretch
- I could stretch a mile if I didn't have to walk back! (muscle stretch)
- Now that's a stretch of the imagination. (hard to believe)
- Isn't that stretching it a little? (exaggerating the truth)

strong
- He's strong as a bull.
- He's as strong as a horse.
- He's as strong as an ox.
- Something smells strong. (spoiled)
- Only the strong survive.
- This coffee is so strong it could get up and walk out.

stubborn
- He's the mule headedest thing I ever saw!
- You are just plain pig headed.
- Once she's made up her mind, nobody is going to change it. (rigid; unbending)
- He wouldn't budge an inch if his life depended on it!
- She's a hard head.
- That girl always "gees" when you say "haw."

- He's the orneriest thing I've ever seen!
- He puffs up like a toad frog and won't give an inch.
- She's fixed in her ways.
- If you stick that lower lip out any further, you're going to step on it!

stupid
- That's the stupidest thing I ever heard in my life!
- You can't get any stupider than that.
- That's the stupidest idea anyone has come up with since the beginning of time.
- I hate to see a kid go stupid. (do something really dumb)

stutter
- Mush mouth (one who stutters)

success
- That's killing two birds with one stone!
- There's nothing sweeter than success.
- Now we're cooking with gas!
- He made out like a bandit!
- He's riding the gravy train.
- He's got it made in the shade.
- She's got it good.
- We're living the good life.
- It's all good.
- They're living high on the hog.
- He's stepping in high cotton.
- He's got it made.
- She's walking in high cotton.
- He's picking high cotton. (refers to the easiest picking of cotton)

- He has the Midas touch. (all turns to gold)
- She's a golden child. (preferred; privileged)
- She's always been a princess. (spoiled; catered to)
- He lives a charmed life. (has good fortune often)
- Hard work equals success.

suitcase
- Pack your bags.
- I've got my luggage ready to go.
- Her suitcase is the size of a steamer trunk!
- Get your budgit packed.

sun/sunshine
- The sun is like a big ball of fire.
- The sun ball is bright today.
- Will there be sun or not?
- You are my sunshine.

superior
- She thinks she's above it all.
- He is top shelf.
- He thinks his poop don't stink.
- She acts like she's been dipped in 24 karat gold.
- He's gone all hoity toity on us.

suppose
- I never allowed you did.
- I changed my mind.

surprise/surprised (expressions)
- They Lord God!
- Law, goodness!
- Well, lookey here!
- Well, doggies!
- By doggies!

- Who'd a thunk it?
- L I B!
- L I B jiggered!
- Well, I'll be!
- We'll I'll be switched!
- I'll be dithered!
- I'll be diddled!
- They law!
- Gee whiz!
- Well, I'll swan!
- I'll be diddled!
- Good land of Goshen!
- Landy Goshen!
- Lawsy day!
- Good night!
- Lawsy daisy!
- Holly Toledo!
- By golly!
- By gum!
- Geezo Petes!
- Gee whillackers!
- Fancy that!
- Well, I'll be jiggered.
- I'll be dipped!
- Heavens to Mergatroid!
- I declare!
- Heavens to Betsy!
- I'll be gummed!
- I'll be dad gummed.

- I'll be dad goned!
- I'll be jiggered!
- I'll be jimmed!
- Well, I'll be Jimmied!
- Dad Jim it!
- Dad gum it!
- Dog gone it!
- You don't say!
- By gum!
- Lord, holp me!
- Well, bless my time!
- Looky here!
- Well, bless my soul!
- Well, I never!
- Holy cow!
- Hot diggity dog!
- Never in a blue moon!
- I got the shock of my life.
- Lordy mercy!
- Lordy day!
- Well, lawsy days!
- I'm dumbfounded!
- Boy, oh boy!
- Well, bust my briches!
- Golly bum!
- I don't believe it!
- Crimanently!
- You've got to be kidding me!
- What do you know about that?

- If that don't beat the cats hopping!
- You look like a deer caught in the headlights.
- What do you think of that?
- Who would have ever thought it?
- Take a feller by surprise!
- Well, shut my mouth wide opened!
- Well, what do you know about that!
- Low and behold, there he stood!
- Well, I'll be dipped in cow butter.
- Well, I declare! (pronounced dee-klar)
- I never thought I'd live to see the day!
- If that doesn't take the cake!
- If that doesn't beat all.
- Well, I wish to my never!
- I've never seen the beat!
- That really takes the cake!
- If that ain't the beatin'est thing I ever heard of!
- I never heard of such a thing.
- You could have knocked me over with a feather!
- You could have bowled me over.
- His eyes nearly popped out of his head.
- That beats all I ever crawled in bed with!
- If that doesn't take the cake!
- I was so shocked I nearly wet my britches!
- Well, I'll be a monkey's uncle!
- Ain't that the beatinest thing?
- Did you ever hear the like?
- Well, dip me in batter and fry me!
- You've got to be making that up!

- If that don't beat the band

swarp/swarping
- I'll swarp you a good one. (slap)
- I'll cut a switch and swarp your legs! (spank)
- He's out warpin' and swarpin'. (drinking; partying)

swear
- Don't be using those by words in here! (curse words)
- By crackies! I will if I want to!
- By jeminies! He makes me so mad I could spit.
- I'll be jiggered!
- I swan! (swear; declare)
- I swanny, that boy doesn't know what he's talking about.

sweat
- I'm sweating like a pig! (miserable)
- You're sweating like a big dog. (panting)
- My sweat is running like a river. (sweat dripping)
- I'm sweating bullets! (very hot)
- He was sweating blood. (working hard)
- My palms are sweating. (nervous)
- That job is hard enough to make a fish sweat. (very difficult)
- I'm sweating like a donkey.
- I'm sweating like a Democrat (or Republican) on Election Day! (great stress; tension)

sweet
- Her smile was as sweet as sugar.
- His kiss was as sweet as candy.
- You're as sweet as blueberry pie.

- The scent was as sweet as sorghum molasses.
- Her lips were as sweet as honey.
- She talks so sweet honey bees were swarming around her mouth.
- I have a sweet tooth.
- Revenge is sweet.
- Victory – oh, how sweet it is!
- The fruit of your labor is always sweet.

swimming
- He swims like a fish. (well)
- She's swimming against the tide. (trying to attain something difficult)
- He's swimming with the fishies. (dead - probably murdered)
- He always swims with the tide. (takes the easy route)
- She takes to water like a fish.
- She's half mermaid.
- He's half fish!

T

table
- The tables have turned. (things have changed)
- Put your cards on the table. (tell the truth)
- Keep your hands on the table. (no funny business)
- We can sit at the table together. (get along)
- Bring it to the table. (discussion)
- We tabled that idea. (rejected)

tag/tagged
- He's been tagged. (earned a reputation)

- She's got him tagged. (She has a particular romantic interest in him.)
- He's been tagged by the law. (arrested or being watched as a suspect)
- Tag me sometime. (Give me a call.)
- I can't put a tag on it. (can't remember what it's called)
- What the price tag? (cost – literal or figurative)
- He's wearing a toe tag. (dead)
- Stop tagging along behind! (catch up)
- Do you mind if I tag along? (go with you)
- He's a tag along. (invited himself to go with someone else)

tail
- He tucked tail and ran. (ran because of fear; left quickly because he had been embarrassed)
- You do everything tail backwards! (don't do the obvious or the easy thing)

take
- I can't take her! (she gets on my nerves)
- Take it with a grain of salt. (not too seriously)
- Be a man. Take it on the chin. (accept your responsibilities)
- Take it to the limit. (100% effort)

talk/talkative/talking
- That's the talk around town. (gossip)
- I've got business with you. (We need to talk.)
- She can talk your head off. (a lot)
- Please stop the chatter.
- He can talk 90 miles an hour.

- She's a regular chatter box. (talks constantly)
- Let's talk turkey! (honestly and open)
- He's the talk of the town. (exciting event in someone's life; scandalous involvement; surprising turn of events)
- He loves to pontificate. (talk on and on; talk too much)
- Talk is cheap. (It's easier to say than do)
- She can talk the back legs off a donkey! (talks a lot)
- Come sit down and let's jaw a spell.
- That girl shore knows how to talk.
- You can talk to that kid 'til you're blue in the face, but he never listens.
- Stop that yammering! (endless talking; whining)
- I might as well be talking to the wall. (being ignored)
- We were just sitting around chewing the fat.
- Her tongue is fastened in the middle. (tells lies; talks fast)
- May I bend your ear? (have a talk)
- He's rattling on about something. (complaining)
- You're talking out both sides of your mouth. (don't know what you're talking about; adapting the attitudes and opinions of whatever company you are with)
- Let's talk shop. (about work)
- He can sure talk up a storm! (a lot)
- Lend me your ear. (listen to my idea)
- What are you prattling on about? (fast talking, unintelligible)
- He can talk a blue streak. (a lot)

- She talks just to hear herself rattle.
- When he's talking, you can't slip a word in edgewise!
- He could talk the rattles right off a rattlesnake.
- I might as well be talking to a tree stump as to talk to that boy. (doesn't listen)
- With her, what I say goes in one ear and out the other. (doesn't take heed)
- He'd talk to a brick wall if he thought it would listen. (talks to anyone who will listen to him.)
- She has a way with words. (her words are pleasing)
- That woman would talk to a brick wall! (speaks to strangers)
- She's got the gift of gab.
- She's a real jabber jaws.
- Her lips are unhinged.
- Stop talking that jibberish! (unintelligible words)
- She wore my ears out. (talked incessantly)
- She can talk a mile a minute.
- She works her mouth more than anything else.
- We don't talk plain. We like to dress it up. (use euphemisms)

tall
- He is as tall as a Georgia pine.
- He stands head and shoulders above the rest.
- She's as tall and slender as a willow tree.
- He's a long shanks.
- He'd stand shoulder to shoulder with a Zulu warrior.

tangle/tangles
- Will you retten out my hair, please? (comb it)
- Your hair is like a bird's nest! (messy)

- It looks like a rat built a nest in your hair.
- She would have done just fine if she hadn't got tangled up with that fella from over the mountain. (got involved with someone who turned out to be an unfortunate choice)

tanned
- You're brown as a biscuit
- You're turning yourself into beef jerky.
- Nobody would want to be that color on purpose.
- You're about toasted!

tantrum
- He really cut a rusty!
- He cut hisself a shine.
- She pitched a fit, but it didn't do her any good
- She threw a conniption fit!

tar
- You made that tar baby. Now you can nuss it! (created a problem and now you can deal with it)
- What in tar nation are you up to? (to emphasize the question)
- He ought to be tarred and feathered! (exposed and humiliated)
- He ought to be tarred and feathered and run out of town on a rail! (kicked out of town)

taste
- That tastes like cyarn. (bad)
- Now there's a tasty morsel! (attractive person; tempting food)
- We sure don't have the same taste. (don't like the same things)

tattle

- She'll tattle on you. (tell on; turn you in; expose you)
- He's a tattle tale. (tells on others to get them in trouble)
- He's a stool pigeon. (tells on others)
- She's a tattler. (tells people things others have said or done in order to bring discord or get others in trouble.

taxes
- You don't have to do anything in this life except pay taxes and die.
- He taxed his physical limits. (strained)
- He taxed his brain. (thought hard)

teach/teaching
- You can't teach an old dog new tricks. (old people are set in their ways)
- You can't teach what you don't know.
- I'd like to teach him a thing or two! (deflate an ego_
- Someone needs to teach her a lesson! (put her in her place)
- Teaching school is like trying to run a race with jack asses and thoroughbreds and expecting them to finish the race at the same time.

teamwork
- They are in cahoots together. (working on something together)

teasing
- I was only fooling.
- We were only fooling around. (playing)
- Just kidding.
- I was just funning you.
- It was just a bit of Tom foolery.
- It was only foolery.

- I was only deviling you a little.
- We didn't mean any harm. (response to a rebuke for teasing)
- We didn't mean anything by it. (response to a rebuke for teasing)

teeth
- I'll shake you 'til your teeth rattle! (threat)
- He's talking through his teeth. (anger; insincere)
- He's just cutting his teeth. (a baby; someone new to a job)
- I'd like to sink my teeth into it. (try to accomplish a specific task)
- He's got a mouth full of teeth! (big smile)
- Her voice sets my teeth on edge. (irritating)
- Grit your teeth. (be strong)
- His teeth are so yellow, traffic stops when he smiles.

telephone call
- Give me a dingle.
- Give me a ring.
- Give me a shout out.
- Give me a buzz.

tell/telling
- Dead men tell no lies.
- It's untelling. (hard to say)
- Tell me no secrets; I'll tell you no lies.
- The truth tells in our eyes.
- Her true age is telling on her.
- There are tell tale signs. (evidence; clues)
- Don't tell me you love me unless it's really so.

- I'm here to tell you… (a phrase said before a statement to give it emphasis – I'm here to tell you, that was the best dinner I ever ate!)

temper
- He's a hot head.
- He's a loose canon.
- He's like a keg of dynamite waiting to blow.
- She's always set on boil.
- She's meaner than a striped cat.
- He's meaner than a striped snake.
- Don't let that mild manner on the outside fool you!
- His temper is like flipping a switch.
- You always have to walk on eggshells around her if you don't want to set her off.
- She's prone to hissy fits.
- You never know when he's going to blow.
- She's like a storm cloud waiting to burst.
- She's always in a dark mood.
- He's a fiery one.
- She's like a firecracker all the time. You never know when she's going off.
- She's got a temper like a kitchen match.
- He's like a keg of dynamite with a short fuse.
- His bark ain't half as bad as his bite.
- Her bite isn't half as bad as her bark.
- He was fit to be tied! (very angry)

temper tantrum
- He cut a rusty when he didn't get his way.
- She pitched a fit, but it didn't do her a bit of good!
- She threw a hissy fit.

- He cut a shine!
- He threw a good one.
- He really cut a rusty!
- He cut hisself a shine.
- Don't throw a cow!
- She threw a conniption fit!

temptation
- You can't keep a bird from flying over your head, but you can keep it from building a nest in your hair.

testing
- They try to push the limits.
- They are pushing the boundaries.
- He's pushing the envelope.
- They will try your patience.
- She pressed every button.
- The students are testing the waters with the new substitute teacher. (seeing what they can get away with)

tether
- Don't tether your heart to the wind. (count on false hopes)

thanks/thank you
- Would you turn thanks, please? (say grace)
- Thank you don't put no gas in my tank, boy!
- Thank you kindly.
- I'm much obliged.
- In everything give thanks. (gratitude)

thin
- He's as thin as a rail.
- She's so thin, a hard wind could blow her away.
- That blouse is as thin as an onion skin.

thing (Also see unidentified **object**)
- thingamabob
- thingamabobber
- thingamajib
- thingamajigger
- thingamadoodle
- doomaflochey
- whirlymajigger
- doohickey
- thingy
- whatchamacallit

think/thinking/thought
- I'm studying about it.
- My wheels are turning.
- My thoughts are churning.
- I'm sitting here pondering.
- I'm having writers' block.
- I have wracked my brains trying to come up with an idea for the talent show.
- If you think I'm going with you to see that movie, you'd better think again! (absolutely not)
- I'll make you think go to town! (in total disagreement; forbid)
- It never even crossed my mind.
- I had a passing thought.
- I had a notion the other day about it.
- It never entered my upstairs window.
- Where did that come from?
- Who'd a thought it?

- What was I thinking?
- It will surely make you stop and think. (said after hearing bad news about someone like a car wreck)
- I thought better of it. (changed my mind)
- She never has a thought in her head. (scatterbrained)
- I thought and thought about it, and now I'm done thinking. (come to a decision; given up)
- Don't give it a second thought. (don't worry about it)
- I thought to myself, "I believe I'll go over and visit granny," and here I am. (internal conversation with one's self)

thirsty
- I'm so thirsty, I'm spitting cotton!
- I'm dry as a bone.
- I'm parched.
- I'm bone dry.
- My mouth feels like I've been sucking sand.
- My tongue is shriveled up in my head.
- I'm as dry as a desert.
- There's a drought in my throat.
- I need a drink of water before I expire.

threats
- I'll knock you into the middle of next week.
- Why don't you come over here and say that to my face?
- I'll knock you into next year.
- You are cruisin' for a bruisin'.
- Do you want to see the back of my hand?
- I'll knock your teeth down your throat!
- I'll make you swallow your teeth.

- I'll punch you so hard your momma will feel it.
- If you've got something to say about me, at least have the guts to say it to my face!
- I'll knock the white (or black) out of you!
- You are asking for it!
- He'll drop you like a sack of taters.
- I'll send you to meet your Maker!
- I'll reach down your throat and turn you inside out.
- I'll dot both of your eyes.
- I'll bash you up one side and down the other.
- I'll make you wish you'd never been born.
- I'll make you sorry one way or the other.
- I'll knock your block off!
- I'll come down on you like a righteous hammer!
- I'll cut you down so low you could bunji jump on a rubber band.
- I'll cut you so low, you could sky dive off a piece of paper.
- You'll hit the ground like a ton of bricks!
- I'll be on you like a duck on a June bug!
- Pick on somebody your own size, not your I.Q.
- If you think you're big enough, why don't you come over here and make me!
- I'll wipe the floor up with you.
- I'll be on you like a duck on a June bug!
- I'll be on you like white on rice!
- I'm going to break bad on you.
- I'll turn you every which way but loose!
- I'll turn you inside out.
- I'll reach down your throat and pull out your gizzard!

- I'll ram my hand down your throat so far, I'll grab your tail bone and turn you inside out.
- I'll whip you like a red headed step child!
- I'll snatch you bald headed.
- I'm going to beat the living daylights out of you!
- I'm about to whip somebody!
- I'll knock the heck out of you.
- I'll beat you black and blue.
- I'll beat you silly!
- Don't you make me hurt you!
- I'll lay you out! (kill you; knock you out cold)
- I'm going to break bad on you!

threw/throw
- She threw me for a loop. (surprised)
- He threw me a curve ball. (unexpected news)
- Will you deep six this for me? (throw something away)
- We are going to have a throw down. (party)
- I'll throw you over my shoulder and pack you home. (make someone leave a situation that is bad for them)
- People who live in glass houses shouldn't throw stones. (Don't criticize others when your own faults are obvious.)
- Don't throw the baby out with the bathwater. (Get rid of the bad and keep the good.)
- Throw me a line. (Help me.)
- I don't need you to throw me any crumbs from your table. (Don't feel sorry for me.)
- He threw me the prettiest smile. (smiled at me

- A sorry wife can throw out more with a teaspoon than a good man can bring home with a shovel. (A wasteful woman is impossible for a hard-working man to provide for.)
- Throw that bum out the door! (Get rid of a husband or a man who is hanging around but won't work.)

thrift
- Use it up, wear it out, make do, or do without!
- She'll be a frugal wife.
- That pair of overalls sure had all the good used out of them!
- We always lived on hand-me-downs.
- Frugality is a sign of good sense.

thunder
- She walks around like a thunder cloud, ready to strike. (angry; ill tempered)
- He's as mad as thunder! (very mad)
- He couldn't hear thunder! (hard of hearing)
- Where in thunder did you put my shoes? (explicative)
- You have to have lightning before you have thunder. (in altercations, someone has to start the process)

tick
- I swelled up like a tick in a coon dog's ear.
- I'm full as a tick.
- I'm as full as a big dog tick.
- If I was a tick, I'd pop.

tickle
- That really tickled me. (made me laugh)
- I have something here that might tickle you fancy. (please you)

- She was tickled pink. (very happy)
- That tickled my funny bone! (something made me laugh)
- Ouch! I just hit my funny bone. (pain in the elbow after hitting it on the edge of something.)
- I'll tickle you 'til you pee on yourself!
- I'm tickled to death. (extremely pleased)
- That notion tickled me. (amusing thought)
- He sure tickles my fancy. (arouses sexual desires; infatuation with a stranger)

tie
- Tether your horse to the post.
- Blessed be the ties that bind.
- They have strong political ties.
- I have no previous ties to anyone. (am not engaged and have never been married)

time
- A stitch in time saves nine. (Do things in a timely manner.)
- Time waits for no one. (opportunity passes; time passes)
- Time marches on. (Time continues forward.)
- Long time no see. (I haven't seen you in a long time.)
- It's time to face the music. (pay the consequence)
- A good time was had by all. (Everyone had fun.)
- Time flies when you're having fun.
- Time flies by! Oops! There it went!
- His time is up. (death)
- Your time is running out, (almost dead; deadline)
- Time will endure until it ends.

- I will love you as long as time endures.
- It's been a time and a time since I've seen your face. (long time)
- Times were hard and things were bad. (usually refers to the Depression years; extreme poverty)
- I've not seen him since Job was a pup. (long ago)
- We're having a time trying to put this thing together! (difficult)
- What time is it? It's a freckle past a hair.
- It's time to chase the chickens. (get work done; prepare a meal)
- Betimes they would walk the long way home. (sometimes)
- We were having the awfulest time that ever was. (difficult; terrible; hardships)
- I've not seen you in a coon's age. (long time)
- It's pert near time to leave. (almost)
- It's about time for all dogs to be dead. Aren't you glad you're a cat?
- Gin we get there, the store will be closed. (By the time.)
- Question: What time is it?
  Answer: Time for you to get a
- We're goin' to have a time! (fun)
- She's really having a time with him. (trouble)
- Time flies when you are having fun.
- She waited a respectable time before she had guests in. (usually refers to a period of mourning)
- I haven't seen you in a month of Sundays.
- I haven't been over to see her in a blue moon.

- She's having the time of her life. (a lot of fun)
- Long time no hear.
- There's no time like the present! (do it now)
- There's no time to lose! (hurry)

tiny
- It's an itty bitty bug.
- I'll take a little bit of cream.
- That baby is teeny.
- She has a teensy waistline.
- The pup is teensy weensy.
- That girl is tinesy.
- There is a teeny tiny speck on it.
- He has teeny weeny eyes.
- That baby is his daddy in miniature.
- Let me taste a tiny bit of the cake so I can decide if I like it.
- She was just a little slip of a woman.

tired
- I'm completely frazzled. (exhausted)
- I'm worn to a frazzle. (exhausted)
- I'm done for. (can do no more)
- I'm pooped. (tired out)
- I'm whipped. (have no more to give)
- I'm dog tired. (very tired)
- I've fizzled out. (run out of energy)
- I'm all in. (can do no more at present.)
- I'm running on empty. (need some food or drink)
- I'm running on fumes. (need some fuel for energy)
- I've run out of steam. (exhausted)
- I'm run down. (may refer to health issues)

- I'm worn out. (all used up)
- I'm wiped out. (can't do any more)
- I'm plumb tuckered out. (spent after a lot of work)
- I've had the lick. (can't do any more)
- I'm sprizzle-sprung.
- I feel like I've been shot at and missed, spit at and hit all over!
- I'm so tired I'm getting slap happy. (giddy)
- I'm so tired I'm getting punch drunk.
- I'm falling over asleep.
- I'm so tired, I can hardly hold my eyes open.
- He looks like he's been rode hard and put up wet.
- What doesn't get done today will be waiting to be done tomorrow.

toad
- That toady frog can jump.
- He thinks he's a prince, but he looks like a toad!
- Before you find your handsome prince, you gotta kiss a lot of toads.

toe/toes
- I stumped my toe.
- I stubbed my toe.
- I wouldn't swap it for my big toe!
- What a cute little toe head you are! (white-blonde hair)
- Your toes look like turtle heads.
- That preacher stepped on my toes. (preached about something that was uncomfortably relevant to my life)

together
- We're on the same page.
- We are hand in hand on this issue.
- We're all in one mind and one accord.
- We'll be together forever.
- We'll be stuck together like glue.
- Two is company, three is a crowd.

tongue
- Her tongue is hinged in the middle. (gossiper)
- My tongue is as dry as powder. (thirsty)
- She has a wagging tongue. (gossiper; bossy)
- Her tongue is about two sizes too big. (talks too much)
- Her tongue is about two feet long. (talks too much)

toothless
- He'll be gumming it since he had his teeth pulled.
- There comes old Snagglepuss!
- I feel like old Snaggletooth!
- You're a regular gummy bear!
- If you try to kiss him, he'll gum you to death!

touch/touchy
- Don't touch my stuff! (hands off!)
- I wouldn't touch that with a ten foot pole! (dangerous or controversial situation to avoid)
- No one can touch her heart. (emotionally cold; unfeeling)
- You're awful touchy today! (irritable)
- He's a touchy man. (easily offended)
- She's all touchy feely when she talks. (reaches out a hand to touch the person she's speaking with)

- You couldn't touch him! (not as good as)

toy
- Oh, momma! Can I have a new play pretty?
- Go over there and get your play purdy.
- His daddy brought him a new play diddle.

town
- When are you going to town? (visiting; grocery shopping)
- He was really going to town on it! (working hard at something)
- We live in a regular whistlestop. (town big enough for the train to make regular stops)
- She's an uptown girl. (high society)
- This place is little more than a hole in the wall. (small town)
- He's a small town guy. (simple ways; unsophisticated)
- This is a one horse town. (very small)

traffic
- Move over slow poke! (Get out of the passing lane.)
- I got behind every slow thing comin' and goin'.
- If you don't know how to drive, get off the road.
- She must have got her driver's license in a Cracker Jacks box. (an insult to a bad driver)
- Cars are whizzing by me like I'm sittin' still. (speeding)
- We're jam packed in here like a can of sardines. (traffic jam; too many occupants in one vehicle)
- Tail lights are stringing into the distance as far as the eye can see. (bumper to bumper traffic after dark)
- There was nowhere to pass. (behind slow traffic)

- I cut around him as soon as I had the chance. (passed)
- Traffic is flowing pretty good. (moving steadily)
- He traffics drugs. (illegally smuggles)
- He traffics in pornography. (buys and sells)

train
- We're all riding on the same train. (common goals)
- I'm getting off this train before it derails. (trouble anticipated in a project or situation)
- This is a train wreck waiting to happen. (unsafe; volatile)
- Train your children up in the way they should go and they will not depart from it when they are older. (teach morals, manners, values, work ethic, etc.)
- You can't potty train an old dog. (hard to change old people or old habits)
- Train your eyes on this and tell me what you think. (look closely)
- It's as unsullied as a bridal train. (pure)

trapped
- I've got my back against a wall.
- He's pinned in a corner.
- She had me over a barrel.
- I was caught between a rock and a hard place.
- She was betwixt a rock and a hard place.
- I was betwixt and between.
- You are trapped like a possum up a gum tree! (refers to being hunted and located by dogs)
- It's hanged if you do and hanged if you don't.
- There's no way in and no way out.

tricked
- I've been hoodwinked
- I've been had.
- He sure put one over on me!
- He got burnt on that deal.
- I've been hornswaggled.
- I've been jiggered.
- I've been diddled.
- He'd believe that roosters lay eggs if you said it was so.

trouble
- Now you are up a creek without a paddle!
- Don't borrow trouble. (Worry about your own troubles.)
- Our sub has sunk. (refers to military defeat of navy sub)
- You are in a heap of trouble. (a lot)
- You are in a peck of trouble. (a great deal)
- Don't give me any flak! (no quarreling or back talk)
- We've hit rock bottom. (Things can't get worse.)
- We are in a fine predicament! (difficult situation)
- What goes around comes around. (trouble comes to all)
- You are in a boat load of trouble. (a lot of trouble)
- You're in a heap of trouble. (big trouble)
- You are in deep doo-doo. (a mess)
- She's in a peck of trouble. (difficulty)
- That's a recipe for disaster!
- The more you stir in poop, the more it stinks.
- Let sleeping dogs lie. (Leave well enough alone.)

- You're digging yourself a hole you'll not easily get out of.
- You've taken the lid off the devil's box.
- You've just opened a can of worms.
- He's getting ready to open a can of whoop arse.
- Just wait until that crap hits the fan!
- We've hit rough weather. (a difficult time)
- Now it's going to hit the fan! (negative reaction)
- Keep it between the lines. (Don't read more into a situation than is actually there. Take it for face value.)
- Don't open Pandora's Box. (refers to Greek mythology)
- Don't open that can of worms. (leave it alone)
- Leave well enough alone. (Don't create trouble.)
- We are in a pickle. (complicated situation)
- We are in a jam. (hard situation to get out of)
- We are in hot water now! (disciplinary action)
- We're in over our heads. (can't handle a situation)
- You're in the dog house. (in trouble with a spouse)
- What a debaucle.

true/truth
- To thine own self be true. (Don't compromise.)
- Be true to yourself. (faithful to your own values)
- That's the truth and it ain't no lie!
- I'll get to the bottom of this! (discover the truth)
- Sometimes the truth hurts. (is undesirable)
- Some truths will raise the hackles on a dog's back. (make a person angry when they hear it)

- The truth never passed his lips! (liar)
- The truth will stand when the world is on fire.
- The truth will set you free.
- Mark my word… (Count on it.)
- That's the unvarnished truth! (no embellishments)
- Mark my word down. (believe me_
- That's the Lord's truth. (emphasizes honesty)
- I'll stake my word on it. (risk my reputation)
- Now that's the honest to God truth! (emphasis on truth)
- Above all others, be true to yourself. (no compromise)
- That is a far cry from the truth. (a lie)
- That's the honest truth. (for emphasis)
- I'll stake my name on it. (reputation)
- I'll stake my life on it. (absolute truth)
- If that's not the truth, may the Lord strike me down right here where I stand! (said for effect)
- She is true blue. (loyal)
- Show your true colors. (be yourself)
- I'll pin him down and get the truth out of him.
- I won't rest until I uncover the truth.
- That's the gospel truth!
- That's the God's honest truth.
- I'll stake my life on it being the truth.
- It is the truth and nothing but the truth, so help me God

tub

- Every tub must sit on its own bottom.
- He's a regular tub of lard! (obese)

turkey
- Who killed the turkey? (who cooked?)
- You turkey! (jerk)
- Let's talk turkey. (honestly; frankly)

turtle *(also called turkle in some regions)*
- I saw a big mud turkle crossing the road.
- She's slower than a turtle.
- Every time trouble comes along, she acts like a turtle and sticks her head in her shell! (doesn't want to face reality)

twilight
- Round about dusky dark the lightning bugs come out.
- In the gloaming part of the day is what I like best.
- It was the shadowy time of evening.
- It's dark thirty. (just after dark)
- The birds sing saddest at evensong.
- We'll light the candles at eventide.

U

ugly
- She is uglier than a mud fence.
- She's uglier than a mud pie.
- She's so ugly she looks like she's been hit with a sack of wet kittens!
- He's as ugly as homemade sin.
- Remember that the ugliest ducklings often make the prettiest swans.
- The ugliest cow in the barn might give the sweetest milk. (don't judge by outside appearances)

- God made him as ugly as he could and threw the rest in his face.
- Beauty is skin deep, but ugly goes all the way to the bone!
- She's so ugly, she must have fallen off the ugly tree, hit every branch on the way down, and then sucked on the roots.
- She's ougly.
- She's so ugly, she could scare a mud puddle dry!
- He's so ugly, he'd make your toes curl!
- She's so ugly, Peepin' Tom pulled the shade.
- Her face could stop a Mack truck.
- He is as ugly as a dog's behind.
- She's so ugly a cow wouldn't walk with her.
- She's so ugly, she's oogled.
- She's pretty ugly and pretty apt to stay that way.
- He's so ugly, he looks like he caught fire and someone tried to beat it out with an ugly stick.
- She looks like the south end of a north bound mule.
- He's so ugly, he'd have to tie a pork chop around his neck to get the dogs to play with him.
- That boy looks like he's been beaten with an ugly stick.
- You're so ugly, if you looked in the mirror, it would probably scream.
- You're so ugly, if you looked in the mirror, it would crack up!
- He's as ugly as a mud fence daubed with tad poles.
- Ugly girls often make the best wives.

- Kiss an ugly girl and everyone will know it by the morrow.
- She's a real battle axe.
- She's as plain as dishwater.
- She's as ugly as an eight day clock.
- Looking long at her would hurt your eyeballs.
- She looks so sour, she must have been weaned on a pickle.
- He's uglier than sin!
- I'd like to have two of those ugly hats… one to use the toilet in and another one to cover it up with.
- He's so ugly, they had to tie a pork chop around his neck when he was a baby, just to get the dog to play with him!
- You're so ugly if you looked in the mirror, it would run away!
- He's so ugly when he was born the doctor smacked his mom instead of him.
- Your sister is so ugly that after she went swimming in the lake, someone started a rumor that there's a monster in the lake.
- Your sister is so ugly, Freddie Cruger has nightmares of her.
- You're so ugly, you have to sneak up on a mirror to get a look at yourself.

unacceptable
- That is a deal breaker. (something not to be tolerated)
- I think not. (I don't think so.)
- No way, Jose. (disbelief; rejection)
- You have it your way, and I'll have it mine.

- That just won't do. (unacceptable)
- That won't fly. (won't be accepted)

unbearable
- I don't think I can live and stand it.
- I feel like I'm in a vacuum.
- I might as wells to dry up and die and get it over with right here and now.
- I've had all I can stands and I can't stands no more!
- That's the last straw!
- That was the straw that broke the camel's back!

unbelievable
- That's outlandish!
- I don't think so!
- Do I look like I've got stupid written all over my face?
- Do I look that stupid for you to think I'd fall for your bull?

uncertain
- I don't know, right off hand.
- I can't say, right off hand.
- It's hard to say, right off hand.
- We'll have to see which way the wind blows.
- I can't say for sure.

undecided
- I can't make up my mind.
- Don't leave me hanging.
- I have half a mind to go ahead and do it!
- Don't leave me dangling.
- I'm leaning 50% yes, and 50% no.
- Well, I might and then again I might not.

understand
- I take your meaning. (I understand your hint.)
- She doesn't cull nothing about men!
- Gotcha! (I understand what you're saying.)
- Got it! (I comprehend)
- I get your drift. (understand your reasoning)
- Your meaning is plain. (clear)
- We understand each other. (mutual consent)
- I take the hint. (understand something unspoken)
- I catch your meaning. (got the hint)
- I get the message. (understand what is being said)
- We're on the same page. (in agreement)
- I've got your number. (I understand you.)

underwear
- Stop leaving your drawers in the bathroom floor!
- Granny wears those old timey bloomers.
- I have to wash my unmentionables.
- I'm in need of some new unspeakable.
- My under things are still wet from washing.
- I've packed my undergarments in the trunk.

undoubtedly
- Beyond a shadow of doubt.
- For sure and certain.
- Indubitably, my Dear Watson.

unexpected
- Out of the blue, he asked me to marry him.
- The news came like a shot in the dark.
- You could have knocked me over with a feather when I heard they had run off together!

unfortunately
- I wish you could go with us. More's the pity you can't.
- Tough noogies! You don't always get your own way.
- Too bad! Better luck next time.
- Tough luck. I heard about you losing your job.

uninformed
- I've been out of the loop.
- What you don't know won't hurt you.
- She's a little light on the subject.
- Someone left Your juice off. (not very bright)
- You don't know Jack about what's going on.
- You don't know diddly squat.
- You don't know your head from a hole in the ground.
- You don't know your tail from a hole in the ground.
- Don't ask me – I'd be the last one to know!
- I don't know and hope I don't have to find out!
- It's a closed book to me!
- I've been left in the dark.
- He doesn't know a diaper from a dishrag.
- I'm not in the know on that matter.
- You don't know beans about it.
- What I know on that subject wouldn't fit in a thimble.

unity
- A house divided cannot stand.
- We'll stand shoulder to shoulder.
- One for all and all for one.
- We are all one blood.
- We are one body
- We are all in the same boat.

unkempt
- That child is a ragamuffin. (clothing in need of mending)
- I look like a whodee thought. (unmatched clothing; caught off guard to be seen by others in work clothes)
- Her hair was tousled all over her head. (uncombed)
- You're looking a little slouchy. (clothes too big)
- You look scroungy. (as if you don't care about yourself)
- You are very disheveled. (wrinkled; dirty clothes)
- I'm just bumbling around. (comfort clothes)
- He is bummed out. (old clothes)
- Her old house needs a new coat of paint. (cosmetics)
- He's falling apart. (untended clothing; shoes)
- He has really gone to the dogs. (slovenly)
- She let herself go after she got married. (stopped caring about her personal physical appearance and/or clothing)

unlikely
- Don't hold your breath!
- Fat chance!
- Slim chance!
- You've got a chicken's chance of crossing the road.
- You've got a pup's chance.
- That's a long shot.
- Don't bet your bootie on it.
- That would be like finding a needle in a haystack.
- That's very doubtful.
- When Hades freezes over!
- When pigs fly!

- When it snows in July!
- That's just a pipe dream.
- Don't count on it.
- You'll see that when the cows come home.
- That will happen when he sprouts wings and flies.
- Sounds pretty far-fetched to me.
- There's not a snowball's chance in hell of that ever happening.
- There's not a gnat's chance in Hades of ever seeing that come true.
- The odds are against it.
- She's holding out hope against hope.
- You don't have a ghost of a chance!

unpredictable
- It's hit or miss.
- You never know which way the wind will blow.
- She's a crazy as a coot!
- He's a Will of the wisp… here today, gone tomorrow.

unprepared
- You know when somebody's coasting.
- You caught me off guard. (no advance notice)
- He's flying by the seat of his pants. (unplanned, unstructured event)
- He's winging it. (making it up as he goes)
- I hope this is not another one of her last minute meetings – all willy nilly.
- We decided to get together on the spur of the moment.

unprepared
- You know when somebody's coasting.

- You caught me off guard. (no advance notice)
- He's flying by the seat of his pants. (unplanned, unstructured event)
- He's winging it. (making it up as he goes)
- I hope this is not another one of her last minute meetings – all willy nilly.
- We decided to get together on the spur of the moment.

unreliable
- You can't depend on her for nothing.
- She blows whichever way the wind blows.
- He's a double minded man.
- She's mealy mouthed.
- He's tossed on every wind that blows.
- She says whatever she thinks will please people in the moment and never thinks of it again.
- He promises the moon but delivers nothing.

unruly (see **misbehavior**)
- This thing is about to get out of hand.
- He must have been a rounder in his younger days.

unsophisticated
- He's straight off the farm.
- He's wild and wooly.
- She's a simpleton.
- She's underdeveloped.
- He's a diamond in the rough.
- She has potential if someone cared to develop it.
- She has country ways.
- He is plain country.

unstable
- That boy is squirrely.
- He's as nutty as a fruitcake.
- She's a silly goose.
- He's a real goofball.
- Idgit! You never listen!
- She is strung too tight.
- He's liable to short circuit at any time!
- She runs hot and cold. You never know which one you are going to get when you see her coming.
- You never know when he's going to blow.

unwanted
- He always shows up, unwanted and unbidden. (uninvited)
- She was an unwanted child. (unexpected, unmarried pregnancy)

up
- We're up a creek now! (in trouble)
- He's up a creek without a paddle. (in trouble)
- What's up? (what's going on?)
- He's up to no good. (mischief)
- It's not up to me. (not my decision)
- Now you're up a gum tree. (in trouble)
- That decision is still up in the air. (undecided)
- That kid is driving me up the wall. (irritating)
- I'll be up to snuff in no time. (back to health)
- She's up to her neck in housework. (busy)
- That house is up for grabs. (whoever can afford it)
- She's uppity. (thinks she's superior to others)

upset
- Don't get upset.
- I'm discomfited.
- Don't get discombobulated.
- Don't get out of socket!
- Don't get your britches in a wad.
- She is beside herself.
- I'm really put out with you.
- Don't upset the applecart. (cause problems)

urine/urinate
- I have to go pee.
- I have to go pee-pee.
- I have to go wee-wee.
- Don't eat yellow snow. (someone/thing has urinated there)
- I need to tinkle.
- Who needs a potty break? We're making a quick stop.
- Do you have to go potty?
- Don't pee into the wind.
- Always drink upstream.
- They are so poor, they don't have a pot to pee in.
- I knew him before he had a pot to pee in.
- If you sprinkle when you tinkle, be a sweetie, wipe the seatie. (clean the toilet seat if you get it wet)
- I'm bustin' to go. (urgently need a bathroom break)
- If you keep drinking that water, you'll be peeing like a race horse.

useless
- He's as useless as a bent stick.

- It's as useless as a broken stick.
- It's as useless as a broken arrow.
- He's of no use to man nor beast.
- He's not good for much but holding a plumb line.
- You can set it on a shelf and look at it, but that's all it's good for!
- I never did figure out what this gizmo is for.

V

variety
- Variety is the spice of life.
- If the good Lord didn't like variety, he wouldn't have made Saint Bernard and French Poodles.

vision
- He has eagle eyes. (clear sight)
- She's blind as a bat. (poor vision)
- He could count the hairs on a frog's back! (excellent vision)
- He has tunnel vision. (single minded goal)

visit/visitors
- I'd like to pay him a surprise visit. (catch him off guard)
- Visitors and fish are a lot alike. They both begin to stink after a few days.
- Visitors are always welcome, but more so when they are expected.
- Leave people wanting more instead of staying so long they want you to leave.

voice
- Her voice is like the call of a wild bird.
- His voice was like a foghorn.
- She has a voice like an angel.
- He sounds like a flock of crows in a cornfield. (raspy voice)
- Her voice was like fingernails on the chalkboard.
- Her voice was so shrill, it could shatter glass.
- She spoke, barely above a whisper.
- His voice is like a freight train!
- He talks Yankified.
- Your talk is as country as cornbread.

vote
- I voted for the lesser of two evils.
- You'd vote for the devil if you thought it would put a dollar in your pocket.
- The nation started downhill when they gave women the right to vote.
- He'll throw the results of that vote if you give him a chance.   (give a false account to make things turn out the way he wanted)

vulnerable
- He's hanging by a thread.
- She's on the edge.
- She's left herself wide open.

W

wagon
- The emptier the wagon, the more it rattles. (unintelligent people talk more about insignificant things)
- I'll fix your little red wagon! (get even)

waist
- That is a lovely waist you're wearing. (blouse)
- She has a waspish waist. (very narrow)
- He's wearing a waist coat. (short jacket or coat; vest)

wait/waiting
- I've been waiting here a month of Sundays.
- Weight broke the wagon! (a response to someone's instructions to "Wait!")
- I've been here long enough for beans to sprout.
- I've been here long enough for butter to churn.
- I've been here so long, I've forgotten what I'm waiting for.
- He's waiting in the wings. (look for an opportunity to act)
- I'm waiting my time.
- I'm biding my turn.
- Just you wait and see!
- My life is on hold.
- Hold your horses!
- That idea is on ice.

wake up greetings
- Rise and shine.
- Mornin'!

- You'd better hit the floor!
- Mornin' glory!
- Top o' the mornin' to ya!
- How'd you sleep?
- Crawl out of that bed!
- Wake up sleepyhead!
- Time to hit the floor running!
- Time to rise and shine, sleepyhead!
- The day is calling! You don't want to miss it!
- Good morning sunshine!
- Did you get your eyes together?
- That's enough shut eye for one night.
- Off your butt and on your feet, out of the shade and into the heat.

walk/walking
- If you want to go, you'll be flat footing it.
- Looks like we'll be hot footing it. (walking on the road)
- You'll be riding shanks mare.
- You'll be trudging it.
- He wobbles like a penguin.
- She walks like somebody shoved an iron rod up her backbone.
- The way she walks, it's a wonder her thighs don't catch fire!
- This will be a walk in the park. (easy)
- I feel like I'm walking a tightrope. (in a dangerous position)
- We're walking on eggshells around her. (careful not to offend someone)

- He tromped up the stairs. (walked angrily)
- He's a walking encyclopedia. (well informed)
- She could walk the back legs off a hound dog!
- If you can walk away and not look back, then keep walking.
- He has a bounce in his step.
- She walked like she had springs in her feet.
- He walks like he has a cob up his hiney. (straight, stiff; proud)

wallow
- He wallers the bed 'til mid day. (sleeps until noon)
- If you wallow in the pig pen, don't be surprised if people avoid your stink.

walls
- Let there be no walls between us. (be truthful with each other)
- I wish I could hide and be a fly on the wall. (spy on a situation that's going to happen)
- The walls have ears. (someone might be listening or eavesdropping)
- If only walls could talk. (expose secrets)
- I've hit a brick wall. (come to a standstill)
- Don't wall yourself in. (shut people out emotionally)
- Let us tear down dividing walls. (get rid of color, race, religion)

wandering
- He's gone traipsing. (wandering in the woods)
- He's gone walk about. (exploring an area)
- I love to wander over the mountains. (hike)

want
- I am in want of nothing. (I don't need anything.)

- I want for nothing. (Whatever I desire I get.)
- I wanted some ice cream in the worst kind of way. (had a craving)
- I have all my needs met, if not all of my wants.
- God said he'd supply all of our needs according to His riches in glory, but He didn't say anything about wants!
- He is in want of a good spanking. (in need of)

waste/wasteful
- You are piddling our life away. (not accomplishing anything)
- You are squandering yourself (not living to your fullest potential.
- A wasteful wife can throw more out with a spoon than her husband can bring in with a shovel.
- Waste not, want not. (be conservative)
- A mind is a terrible thing to waste. (uneducated; drug abuse)

watching/being watched
- He's giving you the stink eye. (angry look)
- She's giving you the evil eye. (watching you with contempt)
- She's getting an eye full. (staring)
- You better watch him like a hawk! (don't trust him)
- Watch your back. (be careful)
- I'm watching you! (don't trust you; keeping an eye on you)
- He can't take his eyes off of you. (captivated by you)
- She's eyeballing you for some reason. (watching what you're doing)

water
- I need to make water. (urinate)
- That's water under the bridge. (something from the past)
- If you plant, someone else will water.
- Trying to talk to her is like trying to look through muddy water. (difficult; unclear)
- Still waters run deep.
- I'm as weak as a newborn calf.
- She's weak minded. (mentally challenged.
- The weak fall by the wayside.

weak
- I feel as weak as a kitten.
- He's as weak as a newborn baby.

wealth
- He has enough money to burn a wet mule.
- He doesn't even know how much he is worth.
- He's got more money than you could shake a stick at!
- He has deep pockets.
- He's living in the lap of luxury.
- She was born with a silver spoon in her mouth.
- He makes out like a bandit.
- That doctor makes money hand over fist.
- He's made a mint off of that timber.
- He's a man of means.
- She's rolling in money.
- She's rolling in gravy.
- He's a regular rags to riches story.
- She's a Cinderella story.
- He's a sugar daddy.

- He's got money to burn.
- He has so much money he doesn't even have to tie his own shoe laces!
- He has so much money in his wallet, he needs two belts to hold his pants up.
- She has more money than she knows what to do with! (very rich)
- She'll cry all the way to the bank. (wealth that comes from a sad situation, i.e. Death or divorce)
- He came into some money. (inheritance, winnings, unexpected gain)
- I've given up on my first million and decided to start working on the second. (humorous saying)
- Wealth does not cure wanting. (wealthy people still want)

web
- Oh what a tangled web we weave, when first we practice to deceive!
- That little spider needs to get caught in his own web.
- She was trapped in a web of deceit (or guilt).
- She's cast a web to catch him in. (romantic interest)

weed/weeds
- That child is growing like a bad weed! (quickly)
- Weeds, like rumors, are not in need of planting or tending. They grow on their own.
- The weeds are getting away from me. (garden or yard needs tending)
- The weeds are taking over. (can literally mean weeds in a yard or garden; something /group of people undesirable)

weep
- She's a weeper. (cries easily)
- Your wound is weeping. (leaking; oozing)
- She can weep at the drop of a hat.

weight loss plan
- "Have you noticed that I've lost weight?"
- "How much have you lost?"
- "How much have you lost?"
- "About as much as you've gained!"
- I'm on the see food diet. I see it, I eat it.
- The only way I could lose weight is to have my lips sewn together.
- Over the lips and past the gums, look out thighs, 'cause here it comes.
- There's no need for me to swallow my food. I might as well rub it on my hips because that's exactly where it ends up.
- I can look at food and gain weight.
- I can smell of food and gain weight.
- I've tried every diet known to man (and woman, too).

welcome
- You're welcome. (in response to thank you)
- You're just as welcome as you can be. (in response to thank you)
- You're welcome any time. (come for a visit; drop in)
- We'll roll out the welcome mat. (want you to come)
- We'll throw out the welcome mat. (want you to come)
- He showed up unwanted and unbidden. (unwelcomed)

- You're as welcome as a warm hearth stone. (warm spot at a fireplace)

wellness (in response to the question: How are you?)
- I'm finer than frog hairs. (great)
- I'm fair to middlin'. (okay; alright)
- I'm middlin' well. (okay; alright)
- Very well, thank you. (good)
- I'm feeling froggy. (very well; energetic)
- I'm bright eyed and bushy tailed. (feeling very well)
- I was better, but I got over it.
- I'm doing as well as a body could expect to be doing at my age. (response from an elderly person in average health)
- I'm better than I have a right to be.
- I've made it through another day and hope to make it through the next one. (one day at a time approach)
- I can't complain. (fair health)
- I can't complain and if I did, nobody would listen.
- Well, I thought about it and I decided I'd be just fine.
- Fine, thanks.
- Fine, and thank you for asking.
- I am blessed inside and out.
- If I was any better, I'd have to take a pill for it.
- I'm just fine and dandy!

wet
- It's soggier than a rain forest today.
- I'm wetter than a dishrag.
- He's as wet as a fish.
- You look like a drowned rat.

whack
- Let me take a whack at it. (try)
- I'll whack you up the side of the head! (hit)
- Whickety whack! (hurry)

wheel
- It's the squeaky wheel that gets the grease.
- He's older than the invention of the wheel!
- He's a real wheeler dealer. (makes a lot of business deals

whip/whipping (also see **spank**)
- I'll whip you all over the place.
- That's a whipping I'm laying up for you!
- I owe you a trip to the woodshed.
- Would you like to step out back?
- You are not too big for a whipping!
- I won't be your whipping boy. (take the blame for your mistakes)
- If you don't take your part, I'll whip you when I get you to the house! (said to a child who needs to stand up to a bully)

white
- She turned as white as a ghost. (frightened)
- His face was as white as a sheet. (sickly)
- She's as white as the driven snow. (pure)
- Her hair was as white as snow.
- He's as white as the blue driven snow. (pale complexion)

whittling
- I was making the shivings fly.
- If you're nervous, take up whittling. (calming habit)

who/what/when/where/why
- Who some ever happens to be there will be alright with me.
- When some ever we go visit granny the net time, I'll take her a cake.
- What some ever you think we ought to do will be okay with me.
- Whichy what are you talking about.
- Whichy way did they go?
- Whichy how do you want me to do it?
- Why for did you do that?
- How come you never told me the truth before now?
- What for do you think she did that?
- How's about me and you going to the movies together?
- Who in all did you say would be there/
- Where in all are they from?
- Who'd a thunk it?
- Why in the world would you do that?
- What in tar nation is going on?
- Anyhows, that's the end of that story.
- For because I said so, that's what for!

wife
- She's my little woman.
- She's my little heifer.
- She's my little dough beater.
- She's my better half.
- She's my split apart.
- She's my old ball and chain.

wiggle
- That boy is a pure little wiggle worm.
- She is a wiggle box.
- I'd like to see him try to wiggle his way out of this one! (refers to someone who often gets by with bad behavior)
- She couldn't wiggle into that dress if she had to! (someone trying to fit into a garment that is obviously too small)

wild
- He's wilder than a wet cat. (frantic)
- He's as wild as a drunk Indian!
- He's wild as a buck. (unpredictable)
- She's pretty wild. (promiscuous)
- That idea is pretty wild. (unbelievable; far out)
- He's wild and wooly! (a big partier)
- We'll have a wild and wooly time. (big fun)
- If you don't train up a dog or a cat, it will be wild. If you don't train up a child, they'll be wild.
- He is wild catting. (working independently)

wimp
- He's such a wimp. (weak; easily bullied)
- Are you going to wimp out? (refuse to even try)

wind/windy
- That's a big windy. (lie)
- My gas tank was sucking wind. (completely empty)
- He came in here sucking wind. (completely exhausted from running or playing)

window
- I'm looking through the pane at the blossoms in the yard.

- He's just window dressing. (looks good, but not much substance.
- I'm window shopping. (looking, but not purchasing anything)

wink
- I'll be back as quick as a wink. (quickly)
- He gave me the wink. (go ahead)
- He's winking at me. (flirting)
- I need to catch a wink or two. (short nap)
- I'll see you in forty winks. (long nap)

wish/wishing
- If wishes were ponies, even beggars would ride.
- Wish in one hand, spit in the other. See which one gets full the fastest. (wishes do little good)
- It's a good thing that most of the wishes I ever wished never did come true. (unwise wishes)
- If you are going to wish, you might as well wish big! (fantasize about good things happening)
- If I could wish it all away, I surely would. (undo the past)
- I wish I had been born rich instead of so good looking!

witch
- She's a pure old witch. (unpleasant; and hard to get along with)
- She witched you. (put a curse or a spell on you)
- She's a witch with a capital B. (derogatory comment)

woman/women
- Did you see that old womern? (elderly woman)
- Have you met my old lady? (wife; live in girlfriend)
- She's his old woman. (wife; live in girlfriend)

- That gal lives across the mountain. (unmarried woman)
- She's quite a lady. (elegant; sophisticated; well-bred)
- That Miss would love to turn herself into a Mrs. (unmarried, no matter how old desiring marriage)
- The women folk are working in the kitchen. (adult females)
- She's a good un. (good wife; mother; good reputation)
- Well, lassie. How are you doing? (unmarried young woman; female child)
- Who understands the mind of a woman?
- If you took a string of women and stood them all on their heads, you'd find they were all pretty much alike.
- He's looking for a woman. (girlfriend; spouse; prostitute)
- I'd like to meet the man who's figured out a woman.
- Some women walk around with not enough clothes on to wad a shotgun.
- Some women try to show their makings. (indecent exposure)
- Bad women try to make a point to let everything hang out.
- I don't know about women who wear their skirts so short, if they happened to bend over, you could see Australia.
- She's his old woman. (wife; girl friend)

- When women shed their skirts for britches, men stopped respecting them and treating them like women.
- Women are like elephants. They never forget a bad deed and they never let you live it down. (bring up the past)

word/words
- A word fitly spoken is like apples of gold.
- A word once spoken can never be completely erased.
- The best advertisement is word of mouth.
- Words fail me. (don't know what to say)
- Sticks and stones may break my bones, but words shall never harm me. (ignore insulting comments)
- I've got a word for you, but I'm too much of a lady to say it! (unspoken insult)
- I read the Word every day. (Bible)
- He is going to share the Word with us. (preach)
- May I have a word with you? (discussion)
- Harsh words are worse than a beating.
- I have a word for you. (spiritual knowledge; insight)
- The word got out. (a secret told)
- Get the word out. (let other know something important)
- Spread the word. (pass news by word of mouth; preach the Gospel)

wore/worn
- I wore it out. (got all the good out of something)
- She wore him out! (spanked)
- I'm worn out. (tired)
- I'm worn out with thinking about it. (sick of)

work/working
- He's working up a sweat.
- She's working up a storm.
- He's working up a lather.
- Are you working hard or hardly working?
- She brings home the bacon in that family.
- Ironwork is his stock and trade. (profession; special skill that is marketable)
- He scrabbled out a living off of that little knotty piece of land. (poor existence as a farmer)
- It's time to clock in. (start working)
- She's busy as a beaver.
- It's good to know which side your bread is buttered on. (who supplies your paycheck or your upkeep)
- Time to go back to the salt mines. (go back to work)
- I've been working like a dog.
- Many hands make light work.
- Work is never done that takes place only in the mind.
- He's working around the clock.
- You're going to have to pull your weight around here. (do an equal amount of work compared to others)
- She is not too workified. (she's lazy)
- You're going to have to knuckle down. (work harder)
- He's burning the candle at both ends.
- He's asleep at the wheel. (not doing a good job)
- He's asleep at the switch. (not doing a good job)
- He's on the bread line again. (without a job)
- He's working the graveyard shift. (midnight shift)
- She's working swing shift. (alternating between day shift, evening shift, and midnight shift)

- You need a good dose of working medicine. (laxative)

world
- What in the world were you thinking? (bad choice)
- What is the world coming to? (immorality)
- She's heading for a world of hurt. (a lot)
- He's got the whole world in His hands. (God)

worms
- Let's not open that can of worms! (don't open a discussion on an unpleasant topic)
- You are squirmier than a worm on a hot rock.
- She will worm her way in to a conversation. (force)
- The earlier bird catches the worm.

worry
- She's a regular old worry wart.
- Don't worry about tomorrow, for tomorrow may never come.
- My worries are many and my pleasures are few.
- I'm a prayer worrier – pray a while and worry a while.
- You are worrying me to death. (causing me concern)
- Get off of me. You are worrying me to death. (said to a child who is wallowing in a mother's lap, clinging to her)
- Those dogs are worrying that old cow to death. (aggravating)
- Don't nobody tell me no more troubles! I've already got enough to worry about.
- Worrying never changes a thing.

worthless
- It's only fool's gold. (deceitful worth)

- It's not worth a red cent.
- It's not worth a plug nickel.
- He's about as worthless as teats on a bore hog!

write/written/writing
- The handwriting is on the wall. (obvious)
- The deal is pretty much written in stone. (settled)
- The truth is written all over your face. (guilt)

- X marks the spot.
- He has x-ray vision.
- He's a Xerox copy of his old man.

yank
- Don't try to yank me around. (be deceitfulwith)
- You're yanking my chain. (trying to make me believe something ridiculous)
- I've got a yen for some home cooking. (desire)
- He's a Yank. (someone from the North)

yes
- Yep, I heard what you said.
- Yes, sir. I will do that.
- Yes siree, Bob. I sure did.
- Shore. I'll be glad to help.
- Of course you can.
- Absolutely! I'll be there.

you/your/you're
- You are what you eat.
- This one is mine. That one's yourn.
- What am I going to do with you? (frustration when a child needs to be punished)
- You're too much! (funny; aggravating)
- Bully for you! (Good for you!; Big deal!)

young
- I've known him since he was knee high to a grass hopper.
- I've known him since he was a tadpole.
- He is young at heart. (behaves younger than his age)
- He chases every young thing in a skirt! (likes younger women)
- The old forget more than the young have known.

Z

zero
- We have a zero tolerance policy at this school regarding bullying. (not allowed under any circumstance)
- Zero hour is here. (time to begin)
- How much money do I have in my pocket? Zilch.
- How many trucks do I own? Nada.

Zip
- Zip it. (shut up)
- Zip your lip. (shut up)

Beannachadh

Made in the USA
Charleston, SC
26 March 2016